Celebrations!

A Personal Memoir Commemorating America's Bicentennial Era:

1971-1991

Doug — Thelma
Thank you for your
important role in making
this book possible.

Hollis Cawood

Celebrations!

A Personal Memoir
Commemorating America's
Bicentennial Era:
1971-1991

by
HOBIE CAWOOD

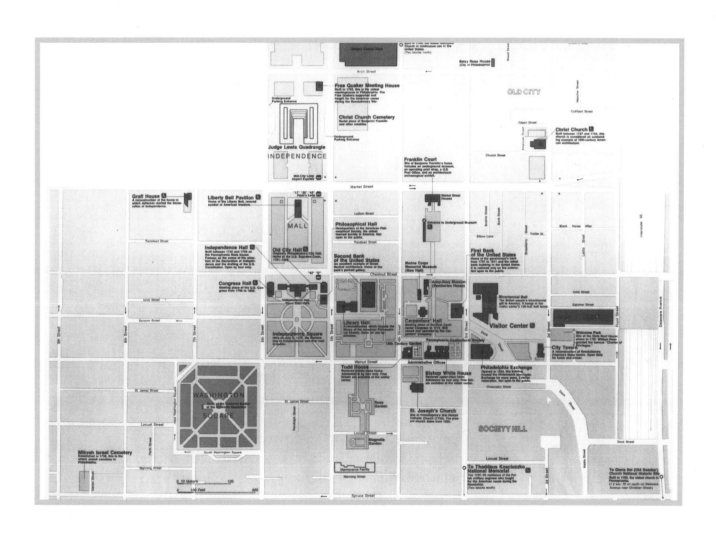

Frontis: Map of Independence National Historical Park.

Published by Diane Publishing Co.
Darby, PA
www.dianepublishing.net
1-800-782-3833

Contents

Acknowledgements

Through the years, friends have suggested that I write a book about my experiences as Superintendent of Independence National Historical Park. I seemed to always have been too busy until 2001, when I retired from my second career as President of Old Salem Inc. in Winston-Salem, North Carolina.

A year or so later, my former boss, Chet Brooks., sent me a few pages of notes about his tenure as Superintendent of Independence (1968-1971). He encouraged me to leave a similar record for the Park. Penny Batcheler, historical architect for the Park, did the same, suggesting that future generations, particularly those involved in the tricentennial, would have an interest in my experiences.

Finally, my wife, Addie-Lou, said that it should be done not only for the Park, but also for our four grandchildren, who might someday want to know about their grandpa. To reinforce the idea, Addie-Lou had clipped everything from the time of our marriage in 1977 which had appeared in Philadelphia area newspapers, plus everything that friends from around the world had sent to us. The clippings filled two medium-sized cardboard boxes.

After giving the project some thought, I discussed it with Gary Albert, Vice President of Publications at Old Salem, and he encouraged me by assisting with the development of an outline and several pages of writing samples. My typing is basic "hunt and peck" so I enlisted Jean Thomas, my assistant at Old Salem, who did work for me at night and on weekends until she retired. Phoebe Thomas at Visit Winston-Salem typed some letters and helped with a picture.

Dennis Reidenbach, Superintendent of Independence NHP, and Roy Goodman of the American Philosophical Society, helped in my search for a publisher. Telephone calls to Kathy Dilonardo, David Dutcher, Bob Gianinni, Mary Jenkins, Susie Montgomery, Peggy Duckett, Toni Butterfield, and Steve Cawood filled in some of the blanks. General conversations with Lita Solis-Cohen, Tom and Jeanne McCallum, Libby and Stanhope Browne, Joan Momjian, Tom Muldoon, Campbell Cawood, and Franklin Roberts improved my memory. Archivist Karen Stevens at Independence Park has been a cheerleader and a helpful worker from the beginning. Her assistance with information, materials, and photographs has been invaluable. Many thanks to Alice and Dick Lonsdorf, Kay and Kauders, and Dorothy Perkins for their general support and enthusiasm.

Lastly I need to thank Herman Baron of DIANE Publishing Company, who has treated me with patience due a veteran rather than an amateur who has written his first book.

Hobie Cawood
Lewisville, North Carolina
September 30, 2007

Foreword

Hobie Cawood was in the cat-bird seat for the greatest public celebrations of United States history ever undertaken. He had one of the best public jobs this country has to offer as superintendent of Independence National Historic Park in Philadelphia. For twenty years he was the steward of the historic buildings and grounds that mark the birthplace of our most cherished founding documents, the Declaration of Independence and the U. S. Constitution. During Cawood's tenure the nation and the world beat a path to his door. He hosted presidents, members of Congress, Supreme Court justices, foreign dignitaries, heads of state, and thousands upon thousands of Americans and visitors from other countries who came to the place where the United States was born.

He has written a personal memoir of those years aptly named Celebrations. It recounts the major celebrations he planned or took part in and it also is about his own sense of wonder, his personal celebrations, which were so tied to these major national events. It is a record of his years as one of the most visible Park Service employees in the entire system that serves this nation so well at historic sites and places of nature's grandeur.

The National Historic Park in Philadelphia is a gem of this system. It is an urban park, a relative rarity in the Park Service, situated in the heart of the fourth largest city in the United States. In this eight square block area walked the giants of early American history, those who drafted our most precious documents and those who launched the government of the United States. New York was briefly the first seat of government under the new Constitution in 1789, but in 1790 the entire government moved to Philadelphia, where it remained for ten years before moving to Washington, DC in 1800.

Hobie Cawood was a seasoned veteran of national celebrations when I first met him shortly after I became the Historian of the U. S. House of Representatives in 1983. My job was to help plan the national celebrations related to the bicentennials of the U. S. Constitution and the U. S. Congress. No plans for these commemorations could ignore Philadelphia, where it all began.

Hobie and I, along with Richard Baker, the Senate Historian, worked closely for several years in planning for these events. We could not have succeeded without Hobie's steady hand and wise counsel. None of these major events were without complications and a host of political considerations. Hobie helped guide us through the minefields of Philadelphia politics and he somehow surmounted every political hurtle that came out of Washington politics as well.

When I first met Hobie I liked him instantly. He had style that was disarming and charming, but always very professional. Hailing from eastern Kentucky, he had an accent that worked well, especially when he told a story. He had a perpetual smile, just a slight one, on his face most of the time, as if he was about to spring a punch line on you that was sure to make you laugh. His handsome, square-jawed features made him appear to be right out of central casting when he wore his Park Service uniform. Nobody looked the part better than Hobie Cawood. But Hobie was the real thing. I cannot imagine a more talented and creative partner for our work together than he was.

Creating large national celebrations does not happen overnight, nor is it ever the work of just a few persons. This is where Hobie's skill as an administrator and network builder came to the forefront. He knew how to motivate people. He knew how to build networks. And, perhaps most important of all, he knew how to make and keep friends.

In this memoir he tells the story of taking President Jimmy Carter up into the bell tower of Independence Hall. It is a little tricky winding your way up those narrow wooden stairs but the view is worth it. This is not something tourists get to do. It wouldn't be safe or practical. But Hobie reserved this special treat for those times when it would serve his purposes and those of the park. I had the good fortune to be able to go up into the tower with Hobie. Only this time, after Superintendent Cawood had me standing inside the bell, he rang the bell and roared with laughter as I stood there transfixed and temporarily paralyzed by the sound. It was one of his practical jokes. It was also something I will never forget and it is one of the many things that made our bond of friendship.

Hobie Cawood loved, and still loves, Independence National Historical Park. He took pride in the place and walked the grounds with an eye for detail. I can recall a number of times when we would be walking together and he would stoop down to pick up a discarded plastic bottle, or some paper. He would do this without breaking stride and without comment and simply deposit the waste in the next receptacle we passed. His genuine feeling for the trust he had been given to operate this special place was apparent at every turn, even in such small details as this.

One of the national leaders of the bicentennial era was Congresswoman Lindy Boggs of Louisiana who participated in all events related to the American Revolution Bicentennial in the 1970s all the way through to the Bicentennial of Congress in 1989. Lindy's daughter Cokie Roberts, of ABC News, once said to her mother that she had quite a racket going for herself. She was in the "bicentennial business and everything was going to be two hundred years old sometime." I was proud to be in that racket and have the honor to work with such a dedicated public servant as Hobie Cawood who helped bring American history alive for generations of Americans.

Raymond W. Smock
Shepherdstown, WV
December 8, 2007

INTRODUCTION

I went to work for the National Park Service quite by accident. After graduating from Emory and Henry College in Virginia with a major in history, I did not have a job. I returned to my hometown of Middlesboro, Kentucky, and found that my cousin, Bobby White, had graduated from the University of Kentucky and was in the same situation. Bobby and I had wives who were working so we decided to start an independent insurance agency. Every commission that we made went back into the business. Bobby's wife, Charlene, became pregnant and had complications so she had to stop working. He needed income but the insurance agency could barely support one of us, certainly not both. One of us had to find a job.

The headquarters for Cumberland Gap National Historical Park was in Middlesboro, so that was one of the places where I looked for a job. I knew that there were National Parks but I knew nothing of the organization that operated them. I was told that to be considered for a job, I had to take a test called the Federal Service Entrance Examination, and I took it at the local post office. A couple of months later I was offered an entry-level position called Park Historian at $3,670 per year.

I found out later that in 1958, most new employees of the National Park Service had grown up wanting to work for that organization. I was able to get a permanent, full time position, which I thought I would keep just until something better came along. The more I learned about National Parks and the National Park System, the more I began to think of the National Park Service as a

career. A three-month basic training course in Yosemite National Park in 1959 convinced me that I had accidentally found a career.

Cumberland Gap National Historical Park was a relatively new unit of the National Park System, with more than 20,000 acres and including the historic gap in the mountains. It was through this gap that settlers passed moving westward and eventually expanded our national boundary to the Mississippi River. It is Daniel Boone and Wilderness Road country. When I started work at Cumberland Gap in March 1958, there was only a two-mile road to the high shoulder of the mountain overlooking the gap. This was a wonderful place to tell the story of this historical and geological feature. A new visitor center was being planned and was opened at the dedication of the Park on July 4, 1959. Besides working on visitor center exhibits and audiovisual programs, I was assigned the job of collecting information about Hensley Settlement, a community that straddled the Kentucky-Virginia line some twelve miles northeast of the gap.

The settlement began in the late 19th Century and lasted until about 1950, when the lands were acquired for the creation of the Park. The people just moved out, leaving their homes, barns, school, cemetery and orchards and, since there were no roads to the mountaintop settlement, a way of life that could have existed two centuries earlier. Because some of those who moved did not go a great distance, they lived nearby and were the best source of information about life at Hensley Settlement. I planned an oral history program and put together a list of prospects to interview.

My first interview was with 80-year-old Sherman Hensley, who lived in a simple house near the park boundary at Caylor, Virginia. His house had no modern amenities, so I had to take a generator to power the tape recorder. That was the least of my problems, because "Uncle Sherm" was not too impressed with the idea of talking to a machine. After I introduced myself, I demonstrated the recorder. He considered our interview for a while and then he told me that he had known a Cawood who married a Pope from Three Star. I told him that my grandfather Frank Cawood had married Mary Pope. He asked if her father's name was "Curl" and I said yes but his real name was Moses and that his father was named Solomon. Uncle Sherm then said that he would be pleased to talk to me.

I had collected questions from everyone on the park staff to ask in the interview. Uncle Sherm talked for five hours about history, genealogy, flora and fauna. He was a storyteller and I was a sponge. I had never in my life had such an experience. Now I was in the history business.

I even asked Uncle Sherm about a story I had heard that he had killed a man, and he told me the whole story. The man was an escaped convict who jumped him, and in wrestling over a shot gun, Uncle Sherm shot and killed him. I played some of the interview back for him and he liked it so well that for as long as he was alive, he sent relatives to Park headquarters to listen to some of the tapes. I interviewed others, and this small beginning led in future years to restoring some of the buildings and daily tours to Hensley Settlement. I was hooked.

By the time I returned from a three month basic training course in Yosemite, I had decided that I was going to be a career employee with the National Park Service. This would require me to move from assignment to assignment in order to maximize my opportunities. In June of 1960 I was promoted to the position of historian at Fort Frederica National Monument on St. Simons Island, Georgia. Frederica (1736) was a fortified town on the southern boundary of the Colony of Georgia and was the primary defense against the Spanish in Florida. From Frederica, Georgia's founder, James Oglethorpe, invaded St. Augustine twice, and he successfully repulsed a Spanish invasion once.

Fort Frederica was a smaller operation than Cumberland Gap, but the job held more responsibility for me, as I was in charge of my own interpretive program. I am sure that my desire to change things was a burden to my Superintendent, Hershal Glover. Frederica was a great learning experience and a great place to live, but I was there only a year.

Again I was given a promotion, and I accepted the job of Park Historian at Fort Sumter National Monument in Charleston, South Carolina. Although I missed the actual date of the centennial of the firing on Fort Sumter (April 12, 1961), I arrived in June of that year and enjoyed the momentum from the event. Because of transfers and military leave, I worked my first 20 days, which included a tour of the fort for 200 people on my first day. I assume there was considerable improvement in the following days.

Having visitors arrive by boat and going to work the same way was a new experience which could be exciting in rough weather. Relatively small Parks such as Fort Sumter had very tight budgets, so when a tugboat severed our underwater telephone line, Superintendent E. J. Pratt and myself dredged the harbor floor with a grappling hook and bound the break. He hired an off-duty telephone company employee to splice it so our budget was not severely impacted. Treatment for sunburn and seasickness was our new problem. Fort Sumter is a well-known visitor attraction in Charleston, so my work there involved me in more activities in the community.

Fifteen months later, Bert Roberts, Superintendent of Castillo de San Marcos National Monument in St. Augustine, Florida, offered me a promotion to a one-year position. The Park Historian was going on educational leave for a year; when he returned, I would have to take whatever position was available in another Park. I composed ten questions, and if he had given me a negative answer to any of them I was going to refuse the job. The answers were all "yes," so I had to learn the Spanish side of the struggle for control of the Southeast. At the Castillo I was involved in managing a larger staff, installing a sound and light show, planning for the 400th anniversary of St. Augustine, and an even closer working relationship with travel and tourism people.

When my year was up in September 1963, I was fortunate to be moved to Chickamauga and Chattanooga National Military Park, where I found myself in the middle of the centennials of the battlefields around Chattanooga. The one at Chickamauga in September went off without a problem. But just as we were about to celebrate the three days of Chattanooga (November 23-25), President Kennedy was assassinated and the activities were cancelled.

I spent four years at Chick-Chatt and loved every minute of it. I worked with a great group of people who did a quality job and often socialized together. During my years there, I spent a total of 12 weeks at the National Park Service Training Center in Harpers Ferry, West Virginia, attending a variety of training courses. National Park Service policy was that its employees should have a great deal of formal training, plus a variety of experiences to prepare them for more responsible positions.

My first five positions with the National Park Service were in the specialty field of interpretation. Although one does whatever is necessary to get the job done, especially in the smaller parks, my position description said that I was to participate in and be responsible for an interpretive program. Interpretation is a National Park Service word that means "providing for the enjoyment or an understanding." With interpretation, one provides information in a way that it inspires and provokes the visitor. The information is provided in a variety of ways through exhibits, publications, audiovisual displays, signs, talks, tours, and so forth. The advantage the National Parks have in creating inspiration is that we are on site where something has happened. It is easier to tell the story of the birth of the United States if you are in Independence Hall or the story of Gettysburg if you are standing in the middle of the battlefield.

My ambition was to become a park superintendent, but there was an understanding that if you are to rise above a certain level, you must have experience in a central office (Region or Washington). In 1967 I accepted a position of planner-historian in the Office of Resources Planning of the Washington Service Center. En route to Washington I spent six weeks at Williamsburg, Virginia, participating in the Seminar for Historical Administrators. This program is sponsored by the American Association of Museums, Association for State and Local History, The National Trust, and Colonial Williamsburg.

All of my experience and training was valuable for the job at the Office of Resources Planning. I served on multi-disciplined teams which prepared master plans for additions to the National Park System that were being considered by Congress. A Bill would be introduced by a member/members of Congress, and before it went to hearing, the National Park Service would do a study of importance and a master plan. This would help us to develop our opinion about the proposal and the costs associated with its acquisition and operation. Often a member of our team who worked on the plan would be a witness before a House or Senate Committee. At other times we re-planned existing parks which had developed problems because of changing conditions.

In 1968, I participated in the planning of a Carl Sandburg Farm National Historic Site. This was a farm that Sandburg had bought in Flat Rock, North Carolina, and the place where he spent his later years. Carl Sandburg did some writing

and received distinguished visitors while Mrs. Sandburg operated a milk goat farm. When we visited the farm, Mrs. Sandburg and their two daughters were still living there, so I had an opportunity to utilize my oral history experience. Mrs. Sandburg and I sat on the front porch in rocking chairs and did some three hours of recording about their life at "Connemara," which is what they called the farm. The Bill passed, the property was purchased, and Mrs. Sandburg moved out, leaving the furnishings in place. Now thousands of Americans visit the site each year and learn about the literary giant Carl Sandburg.

Another wonderful experience was when I was assigned to a three-person team to plan a Lyndon B. Johnson National Historic Site. The site could include some of the ranch, his birthplace, and his boyhood home in Johnson City, Texas. We talked to Lady Bird and former President Johnson at the ranch and it became clear that Mrs. Johnson was the driving force behind the project. She actually spent most of a day showing us the properties. We had access to everything, including the family lawyer and the operations of the Johnson City Foundation.

After we returned to Washington and I was drafting the plan, I decided that we needed additional information, so I called Mrs. Johnson. She said that she was coming to Washington to see her daughter, and if I could pick her up at Dulles Airport, then we could chat until I got her downtown. I took a colleague with me to drive while I sat in the back set with Mrs. Johnson. Secret Service agents were in a car behind us. I was feeling pretty big until she asked me for my telephone number. I couldn't remember it (we had changed numbers recently). I had to ask the driver for his number so the former First Lady could call his line and then be transferred to mine. I was properly humbled.

My career crossed paths with Lady Bird Johnson twice more, once at Richmond Battlefield in Virginia and then in 1976 in Philadelphia. At the latter she was a guest at a reception given by a Philadelphia neighbor of mine, Welles Henderson. He was introducing Mrs. Johnson to those present, and when he came to me, he called me "Hobart Cawood." She grinned and said "Hobie Cawood", and I said "Hi, Mrs. Johnson." The following day I toured the park with her and Mrs. Herman Talmadge.

One day my telephone rang and it was Spud Bill, Associate Director of the National Park Service, who asked me to come by his office to talk about my future! I got there in record time. My supervisor, Ed Peetz, said he would like to promote me and keep me in the planning office. I told him that I wanted to be a Park Superintendent and that if I went any higher as a specialist, I would never make it into management. Spud Bill then told me that there were some superintendent vacancies in the Southeast Region and that I would probably hear from the Regional Director. In a couple of days, Charles Marshall, Deputy Regional Director, called and offered me a lateral transfer to the position of Superintendent, Richmond National Battlefield Park.

Richmond National Battlefield Park included bits and pieces of battlefields of the 1862 and 1864 campaigns to capture Richmond, Virginia, the capital of the Confederacy. There were ten separated parcels of real estate that were parts of the battles of Gaines Mill, Malvern Hill, and Cold Harbor, and several miles of earthworks around Fort Harrison, east of Richmond. Park headquarters was on the site of a Confederate Hospital on Church Hill. In order to visit all the pieces of Richmond NBP, one must drive 90 miles through what had become urban countryside. Not many people made that trip anymore.

I began to think about how we could make the Park more relevant and useful. I went to the Richmond Department of Recreation and Parks and told them that I have several battlefields where we can produce programs, while you have 60 playgrounds and recreation centers where there are youngsters. Can we do a deal? We created a program called Sum-Fun where each playground had an opportunity to visit Cold Harbor for a history day, Malvern Hill for a nature day, and the Defense General Supply Center for a day of fishing. We got people to donate everything we needed, even the fish. The program was a great success and got favorable editorials in the Richmond newspapers. During the second year we dropped fishing but added an overnight campout. The Defense Department had surplus tents, cots, and paper blankets. Everything that was needed was donated and the whole community got excited about the program.

Elbert Cox, former Regional Director for the National Park Service in Richmond, sent the Director, George Hartzog, a copy of an editorial about Sum-Fun with the comment, "The NPS has finally arrived." When George came to Richmond to talk to the Rotary club at the invitation of Elbert Cox, his speech included a great deal about Richmond National Battlefield Park and the job I was doing.

In 1971, Chester Brooks, an old friend from the Washington Service Center, was promoted from Superintendent of Independence National Historical Park to Regional Director of the Northeast Region (Philadelphia). George Hartzog felt that the best way to manage the National Park Service was to select good Park Superintendents, so he personally took part in their selection. He met frequently with his regional directors, and one of the issues they discussed was personnel vacancies.

On the way to one of the sessions in August 1971, George Hartzog said to Chet Brooks that he was thinking of me to be the Superintendent of Independence National Historical Park, and Chet agreed. When they presented the idea in the meeting, David Thompson, Southeast Regional Director, said that he was thinking of me for Natchez Trace Parkway. They decided that Independence was a better match for me. There was one problem with the plan. I was a GS-12 and Independence was a GS-15 and I was not eligible for it, because you can only advance one grade at a time. The solution was that I would advance a grade each year until I reached the GS-15 level. During my first two years at Independence NHP, I supervised staff that had higher grades and salary than I did. There was no problem.

My Regional Director, David Thompson, asked

my future Regional Director, Chet Brooks, if he could give me the news. Thompson knew that I was vacationing at Cape Hatteras, North Carolina, and he was coming down to observe the East Coast Surfing Championship near the Hatteras Lighthouse at Buxton. Dave and Cape Hatteras Superintendent Bert Roberts greeted me as I entered the Pink House (a NPS guest house), "Congratulations, you are the Superintendent of Independence." After a few moments of shock I replied, "That can't be because I can't spell it."

The following week, when I called Chet Brooks I found out that it was really true. We agreed on a move date of early October, but he wanted me to come to a Northeast Superintendents Conference at Cape Cod in September. My wife Shirley, son Stephen, and I would be moving into an 18th-Century house in the heart of the fourth largest city in America. A new adventure had begun.

II.

GETTING READY FOR
THE BICENTENNIAL OF THE DECLARATION OF
INDEPENDENCE (1971-1976)

A. Description of Independence Historical National Park

The park includes some 40 buildings on 40 acres (approximately 8 city blocks) of center city Philadelphia real estate that, when taken together, illustrate the American struggle for Independence and the creation of the United States of America; Philadelphia the capital city, 1790-1800; and Benjamin Franklin, a man of unlimited dimensions. The Federal legislation of June 28, 1948, authorizing the Park and its legislative history, established its parameters. Additional legislation through the years has enhanced the Park's mission.

Independence National Historical Park is arguably the most important historical real estate in America. Within its boundaries our nation was born. The following description underlines the Park's historical resources.

In 1774, the 13 British Colonies in North America decided to discuss their common grievances with the British crown. Philadelphia, located at the mid-point of the Atlantic coast and at the time the second largest English-speaking city in the world, was selected as the site. After meeting for nearly two month in Carpenters Hall, the delegates decided to send King George III a message requesting that he do better by his American colonies. This group, called the First Continental Congress, decided to reassemble the following spring to discuss the King's response.

When the delegates returned to Philadelphia in 1775, they had not heard from the King, but open warfare had broken out at Lexington and Concord.

The Second Continental Congress met in Independence Hall. In June, the delegates created an army and appointed George Washington to lead it. They later created a Navy and a Marine Corps, but they still considered themselves Englishmen, fighting for the rights of Englishmen. They even sent petitions to the King and Parliament suggesting a resolution of the disagreement. But the war continued, and in the Continental Congress on June 7, 1776, Richard Henry Lee presented a resolution that "…these Colonies are of right and ought to be free and independent states." While the delegates were debating the resolution, they appointed a committee to write a declaration or justification in case the resolution should pass. Lee's resolution and independence was voted for on July 2nd and the Declaration of Independence was approved on July 4th.

Thomas Jefferson lived in the Graff House, where he drafted the Declaration of Independence. The house was demolished in the 19th Century, but the National Park Service reconstructed it in 1976 and refurnished Jefferson's rooms on the second floor. The rest of the building includes exhibits about the Declaration of Independence.

Voting for independence did not create a government, so the Second Continental Congress became our ad hoc government until a permanent one could be devised. It actually took until March 1, 1781, before the government formed by the Articles of Confederation was unanimously approved. The Congress usually met in Philadelphia, but the delegates had to leave from time to time for their own safety and convenience. The fighting was concluded later in 1781, but the Treaty of Paris, which recognized the United States of America as a sovereign nation, did not come about until 1783. Pemberton House tells the story of the early years of the U.S. Army and the U.S. Navy, and New Hall is a memorial to the Marines in the Revolution.

The Articles of Confederation was just what is implied: it was a confederation of sovereign States. Each State reserved to itself all powers not ceded to the central government. Taxes were paid on a voluntary basis. This effort at government was so ineffective that criticism began to grow. In 1785, there was a meeting at Mount Vernon to discuss the problems. At another meeting in Annapolis in the following year, delegates proposed that all of the states send representatives back to Philadelphia in May 1787 to make adequate the Articles of Confederation.

This meeting took place in Independence Hall. Over the summer the delegates wrote the

Independence National Historic Park looking West from the U.S. Customs House

Constitution of the United States. On September 17th they signed it and recommended it to the States for Ratification. The Constitution was approved by a sufficient number of States in 1788, and a Federal election was held in January 1789. George Washington was sworn in as President on April 30, 1789.

Congress, which initially met in New York, decided that it would build a capital on the banks of the Potomac, but that it would return to Philadelphia for a decade while the new federal city was being developed.

The Philadelphia County Court House at Sixth and Chestnut Streets became Congress Hall, with the House of Representatives meeting on the first floor and the Senate on the second. It was in this building that George Washington was sworn in for his second term and John Adams became the second President of the United States. The Supreme Court utilized the Mayors Court Room in Old City Hall at Fifth and Chestnut. The President lived in the Robert Morris House (which no longer exists) near Sixth and Market. During two hot summers, Washington lived some 10 miles away at the Deshler-Morris House in Germantown. The First Bank of the United States was constructed in 1795-1797 to be the home of the national bank chartered by Congress in 1791

Two residential properties have been restored and refurnished to provide a look at 18th-Century domestic life. The Todd House is the modest row home of John Todd, Jr., a Quaker lawyer who died of yellow fever in 1792. Congressman James Madison of Virginia courted Todd's widow, Dolley, and they eventually married. Madison served as our fourth president (1809-1817). Just a few doors to the east on Walnut Street is the much larger row home of Bishop William White, the first Episcopal bishop and the rector of Christ Church,

that takes only 10 visitors at a time.

A final theme for the Park is Benjamin Franklin. His home site and five other properties associated with him are called Franklin Court. Franklin lived there while serving in the Continental Congress and the Constitutional Convention, and while he served as President of Pennsylvania; he died there in 1790. The house was demolished 20 years after his death. Today the site includes a steel ghost

Franklin Court (1976). *Image Courtesy of Independence National Historical Park.*

Philadelphia. Bishop White's descendants kept most of the furnishings from this house, and through the efforts of National Park Service Curator Charles Dorman, the family has been persuaded to return most of them to the house. To see these two homes, one must register for a tour

structure outlining the site where Franklin's house stood, an underground museum with displays and a film, an 18th-Century printing office and press, an architectural/archeological exhibit, an operating post office, and a postal museum.
The enabling legislation which created

Independence National Historical Park authorized agreements with the City of Philadelphia to restore and operate Independence Hall, Congress Hall, and Old City Hall; with the American Philosophical Society to include Philosophical Hall and Library Hall in the Park; with the Carpenters Company for Carpenters Hall; and with Christ Church for that historic building. Additional legislation in later years gave the same Park status to Old St. George's Methodist Church, Old St. Joseph's Catholic Church, and Mikveh Israel Cemetery.

The Philadelphia Exchange and the Second Bank of the United States are 19th-Century buildings which were included in the Park because of their architectural merit. These Greek revival buildings serve adaptive uses: Park offices and a Portrait Gallery. Other 18th-Century row homes are used for park residences and for administrative purposes.

Finally, perhaps one of the most important buildings was City Tavern, called by John Adams the "most genteel" tavern in America. It was a gathering place for members of the Continental Congress and the Constitutional Convention, and for officials of the Federal government while Philadelphia was the capital 1790-1800. It has been reconstructed on the original site as an operating 18th-Century tavern serving lunch and dinner daily.

The Superintendent of Independence National Historical Park also serves as the Superintendent of several other units of the National Park System in Philadelphia: Gloria Dei (Old Swedes) Church National Historic Site; Edgar Allan Poe National Historic Site; and Thaddeus Kosciuszko National Memorial.

Besides being a place where significant events occurred, Independence National Historical Park has objects within its collections that are worthy of the label "Of National Significance." The Liberty Bell certainly merits this honor, as does the Syng Ink Stand, which was used to sign the Declaration of Independence, the Articles of Confederation, and the Constitution. The "Rising Sun" chair that was used by Washington while he presided over the Constitutional Convention is of great importance. The portrait collection numbers more than 200 paintings of American political and military leaders from the last quarter of the 18th Century, and they were painted from life. Other treasures of Independence include some of the finest antiques and decorative arts that the nation can boast. And everything is available to the public on a daily basis.

Revenue Sharing Bill Signing

The Revenue Sharing Bill was a major piece of legislation which would return a great deal of money to the state and local governments from the federal government. After Congress passed this legislation in 1972, President Richard Nixon decided that he wanted to sign it into law at Independence Hall.

The first I heard of the plan was when I checked into a hotel at Saratoga Springs, New York, where Assistant Superintendent Doug Warnock and I were attending a conference with other park superintendents in the Northeast Region. When I called back, acting superintendent Charlie Mason told me that he had received a call from the White House informing him that they were sending an advance team to the Park the next day and they wanted to talk to the superintendent and no one else. This was my first Presidential visit so I was pretty excited! I made arrangements to fly to Philadelphia from Albany early the next morning so that I could attend an afternoon meeting with the advance team.

The Park, the Secret Service, and the Philadelphia Police were involved in the planning and agreed that the ceremony should take place on Independence Square behind Independence Hall. There would be a large platform for the dignitaries attending and a semi-circle of low bleachers for an invited audience. The press would be near the Commodore Barry Statue so that the President could sign the bill at a desk with Independence Hall as the background.

On October 20th, the day of the signing, the weather was perfect. I greeted the President as he arrived at the Independence Hall door adjacent to the Liberty Bell. He was to sit on the platform with the Congressional leaders and several governors. The signing went as planned, but the most unusual thing in looking back at it was the people who were there: two Presidents and two Vice Presidents. In attendance on the platform were President Richard Nixon, Vice President Spiro Agnew, Minority Leader Gerald Ford, and New York Governor Nelson Rockefeller. Afterward there was a reception on the second floor of Independence Hall, where President Nixon again said "thank you" for our efforts by giving me a pair of cuff links. A week later, I received a

President Richard M. Nixon and Hobie in Independence Hall (October 29, 1972)

nice letter of appreciation from him.

Little did I realize that he was the first of five Presidents of the United States whom I would greet as Superintendent of Independence National Historical Park.

B. The Bicentennial Projects

Second Floor of Independence Hall

The restoration and refurnishing of Independence

Hall took two decades. There were two reasons for the extended project: the funds were of such magnitude that the National Park Service was only willing to take it in small bites, and the research that it required was complicated and time consuming. Restoration research on historic buildings was in its infancy and the Independence Hall project brought about new discoveries and techniques. The people doing

Independence Hall, Long Gallery (ca. 1897-1923) Photo by C.S. Bradford. *Image Courtesy of Independence National Historical Park*

the research, such as Charles E. Peterson, Lee Nelson, Penelope Hartshouse Batcheler and John Milner, were pioneers in the field. They were not only concerned with returning the building to its original appearance (complicated by previous restoration attempts) but also with its structural reinforcement, and the addition of climate control equipment that would help perpetuate the building and its furnishings. All of this work was accomplished while hosting thousands of visitors

who came through the building.

The refurnishing of an historic building like Independence Hall also requires extensive research to develop a furnishings plan. Even with a plan, acquisition of the objects may take many years. Some of the National Park Service's most prominent historians, such as Edward Riley, Martin Yoelson, Sydney Bradford, and John D. R. Platt, worked on the Independence Hall research. David Wallace, John Milley, and Charles Dorman accomplished the curatorial research. The project received early support from General Federation of Women's Clubs, which provided nearly $210,000 for the furnishings on the first floor.

When I became Superintendent of Independence National Historical Park in the fall of 1971, the second floor restoration had been completed except for some of the flooring and the painting. There were no funds for the furnishings. My predecessor, Chet Brooks, had made a friendship with Mrs. Eleanor Spicer, who was campaigning to become President General of the National Society, Daughters of the American Revolution. Mrs. Spicer's campaign featured "A Gift to the Nation," a $180,000 contribution to the National Park Service to furnish the second floor of Independence Hall. Shortly after her election, she brought several of her advisors to see the space. John Milley and Charles Dorman had some plywood tables made and covered them with green baize cloth. Chairs were brought from other places in the Park, so when the ladies arrived they had an impression of how the completed room would look. Mrs. Spicer and her team went forth to raise the money. Their plan was to ask each State Society and each chapter to raise $1.00 per member; that would total just over $180,000.

One of the issues that we resolved after lengthy discussion was how best to recognize the DAR for their gift. We did not wish to erect signs in this important historic building which had been faithfully restored and refurnished. Neither did we want our staff that was leading visitor tours to digress from the historical story they were presenting in order to tell them about the DAR gift. This could backfire and create negative feelings toward the donor. We finally decided that we would make a leather bound book which would appear to be part of the furnishings: it would lie on the large table in the Governors Council Chamber. We listed in the book all of the vital data about the gift and even listed each DAR Chapter that had participated. Anytime a DAR member, or anyone else for that matter, asked about the gift, we would share the book with them.

In the spring of 1972, I went to Washington to

get the first payment, and this was sufficient for Milley and Dorman to go to work on the project. In fact, by taking things from storage and other furnished rooms, and by draping cloth over plywood, we were able to reopen the second floor on July 4, 1972. The Independence Day speaker was L. Patrick Gray, Director of the Federal Bureau of Investigation (FBI), but the highlight of the day was the reopening. Mrs. Spicer participated in the program, as did William Thornton, who represented the National Park Centennial Commission. This year, 1972, was also the centennial of the establishment of Yellowstone, the world's first National Park. The DAR funding was completed in 1974, when National Park Service Director Ronald Walker and

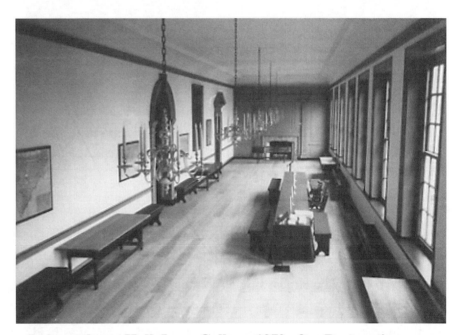

Independence Hall, Long Gallery, 1972 after Restoration. Photo by Warren McCullough. *Image Courtesy of Independence National Historical Park*

myself attended the National Society, Daughters of the American Revolution Continental Congress, where we were able to thank that impressive gathering for their "Gift to the Nation."

After the completion of the restoration and refurnishing of the Second Floor of Independence Hall, it occurred to us that the Long Gallery should be available for use beyond the normal daily guided tours. After all, the Long Gallery of the

Pennsylvania Governor Richard Thornburgh unveiling the New Hampshire Map which completed the Furnishings Plan for the Long Gallery, with Hobie and Addie-Lou

Pennsylvania State House (Independence Hall) is twenty feet wide and one hundred feet long, and was probably the largest single room of any building in the Colonies. Today we would call it a multi-purpose room, and historically it was used for banquets, musicals, meetings, receptions and official functions of all kinds. We could make the room "live" by putting those functions back into the restored room, but we had to be careful not to open it up to any and all activities.

Our staff developed a policy for the use of the Long Gallery that was limited to activities and events that had been held there prior to the year 1800. For example, the Mayor of Philadelphia had held official ceremonies in the room and it had been used by the Masons, so these uses qualified under the policy. Besides the several events that qualified, it occurred to us that there may be an activity from time to time that was so important that it should be held in the Long Gallery. For such an activity, only the Governor of Pennsylvania or the Secretary of the Interior could grant exception to the 18th-Century precedent. Independence Hall was the seat of the Colonial and State government of Pennsylvania, and the Governor's office was adjacent to the Long Gallery, so historically he managed the room. Of course, the Interior Department now manages the building, so the Secretary or his agent (myself) could also approve activities there. None of the modern activities that we might approve could have a detrimental effect on the preservation of the building. Also, any activity that was held would have to be at the expense of the sponsor.

I asked the Independence National Historical Park Advisory Commission to review the policy, and with few changes they recommended it. Even with a policy for the use of the Long Gallery, we did not advertise the fact that events could be held there. It was convenient to have a policy that would prohibit the inappropriate use and it kept the Superintendent from arbitrarily deciding what activities he would approve or disapprove.

One of the first uses for the room was as the place to sign the Articles of Incorporation of the Friends of Independence National Historical Park (FINHP; 1972). During the same ceremony, the agreement between the Friends and the National Park Service was executed. In September 1974, President Gerald Ford attended a small cocktail reception for the Governors of the first 13 states, who had gathered to celebrate the bicentennial of the First Continental Congress.

Afterward, he crossed Chestnut Street to a large tent on Independence Mall for a banquet and speech. During the reception, when President Ford asked his aide for a drink, the aide went to three different bars for the President's drink. He then brought three drinks to President Ford and he selected one of the three. I suppose that this was a security measure that would reduce the possibility of someone giving the President something that he should not have.

for the participants of the filming of the television series, "The Constitution: That Delicate Balance" (1985). In this case, Fred Friendly of Media and Society Seminars (formally of CBS News) requested the Long Gallery for a reception the night before they would begin filming the series. The participants included former President Gerald Ford, Justice Potter Stewart of the Supreme Court, several Congressmen and Senators, Dan Rather, Jim Lehrer, several appellate court justices, and numerous notable lawyers. I could have easily approved the after hours use, but I suggested to Fred that he call Governor Dick Thornburgh and seek his approval, since he would be in attendance. One time, I might have stretched an approval when

President Gerald Ford at the Liberty Bell (September 6, 1974)

Through the years a number of very special events have taken place there, including a reception in 1988 in honor of Lech Walesa, the President of Poland. One of my favorites was the reception

my friend and Park supporter, Isadore Scott, asked if the Board of Directors of Washington and Lee University could meet in the Long Gallery. This Virginia school had a tradition of holding a board meeting periodically in Philadelphia. I suggested that if they could meet between 8:00 – 9:00 a.m. in Independence Hall, then when we opened to the public, they would go to another space nearby; we could work it out. I came in early on Saturday morning and opened up for them. They had a role call and a brief ceremony, and by 9:00 a.m. they were deliberating at another location. The Directors were thrilled and there was no cost or inconvenience for the government. Because I had assisted them with this honor, the Chairman, Jim Balangee, gave me a bottle of 1917 Madeira.

Lech Walesa, President of Poland, with Addie-Lou and Hobie (November 19, 1989)

Second Bank of the United States

During the War of 1812, the United States financial and monetary programs were in such disorder that the Congress authorized the charter of a national bank, called the Second Bank of the United States. Like its predecessor, the First Bank of the United States, it would be the cornerstone of the Federal fiscal policy, serve as the United States depository, and regulate the currency. The charter would last for twenty years and the bank would be located in Philadelphia, with several branches throughout the country. The Second Bank began operation on January 1, 1817. It had two short-term presidents, but in 1823, Nicholas Biddle became the third President and operated it until 1836, when its charter expired. A new bank building was designed by Philadelphia architect William Strickland and built between 1819 and 1824. This building, the Second Bank of the United States, is one of the finest examples of Greek Revival architecture in America.

Under Biddle's leadership the bank became one of the most important financial institutions in the world, but it also became the center of disagreement between Nicholas Biddle and President Andrew Jackson. Jackson vetoed the bill to renew the bank's charter, so after 1836 it ceased to exist. The building continued to serve as a bank under Pennsylvania charter for a time. In 1845 it became the Philadelphia Customs House and, after 1935, a Federal office building, until it was acquired by the Park.

From the early planning of Independence National Historical Park, it was always contemplated that the Second Bank building would be part of the Park. It was important to save the building because of its architectural merit, and the interior could serve an adaptive use. A succession of plans saw it as an office building for park staff, a visitor center, and a museum to display the Park's magnificent portrait collection.

The collection began in the early 19th Century when the City of Philadelphia both commissioned and acquired portraits of famous personalities. Philadelphia had developed an awareness of its place in history and by 1854 the city had purchased the Peale Museum, which included 85 portraits of leaders in the American struggle for independence and the creation of the United States. For 45 years, Charles Willson Peale

South Facade of the Second Bank of the United States. *Image Courtesy of Independence National Historical Park*

had painted portraits of "worthy personages," and they hung on the second floor of Independence Hall during the years that Peale's Museum was there. A second artist, Englishman James Sharples, had toured America in the late 18th and early 19th Centuries, and he also had painted the portraits of the heroes of the new nation. His works were pastels that measured seven inches by nine inches, and they recorded the details of the person sitting for the portrait. A national museum was established in Independence Hall just before the 1876 Centennial celebration, and the Sharples collection and many more works, totaling 113 portraits, were added to the City's collection.

This amazing collection was displayed in Independence Hall when the 1948 legislation authorizing Independence National Historical Park passed. Through the agreement between the

National Park Service and the City of Philadelphia, the buildings on Independence Square and their collections were turned over to the National Park Service for management, restoration, and display. Since that transfer, through gift and purchase, the National Park Service has added significantly to the collection. Today the collection represents more than 200 political and military leaders of the last quarter of the 18th Century. Almost every person the visitor learns about in the other buildings within the Park can be seen in the Second Bank in a portrait painted from life by a well-known artist. The Park, in cooperation with the American Philosophical Society, has published a catalog of the collection.

Restoration of the Second Bank building took 12 years, beginning in 1960. The work went rather slowly because of the lack of money and the complexity of the building. The first problem to be resolved was to stop the deterioration of the Pennsylvania Blue Marble columns of the North and South facades. Because of the quality of the marble and the effect of acid rain, large chunks of stone had fallen off the columns. The introduction of heating, ventilating, air conditioning, and climate control to this 50,000+ square feet stone building was another major problem. Finally, there was the problem of dealing with a large copper roof with a complicated system of rain conductors located within the walls of the building. Some years showed major progress while others almost none. By 1972 the bicentennial funds began to flow, which provided for the interior work required for mounting the exhibit called "The Faces of Independence."

Director of Museum operations John C. Milley took the lead in putting together the exhibition with David Wallace of the National Park Service's Harper Ferry Center assisting. Of course, everyone on the curatorial staff was involved in one way or another. The Collection was organized into subjects, and each category was assigned a room in the building, with the large Main Banking Room reserved for the signers of the Declaration of Independence and the Constitution. As the work progressed, we realized that the gallery was going to be the first of the bicentennial projects completed, so it was important that we plan a significant opening. Milley and I agreed that we should ask the Friends of Independence National Historical Park to assist us in putting it together. We also agreed to schedule the opening during the observances of the bicentennial of the meeting of the First Continental Congress, September–October 1774. The opening reception

and dinner were held on October 13, 1974, with the building opening to the public the following day. The details of this event are included in this book under the heading "Friends of Independence National Historical Park." One of the guests at the opening, Clement Conger, curator of the State Department and the White House, stated after

Second Bank of the United States. "Officers of the Revolution" Gallery. *Image Courtesy of Independence National Historical Park*

viewing the exhibition, "It is the greatest event in American portraiture I can remember."

The Portrait Gallery was a great success, a serendipitous experience for the thousands of Park visitors. Among its admirers were Queen Elizabeth II and Valery Giscard d'Estaing (the

President of France) and many other luminaries. After 11 years, the exhibiting and carpets were beginning to show wear, and John Milley began to rethink the design, so we closed the gallery and utilized the prestigious space for the blockbuster exhibit "Miracle at Philadelphia." Many of the portraits were utilized in this exhibition about the Constitution. "Miracle" would be in place for the Bicentennial of the Constitution, 1986-1987; then we would reinstall the portraits, utilizing all of the knowledge that we had gained from the first installation.

"Miracle at Philadelphia" was a magnificent exhibition and the Second Bank was the perfect venue in which to present it. When "Miracle" was dismantled, the planning was underway for the reinstallation of the portraits that are now in place again.

First Bank of the United States

Our new country had great problems with its financial and monetary system, which led Secretary of Treasury Alexander Hamilton to urge Congress to Charter a national bank. It was formed in 1791 with a charter which would expire in 20 years.

A building for the First Bank of the United States was erected 1795-1797 at 120 South Third Street. The restoration of this neo-classical building was one of the bicentennial projects of the Park. Three sides of the building were brick, but the Third Street façade was marble. The pediment above the tall columns was of carved wood that was painted.

It is interesting that the wooden pediment has suffered less through the years from the elements than have the marble columns.

With all of the projects we had underway, we were only able to complete the exterior restoration of the First Bank; a shortage of time and money kept us from completing the interior adaptive use. The third floor became the Park library and offices for the historical architects, while the second floor served as offices for the curators and historians. The first floor was to have held an exhibition about the Executive Branch of government. An exhibit and film would have told of the beginnings of the cabinet and the development of the executive branch, as Congress Hall does for the Legislative Branch and Old City Hall does for the Judicial Branch. A short film was completed but time and money required that we postpone the exhibits until later.

Nevertheless, the building served us well in a variety of ways. It was the site of a great party by the Friends of Independence at the premiere of the Visitor Center film *Independence*. There was a wonderful dinner with entertainment by Fred Waring and his Pennsylvanians. During 1976, the first floor was the venue for the drama *Spirits of 76*, which was presented three times each day.

After 1976, we did not have the money to complete the Executive Branch exhibits, and we rather enjoyed having a multi-purpose space for programs and activities. The space was used for an exhibit of the gifts given to President Gerald Ford during the bicentennial. The exhibit included treasures given by world leaders, but also quilts from small towns and even a large board of the Declaration of Independence made from letters from alphabet soup. The Gay and Lesbian Task Force had an art exhibition there, as did the Philadelphia Wedgewood Museum. Both *NBC News* and *The McNeil-Lehrer Report* originated from there on different occasions. The building was constantly in use, but the luncheon for Princess Alexandria of Great Britain was my favorite event. The building seemed to serve us and the community well, so we decided to forgo the Executive Branch exhibit in hopes that it would be sufficiently covered in other buildings.

The Film *Independence*

The new Independence National Historical Park Visitor Center, designed by Cambridge Seven Associates, was to be a spacious expo-type building that would serve thousands of visitors each day. It was a modern brick-and-glass structure that was effectively landscaped and certainly would not be mistaken for one of the park's historic buildings.

The principal orientation and interpretive exhibit in the building was to be a film that would be shown in two 350-seat theaters. It could be shown to 1,400 people per hour. The projector equipment was commercial quality and the 35-mm film was projected on a screen the size of a billboard.

The National Park Service was prepared to spend more money on this film than on any audiovisual program it had ever produced. A request for a proposal was sent to established filmmakers and production companies in the industry, and the response was excellent. The actor Gene Kelly was very interested in the project and he invited me to have lunch with him at a friend's house in Society Hill to discuss the project. During our meal, he outlined his thoughts about putting a team together to respond to the proposal.

Film and exhibits planning and production for the National Park Service are managed by its Harpers Ferry Center in West Virginia, so they evaluated the responses to the proposal. Twentieth Century Television Production, under the leadership of Lloyd Ritter, was selected to produce the film. Ritter had written the script with the Park Service's historical guidance. The title *Independence* was given to the film, which would tell the stories of our nation's birth as illustrated by the Independence National Historical Park buildings. The purpose of the film was to provide the public with an engaging introduction to the park's history prior to visiting the buildings. Such an introduction would allow visitors to understand how each building fit in the overall story of American's independence. The film would also allow our guests to experience a virtual 18th-Century setting for the buildings they would soon visit surrounded by 20th-Century people.

One of the reasons that the bid by Twentieth Century and Ritter was successful was because it included the skills of renowned actor-director John Huston. The cast was also superb, with Patrick O'Neil as Washington, Eli Wallach portraying Franklin, Pat Hingle as John Adams, Ken Howard playing Jefferson, Ann Jackson playing Abigail Adams, and other well-known character actors. It was John Huston's involvement that had enticed them all to be a part of our particular project.

Huston's staff led me to believe that to make the film, he would take over Independence National Historical Park, even closing buildings in order to shoot scenes. The closure of buildings concerned me, especially that of Independence Hall. I was acutely aware that many of our guests would be

action came to my mind: I would call him "Sam" and the great filmmaker would be neutralized by the perplexity of not knowing how to deal with a hillbilly who didn't know the difference between Sam Houston and John Huston.

Two days before the filming was to begin, Mr.

Film Director John Huston (Filming *Independence* in 1975) and Hobie

making once-in-a-lifetime visits to Philadelphia, and I did not want the filming to cause them to miss experiencing the place where our nation was born.

A war of wills between Huston and myself seemed inevitable. I was steadfast in my resolve to keep the park open to the public throughout filming. But what could I do to avoid being overwhelmed by a personality and talent as large as John Huston? A plan of what I thought was clever and ingenious

Huston called and invited me to come by his hotel for a drink. "Here it comes," I thought. He's going to ask me to turn the park completely over to him. It was a delightful surprise and relief when he extended me a gracious welcome and described what a privilege it was for him to make this picture. We discussed the schedule and other details of the shooting and he said he would respect our decisions about the use of buildings. In fact, our meeting went so well that I confessed to him that I had been concerned about our working relationship and had planned to call him "Sam." He had a good laugh about my cunning plan and invited me to call him "Sam." Which I did. As it turned out, the entire cast and crew of *Independence* joined Huston in their sense of pride to be involved with such a special project. This extraordinary respect for the story was exemplified during a midnight shooting of a scene in the Assembly Room inside Independence Hall. Eli Wallach, who was portraying Benjamin Franklin, had just finished his fourth take of his comment about the Rising Sun Chair. This is the chair George Washington sat in while presiding over the Constitutional Convention. On the day the delegates signed the Constitution, Franklin referred to the carved half-sun on the back of the President's chair as a rising rather than a setting sun. This was a high moment in the film and Wallach wanted it to be just right. Huston thought that take number four was perfect. Everyone else agreed with the director's assessment because they were tired and wanted to go to bed. But Wallach pleaded for one more take, and the director, cast, and crew finally gave in. Wallach was right. His extra effort captured the weighty moment and produced a performance that would have made Franklin proud.

Despite my original objections to the closure of Independence Hall, I relented after realizing that shooting for weeks after the park had closed at night would not produce the results needed for the film to succeed. We agreed to close Independence Hall for one day of filming. Much to my astonishment, instead of being a disappointment, we were able to turn the closure of Independence Hall that day into a memorable event for our visitors. Arrangements were made for a large television screen to be placed outside Independence Hall with a feed from the film set so that visitors could watch the famous actors performing inside the building. The park's rangers stood beside the screen, giving a running commentary with historical information about the scenes being shot. There were many visitors to the park over the subsequent years who would tell us that they were there on the day *Independence* was being filmed in Independence Hall and explain to us that being there that particular day was a cherished memory.

On the last night of shooting, Huston called everyone together in Congress Hall. He said that filming was almost finished but that there was another half day of work needed to capture one final scene. The National Park Service had exhausted its budget for filming and there were no additional funds to pay for the extra work. Huston made an emotional and stirring appeal to his cast and crew, stating that America had given them all so much. "You are now in a position to give back," he said. He concluded that he was willing to donate his time to complete the film for the bicentennial. Huston's speech worked. The actors involved said that they could make some telephone calls and rearrange their schedules. The crew knew that their union would frown on their working for free, but they would ask that an exception be made for this special situation. The next day everyone was on set and the scene was filmed.

About a year later I tracked down John Huston in London to invite him to Philadelphia for the premiere of *Independence*. I placed a call for him at his hotel. When he answered the phone, I said "Sam." I knew that I had made a friend for life when he replied without any hesitation, "Hobie!"

Old City Hall

This beautiful brick building just east of Independence Hall at the corner of Fifth and Chestnut Streets was completed in 1790. The first floor contains a large lobby, the Mayor's office and the Mayor's Courtroom. The courtroom occupies more than half of the first floor and has a balcony for courtroom spectators. The second floor contains space that was used for municipal offices.

It was in the Mayor's Courtroom that the Supreme Court of the United States heard its first case in 1791. The United States District Court and the Supreme Court continued to use the building until the Federal government moved to Washington, D.C., in 1800.

The exterior restoration of Old City Hall required only a small amount of work. However, the inside needed a greater effort in order to re-establish the original room spaces on the first floor. The second floor was completed as an open space.

When visitors entered the lobby on the first floor, a ranger met them and they could look at the exhibits in the lobby area until the courtroom door was opened. Inside they saw an audiovisual show that utilized slides, film and audio. During the 12-minute program, a supporter and an opponent argued the merits of the court and talked about its early years. At the conclusion of the program,

visitors left the courtroom by way of the Mayor's Office, which contained a few simple exhibits. Over the years I had the opportunity to show the courtroom to several Justices of the Supreme Court, including Chief Justice Warren E. Burger and Chief Justice William Rehnquist.

The second floor was used for exhibits to tell the story of Philadelphia, the Capital City, 1790-1800. Since the space was left open, the exhibits were planned in an effective way so that the visitors felt as if they were walking through the streets of old Philadelphia. The subjects covered included education, medicine, music, religion, and entertainment and community activities. During that decade, Philadelphia was the second largest English-speaking city in the world. The exhibits were removed in 1986 and the space was used for the Magna Carta exhibit in 1987.

During the time that there were no exhibits being shown on the second floor, we used the space for a variety of activities, including a reception by the Prime Minister of Malta, a press conference for former President Jimmy Carter, and a press conference for the Dalai Lama.

About July 12, 1988, I received a telephone call from the State Department telling me that the Prime Minister of Malta was visiting in Washington and that he had expressed a desire to come to Philadelphia. They did not have a clue as to why he wished to come and I told them that I knew. He wanted to see the Liberty Bell, because John Pass, who had helped recast the bell and had left his name on it, was a native of the Isle of Malta. When the party arrived two days later, it included the Prime Minister, Malta's Ambassador to the United Nations, the Ambassador to the United States, and the Minister of Foreign Affairs. With press and dignitaries, I gave the group a brief talk at the Liberty Bell, and then the Prime Minister said that every school child on Malta knows about this Bell because one of our natives cast it. Its message of freedom is ours, as well as yours. Following a visit to Independence Hall, the Prime Minister hosted a reception for invited guests on the second floor of Old City Hall.

President Jimmy Carter was given the Philadelphia Freedom Medal on July 4, 1990, in a ceremony at Independence Hall. With the medal came a stipend of $100,000 which could be used as he wished. After the ceremony, President Carter held a press conference on the second floor of Old City Hall to tell how he planned to use the

award money. While we were killing time after the ceremony, waiting for the time for the press conference, I asked President Carter if he would like to climb the tower of Independence Hall. We went up behind the faces of the clock to the Centennial Bell. While we were taking in the view, he asked if I knew of any other president who had done this. I said no, and when he opened his press conference later, he said that he was thrilled to be the first U.S. President to go to the top of the Independence Hall tower.

One of my favorite visitors to Independence National Historical Park was the Dalai Lama, who came on September 27, 1990. I met him first at the Liberty Bell and gave him a talk in English, which he mostly understands, but he keeps a monk close to him in case he needs clarification with a word. I asked if I could attach

The Dalai Lama and Hobie at the Liberty Bell (September 22, 1990)

a small Liberty Bell pin to his robe and he said certainly. He then turned to the press and flashed a "V" for victory sign with his hands. I was impressed with the size of the crowd behind the barricades en route to Independence Hall. They were probably 90 percent Caucasian. Inside Independence Hall, the Dalai Lama, Mayor Wilson Goode and Philadelphia Archbishop Anthony Bevilacqua joined me behind the railing, while the photographers and the party of monks stayed outside. After I gave the talk and he explored the room, I said that we would now go to Congress Hall. The Dalai Lama asked if he could have a minute and he began a chant with his monks joining him. He was offering a prayer in the room where our nation was born. We all had a lump in our throat.

Then we went to Congress Hall and talked about the decade that the Congress met in this building and the place in which John Adams became our second President. Then in a brief ceremony, Mayor Goode gave the Dalai Lama the Philadelphia Bowl and Archbishop Bevilacqua greeted him on behalf of the Catholic Church. Then the Dalai Lama spoke. This place meant so much to him because he wished to return to Tibet and establish a democracy. This is a major change from the past because all Dalai Lamas have been both the religious and secular leader of their country.

Afterward we went to the West Wing Reception Room to await the time for the press conference on the second floor of Old City Hall. My wife Addie-Lou (my second wife) and I sat beside him during tea, and we asked him if we could have someone take our picture with him. He was delighted and, standing between us, he held our hands in the air for the photo. We used it on our Christmas card that year. I also gave him a number of books of the writings of Thomas Jefferson, whom he liked.

The press conference lasted for a half hour and he mostly answered questions. During my time with him I felt that I was in the presence of someone who is holy.

City Tavern

Built in 1773 by subscription of the "principal gentlemen" of Philadelphia, City Tavern was a proper social center for the second largest English-speaking city in the world. Its patrons could enjoy drinking a punch, dine, join in song and dance, or even transact business. When John Adams came to Philadelphia in 1774 to attend the First Continental Congress, he referred to City Tavern as "the most genteel" tavern in America. The Tavern included several large meeting rooms, lodging rooms, two kitchens, and a bar. It was said to have been furnished in the style of a London tavern with a coffee room that was stocked with English and American newspapers.

City Tavern was soon caught up in the movement for independence when in May 1774 a group of radicals meeting at the Tavern began to push Pennsylvania in that direction. When the First Continental Congress came to Philadelphia in September of 1774, they had their first meeting at City Tavern before adjourning to Carpenters Hall. It has been suggested that for the next 26

Bank of Pennsylvania, on South Second Street, Philadelphia (with view of City Tavern). Engraved and published by William Birch, 1804. *Image Courtesy of Independence National Historical Park*

years, decisions were made at City Tavern but only became official later at Carpenters Hall, Independence Hall, or Congress Hall. But whether it was in war or peace, the great and near great enjoyed the services of this most agreeable facility.

After the government moved to Washington, D.C., in 1800, some of the luster was removed from the Tavern. Then a new idea called "hotels" began to be built and the old Tavern went out of style. For a time the Tavern catered to the merchants that were doing business nearby, but the old glamour was now gone. In 1854, the building was demolished.

Beginning in the 1940s, plans for the development of Independence National Historical Park were made and remade. All of the plans included the reconstruction of City Tavern. One plan called for a museum in it because the movement toward independence had progressed from City Tavern to Carpenter's Hall to Independence Hall. Others envisioned it as part of a visitor center complex. When I arrived in 1971, it was seen as an operating tavern serving period food so that the historical experience for visitors in the Park could continue through mealtime.

Certainly enough was known about the historic building to accurately reconstruct it. Over the years, National Park Service historical, architectural, and archeological researchers had

28

ferreted out the location and details of the building. When time came for the design followed by plans and specifications, National Park Service architects were tied up with other projects, so John Dickey, a well-known local historical architect, was hired to do the work. Mr. Dickey did an excellent job, which allowed us to bring the project in on time and on budget. This included rebuilding the tavern and the shop next door, where we placed the kitchen and storage facilities. There was one problem: we had no funds for furnishings.

I became acquainted with Rian Taggart, an interior decorator in Philadelphia, who was a member of the National Home Fashion League. Rian and other members of the Philadelphia Chapter convinced the League to undertake the furnishing of City Tavern as a national project.

Another organization that was looking for a bicentennial project was The Pennsylvania Society of Cincinnati, which had been organized at City Tavern in 1783. The Society of Cincinnati's members are descendents of the officers of George Washington's army. There are fourteen State Societies: thirteen from the first thirteen states and one from France. Since the Pennsylvania Society was organized in the Tavern, we asked them to furnish a meeting room on the second floor. This included their flags and wall hangings, as well as a table and chairs. In 1980, the Pennsylvania Society gave me the honor of granting me honorary membership.

After competitive consideration, the National Park Service awarded Trans World Airlines Services a concession contract to provide food service at City Tavern. TWAS was part of Canteen Corporation. Their contract required that they complete the kitchen equipment and food service requirements. Our curatorial staff helped them select tableware, china, and serving dishes.

In February 1976 we were ready to open City Tavern for business. The plan was to serve an 18th-Century menu in an 18th-Century manner. Some of our plans lasted one day. For example, on the first day there was no ice in the drinks; but there was ice on the second day. We had to make any number of small adjustments in order to appeal to the American public. The City and State health codes required us to make other changes in our food and beverage service. Before adjustments were made, a newspaper food critic gave the tavern a poor review, and that really

City Tavern. Photo by Thomas L. Davies, 1985. *Image Courtesy of Independence National Historical Park*

crippled the local business that TWAS was trying to build. After approximately three years, TWAS sold their contract to a local company called Nilon Brothers. Michael Nilon became the manager and operator of the tavern and was doing so when I retired from the National Park Service in 1991.

City Tavern was a place where tour groups liked to eat as well as the average visitor. One could get lunch, but a candlelight dinner was special. The tavern has hosted many meetings and special

City Tavern interior, 1980. *Image Courtesy of Independence National Historical Park*

events through the years, and I was often invited to address the groups. Bicentennial events such as French Recognition of the United States and the signing of the Articles of Confederation were also held there. On a personal note, my 50th surprise birthday party and my retirement party were also held there.

My favorite story about City Tavern is the night we were having a retirement party for Curator

Charles Dorman. During the course of the evening, my friend Tom McCallum was on his way to the restroom in the basement when he slipped and fell down the steps and landed on a solid brick floor. Tom had recently had cataract surgery, and Jeanne, his wife, was concerned that he had injured his eye. He kept saying that his hip hurt, but we paid no attention to what he said. When the emergency vehicle came to get him, I told Addie-Lou to go to the hospital with Jeanne to help her. Addie-Lou is not good at times like that, so by the time the ambulance pulled away, Tom and Addie-Lou were both lying down in it and Jeanne was trying to help them both.

After I made sure everything was going well at the party, I joined them at Pennsylvania Hospital's Emergency Room. Jeanne and Addie-Lou were in the waiting room when I arrived, but I could hear Tom yelling in the back. The doctor asked Jeanne to come back to discuss Tom's condition and she asked me to accompany her. The doctor explained that Tom had a chipped hip bone and that he would be admitted to the hospital. The antiseptic smell was strong in the room and I began to feel faint. I sat down on a chair and put my head between my legs while Jeanne continued to talk to the doctor. Addie-Lou and I both had been miserable failures in our attempt to help Jeanne.

Before we left to go home, a nurse gave us Tom's clothes in two shopping bags. We walked Jeanne to her car and went home. During the night Jeanne developed a migraine headache. At 6:00 a.m. the next morning Tom called her from the hospital to see if she had taken someone else's clothes with his. She said that she was too sick to check or even talk. Tom called her back about 8:00 p.m. and asked her to please look through his clothes to see if there was a Gucci tie. After a struggle, Jeanne checked and there were clothes which did not belong to Tom, including the Gucci tie and car keys. Tom asked her to bring them in so that the owner could be released from the hospital. Jeanne said that she was too ill, so Tom called a friend, Somers Steelman, and asked him to pick up the clothes and bring them to the hospital.

Now, Somers is a bit of a character, so he loaded his doctor bag (he is certainly not a doctor) with Irish whiskey, picked up the clothes and went to see Tom. He walked into Tom's hospital room and told him that what he needed was a drink and pulled out the whiskey. Tom was in a semi-private room and his roommate was a Damon Runyon-type South Philadelphia numbers runner called "Ponzi," who watched what was happening and told Tom and Somers that he had better stuff to drink than they did. They opened his closet and he had bourbon, scotch, gin, vodka, and lots of wine. Sometime later a nurse broke up the party.

Tom was in the hospital about four days so I was able to meet Ponzi, who was a character.

He gave everyone gifts: watches for the nurses and a pair of diamond earrings for Katie, Tom's daughter.

This was quite an adventure that would not have happened except for City Tavern.

Graff House

During the spring of 1776, Thomas Jefferson rented two rooms in a year-old house owned by Jacob Graff, Jr., at the corner of Seventh and Market Streets. Jefferson had a parlor and bedroom on the second floor of the house, and it was here that he drafted the Declaration of Independence.

On June 7, 1776, Richard Henry Lee of Virginia offered a resolution to the Second Continental Congress declaring "That these Colonies are,

Site of Graff House. Southwest corner of 7th & Market Streets. Photo by Charles E. Peterson, 1947. *Image Courtesy of Independence National Historical Park*

and of right ought to be free and independent States." While the resolution was being debated in Congress, a committee was appointed to draft a declaration "setting forth the causes which impelled us to this mighty resolution." The committee members were Thomas Jefferson, John Adams, Benjamin Franklin, Roger Sherman, and Robert Livingston, but Jefferson was the principal author. On July 2nd the independence resolution passed, and two days later the Congress approved the Declaration of Independence.

One would think that the site where this world-famous and often imitated document was drafted would be worthy of preservation. But the Graff House was demolished in the 19th Century, and at the time of the planning for the Park, there was a small hot dog stand on the site. Since there was no original fabric left of the Graff House, it was not included in the 1948 legislation that authorized the creation of Independence National Historical Park. This was disappointing to Judge Edwin O. Lewis, the principal leader in the creation of the Park, and the Independence Hall Association, because the Graff House was important to their image of the Park. They continued to lobby for its inclusion, and in 1952, additional legislation was passed that authorized the inclusion of the Graff House site in the Park. However, no funds were appropriated to acquire it, which was in large part because the National Park Service was cool toward the project.

By 1964, the Park Advisory Commission and the Independence Hall Association had convinced the Congress to appropriate funds to purchase the property, and in return the Independence Hall Association would raise private funds to

reconstruct the building. Judge Lewis, who was nearly 90 years of age, retired and was succeeded as Chairman of the Independence Hall Association by Arthur Kaufmann. He had been the manager of Gimbels Department Store and was a marketing whiz. He put together a major fundraising effort for the reconstruction of the Graff House.

Graff House, 1976. *Image Courtesy of Independence National Historical Park*

One of Arthur's plans to raise funds was to utilize the estate of Emily Balch, who had left a bequest of several million dollars to create a library within a certain geographic distance of the center of Philadelphia. The trustee of the estate was

32

convinced by Arthur Kaufmann that to create a library of "freedom and independence" adjacent to the Graff House was an appropriate use of the funds. Naturally, government funds for land acquisition and private funds for shared facilities would be commingled in order to get the project completed. As construction of the library neared, its board of directors decided that it should be the Balch Institute and Library and that it should be devoted to the study of ethnic history, particularly the migration of immigrants to America. To everyone concerned, this seemed to fit very nicely with Jefferson's words in the Declaration of Independence.

The firm of John Milner Associates, with Robert A. DeSilets, Jr., as project architect, did the design, plans and specifications, with historical, architectural, and archeological research accomplished by the Park. John McShane was the successful bidder for the construction and did an excellent job.

During construction of the Graff House, I met my pastor, Robert L. Curry of Old St. George's Methodist Church, for lunch at the Union League. We just happened to encounter John McShane there and exchanged greetings and information about the project. John gave me a story about being slightly behind and that he may need some extra time to complete the job. I quickly let him know that 1976 was getting closer and that there was no extra time, so therefore I expected his company to finish the work on time and within budget. Bob Curry was impressed with my firmness with this well-known Philadelphia businessman. This was an attitude that was

necessary to maintain if we wished to meet the bicentennial deadline. Graff House was ready and on budget.

When the visitors came to the Graff House, they entered through the garden between the house and the Balch Institute. They were then directed to a simple theater with carpeted step seating where a ten-minute film about the drafting of the Declaration of Independence was shown. Upon conclusion of the film, they were directed upstairs to see the refurnished parlor and bedroom where Thomas Jefferson had lived. Then as they exited Jefferson's rooms, they walked through an exhibit space showing exploding fireworks, people eating watermelon, patriotic parades, and all manner of things that we do to celebrate Independence Day. Finally, they went downstairs and out of the building. The third floor was office and storage space.

We opened the Graff House in time for the April 6, 1976, visit of Karl XVI Gustav, the King of Sweden.

Thaddeus Kosciuszko National Memorial

Thaddeus Kosciuszko was a young Polish military officer who came to America to volunteer his services to the American Army during the Revolution. George Washington used him to great advantage as a military engineer. His best-known contribution to the American cause was to design the defenses at West Point on the Hudson River. Later, during the American Revolutionary War Kosciuszko became a commander of troops, but his service had a negative impact on his health.

This did not keep him from later participating in the French Revolution, but in the fall of 1797 he returned to Philadelphia. He took a room from Mrs. Relf in a small boarding house at Third and Pine Streets and petitioned the Congress to grant him a pension. During this period he was often confined to his bed and was visited on several occasions by his friend Vice President Thomas Jefferson.

In the spring of 1972, the Director of the National Park Service, George Hartzog, notified me that I should come to Washington to participate in a hearing before the Senate Interior Committee concerning a Thaddeus Kosciuszko National Historic Site. If it became a unit of the National Park system, the site would be managed by the Superintendent, Independence National Historical Park.

Like many of the 18th- and 19th-Century row homes in Philadelphia's Society Hill neighborhood, the house at Third and Pine had deteriorated through the years. Sometime in the 1960s an individual had purchased the house in hopes of turning it into a visitor attraction honoring Kosciuszko. The gentleman was unable to secure funding for his project, so he agreed to sell it to Edward Piszek, owner of Mrs. Paul's, a seafood company in Philadelphia. Ed Piszek was a self-made man who was extremely proud of his Polish heritage. He reasoned that the Third and Pine property should be part of the National Park system and convinced 18 U.S. Senators and 45 Representatives to sponsor a bill in Congress to create a National Historic site.

When a Bill is submitted to Congress and is likely to come to hearing, the Secretary of the Interior has an advisory board that researches the project and advises the Secretary concerning the matter. In this case, the board said that Thaddeus Kosciuszko did make a significant contribution to the American cause during the Revolution, but that the house where he rented a room for five months after the fact did not illustrate those accomplishments. Therefore, the National Park Service would not approve the project. This was the position that George Hartzog and I would present at the hearing.

As we were walking down the hall toward the room where the hearing was to be held, I began to recognize people. I said, "George, there is a crowd here from Philadelphia." He then suggested that I sit behind him and not with him at the witness table. This, he assumed, would keep me out of the fight in case a battle ensued and would protect me against hard feelings with the Philadelphia people.

You would not think that this hearing would draw a crowd, but the room was full and there were an impressive number of witnesses. This was because 1972 was a Federal election year, which also included a Presidential election. So not only were we taking a position against the sponsors of the bill, but the witnesses for support of the bill were everyone who was running for reelection in Congress who had Polish-American votes in their district. At the time there were several candidates in the running for the Presidential nomination and they also wanted to appeal to the Polish-American voters. How could we be so dumb! George Hartzog immediately sized up the situation. He testified that the National Park Service had done some evaluation of the project that was negative but that our work was incomplete and we would like to report back to the Committee in a couple of weeks.

As we were driving back to the Interior Building, George said that we were going to get this building no matter what we say. Since we have said that Kosciuszko made an important contribution to our independence, but we opposed it because it did not meet the criteria for a National Historic Site, what if we went back to them and said it should be a National Memorial and not a National Historic Site. Then we could all be happy. He asked that before he went back to the committee with a report, could I go to Mr. Piszek and propose the name change. During the hearing, Mr. Piszek had said that he would give the 15 x 30 foot property to the NPS. This was too small to accommodate many visitors, so George suggested that he buy the house next door and contribute it also. I went to Ed Piszek with the proposal and not only did he agree but I made a wonderful friend. I also got a lesson from George Hartzog on how the system works. Thaddeus Kosciuszko National Memorial was authorized by Act of Congress on October 21, 1972. Its acreage was .02, the smallest in the National Park System.

Since it was part of the American Revolution, we

immediately requested bicentennial funding. On examining the house after we acquired it from Ed Piszek, we found that there were serious structural problems which required the rebuilding of portions of the walls. Henry Apadaca from the Denver Service Center became the project supervisor. Upon entering the building from Pine Street, visitors would find themselves in a memorial

Ed Piszek and Hobie at the Thaddeus Kosciuszko House

room the size of the first building. The display included flags and a large portrait of Kosciuszko with a label spelling out the purpose of the Memorial. A stairway leads to the second floor and Kosciuszko's bedroom. Museum Curator Bob Giannini did a great job of documentation for the refurnishing of the bedroom. He found a historical painting of Kosciuszko done by Benjamin West in London just before he returned and matched that to an inventory taken during his time there. For example, a crutch, a sofa, and a tablecloth appear in both sources.

After leaving the bedroom, one crosses into the second floor of the second house, where a brief audiovisual program about Kosciuszko is presented to a standing audience. From there, one descends the stairs to an exhibit area that shows genealogical features and man-made structures around the world that were named for Thaddeus Kosciuszko. There are an amazing number of things, such as mountains, bridges and towns named for this freedom-loving Pole. From this room one exits onto Third Street.

We decided that we would open and dedicate the National Memorial on Kosciuszko's birthday in February 1976. I was inside the house in my National Park Service uniform greeting people as they gathered for the outside ceremony. Almost everyone you saw was a celebrity, but I recognized Stan Musial, the Hall of Fame Baseball player, who was of Polish heritage. He was a childhood hero of mine, so I walked over to "Stan, The Man" and introduced myself and told him of my connection to the National Memorial. I was excited, and after a moment he asked me if I would stay where I was for a few minutes. Sure enough, he came back with his wife and said, "Honey I want you to meet this guy, he is in charge of this house, and Independence Hall, and the Liberty Bell...." It was a big deal for me to meet him but he turned it around and made a big deal of me.

Everything went well with the ceremony, and afterward Mr. Piszek provided a wonderful reception at the First Bank of the United States. About six months later a reporter asked me who,

among all the people I had met in 1975, gave me the most pleasure. Without thinking, I said Stan Musial, whom I had known about most of my life. I knew him before I knew of Kings and Queens, and Presidents. The article was printed.

During the fall of 1976, Addie-Lou and I were invited to Ed Piszek's birthday party, which was held in an enclosed tennis court at his home in Fort Washington, PA. I was standing in line to get a drink when I realized that the person standing in front of me was Stan Musial. I touched his shoulder and reintroduced myself. The first thing he said to me was, "I hope that you will forgive me." He said that someone had sent him a newspaper article where I had said that it had been a pleasure to meet him. He had meant to write me a letter. He had forgotten it but he was reminded of it when he saw me. He did it to me again. I wanted to flatter him and he turned it around on me. One hears great things about him being a family person who supports his community. From my brief impression he is the best.

C. Moving the Liberty Bell

In 1751, the General Assembly of the Province of Pennsylvania authorized the purchase of "a good bell of about two thousand pounds weight" for the tower of the new State House, which would be completed within the next year. Even though there was a small bell tied to a tree in the State House yard, Philadelphia needed a larger bell in order for it to be heard throughout the rapidly expanding capital city.

For centuries, bells were used as quick and efficient ways to communicate. A bell could tell the inhabitants when the government would meet, that there was a fire in the city, when an important personage had died, or even call the citizens together to hear the news of the day.

On November 1, 1751, Isaac Norris, Superintendent of the State House, wrote to Robert Charles, an agent for Pennsylvania in London, requesting him to procure a good bell as soon as possible. The reason for the rush was that Norris anticipated the tower to be completed by the following summer and he wished to be able to hang the bell before the construction scaffolding was removed. Inscribed around the bell was to be: "By order of the Province of Pennsylvania for the State House in the City of Philadelphia, 1752." Underneath the inscription was to be: "Proclaim Liberty thro all the land to all the inhabitants there of. Levit XXV 10."

The biblical quotation on the bell was appropriate because Pennsylvania was celebrating the 50th anniversary of William Penn's Charter of Privileges, a government that had produced peace, prosperity, religious liberty, and civil liberty to the colony. Of particular interest was Pennsylvania's tolerance of religious liberty, of which its diverse inhabitants were so justly proud. The entire verse of Leviticus XXV:10 reads "And ye shall hallow the fiftieth year and proclaim liberty throughout the land unto the inhabitants there of; it shall be a jubilee unto you and ye shall return every man unto his possessions and ye shall return every man unto his family" (King James translation).

The bell ordered by Philadelphia's agent, Robert Charles, was cast at the Whitechapel Foundry in London, a firm with a long history and an excellent reputation for making bells. The Pennsylvania bell probably arrived in Philadelphia by ship in late August 1752. Excitement was so great that it was decided to test the bell before it was hoisted up the State House tower. A scaffold was erected and the bell was struck. For some undetermined reason, the bell cracked. Whether it was the fault of the maker or the ringers we may never know, but one thing is for sure: the bell would not ring.

The community's first impulse was to send the bell back to Whitechapel for recasting, but upon checking with the next ship sailing for London, Superintendent Norris found that it was filled with cargo and there was no room for the bell. He then turned to "two Ingenious work-men," John Pass and John Stow, who would undertake to recast the bell in Philadelphia. John Stow was an identified Philadelphia brass founder, but all we know about John Pass is that he was a native of the Isle of Malta.

The bell was broken apart and recast but the sound that it made was not acceptable, so Pass and Stow had to recast it again. This time they added some more copper to the alloy. By the first week in June 1753 the bell was in its place high above the State House.

The inscription on the final casting was much the same as the original, if one allows for abbreviations and misspellings (for example, "Pennsylvania" has only one "N"). There was also an addition on the face of the bell: "Pass and Stow,

PhiLad^A, MDCCLIII" (1753).

The State House bell seems to have settled into a normal routine that one would expect for service in the prominent building in the largest city in America. Certainly the bell was in place when the First Continental Congress met in Philadelphia in 1774. This was the first gathering of representatives from the American colonies to discuss their common grievances against the British Crown. Their meetings were conducted in Carpenters Hall, two blocks east of the State House. There is no record of the bell ringing on that occasion; however, it did ring on April 25, 1775, to summon the people of Philadelphia to hear the news of the battles of Lexington and Concord which began the American Revolution.

Less than a month later, the bell announced the convening of the Second Continental Congress in the State House. These representatives of the 13 American colonies responded to the military engagements in Massachusetts by creating an Army with George Washington as its commander. Later in 1775 they created a Navy and a Marine Corps, but most of the delegates were more willing to fight for their rights as Englishmen rather than as independent citizens of a separate nation. Finally, after a year of frustration, on June 7, 1776, Richard Henry Lee of Virginia presented a resolution that began:

> These United Colonies are, and of right ought to be, free and independent States; that they are absolved of all allegiance to the British Crown and that all political connection between them and the State of Great Britain ought to be totally absolved… .

Lee's resolution was debated throughout June, and on July 2nd it was unanimously passed. A declaration that would justify to the world the reasons for the independence vote was debated and passed on July 4, 1776. The Declaration of Independence was printed that night and distributed to the colonies and the army in the field. On July 8th the State House bell summoned the citizens of Philadelphia to hear the first public reading of the Declaration of Independence.

During the last quarter of the 18th century, the city of Philadelphia and its State House were central to the American struggle for independence and the creation of the United States of America. There were many occasions when the old bell communicated with those involved in momentous events. Before British troops occupied Philadelphia in September 1777, everything that might be useful to them, including the city's bells, was removed and sent into hiding. The State House bell was given refuge in the basement of the Zion Reformed Church in Allentown, Pennsylvania. There it remained until the British evacuated Philadelphia the following June and the bell was returned to the State House.

The bell continued to announce important moments in the life of the city, state, and nation. The conclusion of the Constitutional Convention (1787) and Washington's trip through the city en route to New York to be sworn in as the first president of the United States (1791) were certainly high occasions for the bell. In 1799, the bell's importance was diminished when the Pennsylvania capital was moved to Lancaster; in 1812, the state capital was moved again, to its current location in Harrisburg. Eventually the State House was purchased by the City of Philadelphia. Under new ownership, the old bell continued to ring until it cracked on July 8, 1835, while tolling the death of Supreme Court Chief Justice John Marshall. The bell was used sparingly until 1841, when it cracked further while tolling the death of President William Henry Harrison and was taken out of service.

An attempt was made to restore the bell's voice to enable it to mark George Washington's birthday in 1846. The bell's hairline crack was drilled out so that the rough edges would not rub against each other. This treatment seemed to work for a time, but the bell completely lost its voice when the crack extended into the crown of the bell. By this time the newspapers were referring to it as "The Old Independence Bell."

On the centennial of the bell's arrival in Philadelphia, it was removed from the tower and placed on exhibition in Independence Hall, as the State House became known after the state capital was moved from Philadelphia. A new bell, known as the Centennial Bell, was cast and installed in the tower. The first use of the term "Liberty Bell" for the old bell came from the Friends of Freedom, an abolitionist group that adopted the bell as their symbol of liberty from slavery. The group published many materials utilizing the bell and its inscription to make their point.

For the next several years the Liberty Bell was displayed in a variety of ways in the Independence Hall Assembly Room, the Pennsylvania Supreme Court Chamber, and the room immediately below the Independence Hall tower. In 1885, the bell was taken outside Philadelphia to New Orleans for the World Industrial and Cotton Exposition. It was shipped by train and made stops along the way. Each stop included an elaborate ceremony. When it stopped in Richmond, Virginia, even Jefferson Davis, former president of the Confederacy, got out of his sick bed to see it. In New Orleans, the Liberty Bell was the hit of the Exposition, which only increased its popularity on the return trip to Philadelphia. In following years the bell made trips to Boston, Charleston, and St. Louis. Each trip added to the Liberty Bell's fame. Its final trip outside Philadelphia was to San Francisco in 1915. Moving about the country had taken its toll on the bell's condition. One of its last journeys was to be moved just outside Independence Hall for display on Chestnut Street in May 1919 as a greeting to soldiers returning home from World War I.

The inscription "Proclaim Liberty" cast on the crown of the Liberty Bell has proven a versatile theme. It was selected to celebrate the religious liberty enjoyed by Pennsylvanians. It became a symbol of political liberty because it was a sentinel high above the building where we declared independence and wrote the Constitution. To some, it had a special meaning as a symbol of liberty for those in bondage. As time has passed, the Liberty Bell has become not only one of the best-known symbols of America, but also an important symbol of liberty and freedom throughout the world.

An effort to include Independence Hall and other historic buildings as part of the National Park Service had begun before World War II through an initiative of the Independence Hall Association under the leadership of Judge Edwin O. Lewis, a Philadelphia municipal judge. The war had delayed the effort, but it was resumed immediately after peace was achieved. The endeavor resulted in federal legislation being passed in 1948 that required an agreement between three levels of government: Independence National Historical Park would comprise the equivalent of five city blocks east of Independence Square; the State of Pennsylvania would create Independence Mall State Park, which brought about the demolition of buildings in the three blocks north of Independence Square in order to create an appropriate landscape; and the City of Philadelphia turned Independence Hall and its historic contents over to the National Park Service for restoration and management. This included the Liberty Bell.

Inclusion in the National Park System created an increased awareness for Independence Hall and the Liberty Bell. Since 1917, the Liberty Bell had been displayed on the ground floor of the Independence Hall tower on a Victorian-style iron structure that was shaped like a wishbone. This location worked very well when there were just a few visitors, but as crowds increased, the 20-foot by 20-foot tower room was too small. Additional problems were posed by the tower room serving as a crossroads for visitors navigating Independence Hall while simultaneously learning about the Liberty Bell.

Anticipating major logistical difficulties with the

The Liberty Bell inside Independence Hall, March, 1967. *Image Courtesy of Independence National Historical Park*

setting of the Liberty Bell, Park Superintendent Chester L. Brooks (1968-1971) began planning to move the Liberty Bell out of Independence Hall. Through the cold, logical thought processes of a site planner, the need for the move was obvious. By separating Independence Hall and the Liberty Bell, a better job of interpreting them both could be accomplished. However, because these two popular American symbols had existed together since 1752, separating them was emotionally difficult for the general public to understand and accept.

Chet Brooks's plan called for the Liberty Bell to be placed in a visitor center to be built three blocks to the east of Independence Hall. This location would put the Hall on one edge of the park and the Bell on the other, with many of the park's historic buildings located between its two most popular attractions. The firm of Cambridge Seven was engaged to design the visitor center, with Peter Chermayeff as the lead architect.

The National Park Service promoted Chet Brooks to Northeast Regional Director and on October 3, 1971 I replaced him as Superintendent of Independence National Historical Park. During my first week, I went to the design office at the Washington Service Center for a briefing on the new visitor center, which included space for the Liberty Bell. The building was a quarter of a city block in size, with a mammoth reception and information area, two 350-seat theaters, a sales area and bookstore for interpretive materials, and huge restroom facilities. In front of the building was a 100-foot-high brick tower. The Liberty Bell was to be at the base of the tower, which was connected to the building by an enclosed walkway.

My first major undertaking was to sell the visitor center design to the Independence National Historical Park Advisory Committee and get them to help us secure general acceptance for moving the Liberty Bell. The advisory committee was created by 1948 legislation that authorized the establishment of the park. It had three members recommended by the mayor of Philadelphia, three by the governor of Pennsylvania, three by the U.S. Secretary of the Interior, one from the Carpenters Company, and one from the Independence Hall Association. The purpose of the advisory committee was to advise the National Park Service

on matters that may be referred to them. Since the advisory committee had functioned almost as a board of directors since the park's creation, it had not occurred to them that we might not take their advice!

An advisory committee meeting was called and I asked their opinion on the visitor center project. Peter Chermayeff came to the meeting and gave a presentation on the design. The response was less than enthusiastic, to put it mildly. Some committee members didn't like moving the Liberty Bell so far away from Independence Hall. Others did not like the modern design of the building and thought that it should be "colonial." The committee's chairman, Arthur Kaufmann, did not like Peter Chermayeff and vice versa. In Chermayeff's defense, he was outlining a project that his client, the National Park Service, had already approved, and probably gave the committee the impression that he was presenting a final design for the visitor center rather than asking for their thoughts on a proposed design. For the next several months I served as a very uncomfortable middleman between the advisory committee and Chermayoff as small adjustments were made to the visitor center design.

While we were debating the details of the visitor center, 1976 and the Bicentennial of the Declaration of Independence was drawing ever closer. To best move forward with our plans, we made a public announcement about the visitor center project and the plan to move the Liberty Bell from Independence Hall. The heated debate that was going on within the advisory committee very quickly became a nationwide issue. The question of whether or not to move the

Liberty Bell appeared in newspapers, national news magazines, and even as a questionnaire in the monthly billings sent to members of the American Waterworks Association. Counting the Waterworks questionnaire, I received over 20,000 opinions on the situation, both pro and con.

Because the Liberty Bell actually belongs to the City of Philadelphia, I met with the new mayor, Frank L. Rizzo, and the city representative (a member of the mayor's cabinet who is responsible for commerce, including tourism), Harry Bellinger. The mayor gave tentative approval to the moving of the bell from Independence Hall. Bellinger not only approved of our plan but became a valuable ally and even tried to assist me with the advisory committee. The congressional delegates from Philadelphia in Washington, D.C., were also supportive and we kept them informed as the project moved forward. Also, as a courtesy we briefed Pennsylvania Governor Milton Schapp, Lt. Governor Ernest P. Kline, and members of the Pennsylvania General Assembly.

On April 14, 1972, Isidor Ostroff, a private citizen who had been active in the Independence Hall Association in the 1940s, filed suit in federal court to prohibit the National Park Service from moving the Liberty Bell out of Independence Hall. The suit was filed against the U.S. Secretary of the Interior, the director of the National Park Service, its regional director, and myself, the superintendent of the Independence National Historical Park. By some odd stroke of luck, I was the only one who had to appear in court. One of the most amusing moments of the proceedings was when one of Ostroff's witnesses testified that the crack in the

Liberty Bell represented the Mississippi River and that if we moved the bell the eastern half of the United States would slide into the ocean. This bizarre argument may or may not have influenced District Court Justice John Fulham's ruling that Ostroff could not prohibit the move.

Summer and autumn came and went but the issues surrounding the moving of the Liberty Bell were not resolved. My relationship with the advisory committee chairman and some other members of the committee suffered. Mr. Kaufmann complained to George Hartzog, director of the National Park Service, about my attitude, and a member of the committee told me that I should resign. These were very real and scary threats to a career employee of the National Park Service who dearly loved his job. But I stood behind our plans to move the bell.

The design development for the new visitor center by Cambridge Seven continued because any delay would cause us not to be ready for the bicentennial celebrations. We decided that if we had to eliminate moving the Liberty Bell from the project, we could address the issue later. So in late 1972 we bid the visitor center construction project and awarded it to the winner, Wintz Brothers Construction of Philadelphia.

The National Park Service sent Fred Spencer to the park to serve as the visitor center project construction supervisor. Fred eventually became the lead supervisor for all of the projects that would be completed in the park before 1976. He also became a good personal friend and someone I spoke with almost daily for three and a half years.

We made a good team, maintaining excellent relations with contractors, politicians, and unions to keep the projects moving.

On December 16, 1972, *The Philadelphia Inquirer* printed an editorial that said that the Liberty Bell must be removed from Independence Hall but that it should be moved to a facility on Independence Mall, not to the visitor center. The problem with that idea was that the three-block-long Independence Mall was a State Park and was not managed by the National Park Service.

After a year of public debate about relocating the Liberty Bell to the new visitor center, I received two telephone calls on February 8, 1973: one from my congressman, Bill Green, and the other from Ken Davis in Senator Hugh Scott's office. Both men told me that the Philadelphia congressional delegation had met and decided that the Liberty Bell should not go to the new visitor center. In giving me this news, both callers expressed confidence in me personally, but instructed me that if the bell is moved out of Independence Hall, it must be located in close proximity to the building for which it was cast.

By this time the visitor center with its tower was under construction. What would we do with the space reserved for the Liberty Bell? Architect Peter Chermayeff came up with the idea of a Bicentennial Bell, a gift of the people of Great Britain to the people of the United States on the 200th anniversary of the Declaration of Independence. This Bicentennial Bell could even be cast by the Whitechapel Foundry, the company that originally cast the Liberty Bell. I discussed the idea with the British Counsel General in Philadelphia, Charles Thompson, who was being transferred to London but agreed to pursue the idea when he got home. Chermayeff had once lived in London and had a number of good contacts who were helpful. Even the office of the U.S. Secretary of the Interior got involved. After a few months of urging, the project went forward. Chermayeff then raised the tower to 130 feet and worked with the Whitechapel Foundry to have the ringing equipment installed.

There were two logical sites for a new facility for the Liberty Bell closer to Independence Hall: at the center of Independence Square to the rear of Independence Hall, and somewhere in the first block of Independence Mall in front of Independence Hall.

The main issue against choosing the Independence Square site was that it was the location of the Commodore John Barry heroic-size statue. Barry is called the Father of the American Navy. While the new site for the Liberty Bell was being debated, I was invited by Michael Bradley to attend the annual meeting of the Friendly Sons of St. Patrick. Bradley was a former congressman and a member of the Independence National Historical Park Advisory Committee. He had been a good friend to me during my first two years as the park's superintendent. During the annual meeting's festivities, the dignitaries present were introduced. When it came to Michael Bradley, his offices and accomplishments were mentioned, but his introduction concluded by calling him "the defender of John Barry on Independence Square." The audience of several hundred Irish-Americans went wild. During the applause, the standing Michael Bradley looked down at me and smiled. When he sat down, I whispered to him, "Michael, I got the message." The Irish did not want the statue of their man removed from Independence Square, even for the Liberty Bell!

On June 27, 1973, the National Park Service announced that it favored the Independence Mall site, and on August 30th, Mayor Rizzo announced that he also favored the first block of Independence Mall as the site for the Liberty Bell. After a tour of the site with local leaders and city and state officials, a task force was put together, with Michael Bradley as the chairman, to examine the requirements necessary to move the Liberty Bell across Chestnut Street to Independence Mall.

The three blocks of Independence Mall belonged to the State of Pennsylvania, and the state offered to give the National Park Service permission to build a pavilion for the Liberty Bell. But the National Park Service, as part of the federal government, could not spend money to erect a building on someone else's property. The State of Pennsylvania then offered to give the National Park Service all three blocks of the mall, but it was soon found that bonds had been issued when the mall had been developed to accomplish the work and that the property was put up as collateral for the bonds. The bonds would not be completely retired for 15 years, so the property could not be transferred yet. The solution was to sign an agreement that the National Park Service would manage Independence Mall State Park until such time as the bonds were retired and then the property would automatically transfer in fee.

Meanwhile, a sufficient amount of the bond debt was retired so that the State could transfer in fee the center portion of the first block of the mall, and there the National Park Service could build a separate building for the Liberty Bell.

The way was now clear to move the Liberty Bell, but since a separate building for that purpose was not anticipated, funds had not been appropriated. I huddled with my boss, Regional Director Chet Brooks, and between the two of us and the Washington office the funds were found to design the building. The Philadelphia firm of Mitchell/Giurgola was selected to design the Liberty Bell's building. The design, plans, specifications, and bid documents took approximately a year to complete, but still we did not have the funds to erect the building, which would become known as the Liberty Bell Pavilion.

We had $225,000 appropriated to move the Liberty Bell that we could use to construct the Pavilion. A grant of $93,000 from the William Penn Foundation was awarded for the project. The Independence Hall Association had raised $500,000 toward the construction of the Graff House (where Jefferson lived when he drafted the Declaration of Independence), but we already had that building under contract, so we asked Chairman Kaufmann if he would give us the cash for the Liberty Bell Pavilion and we would give them credit for the Graff House construction. Also, the Knights of Columbus were looking for a project to sponsor, so we asked them to fund $8,000 for the hardwood floor. Little by little and piece by piece we put together the $900,000 needed to erect the Liberty Bell Pavilion. The successful bidder for the construction contract was J.J. White of Philadelphia, who also won the bid to move the bell to its new home.

The Pavilion was modern in design and rectangular in shape. It was mostly glass, granite, copper, and brick with a hardwood floor. It was positioned near Market Street and lowered as

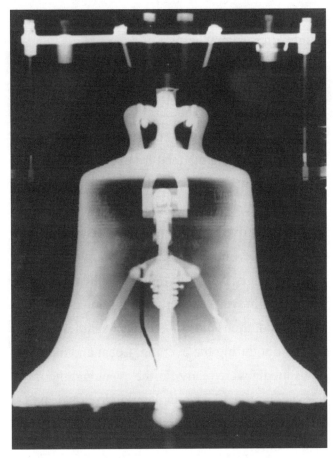

The Liberty Bell; X-Ray Prior to Moving (1975). Photo by Kodak. *Image Courtesy of Independence National Historical Park*

much as possible so as not to interfere with the view of Independence Hall from the second and third blocks of Independence Mall. The inside was shaped similar to a barbell, with the Liberty Bell in the southern room and a staging room of equal size on the northern end. As one walked through

the space connecting the two rooms, one saw the Liberty Bell in the foreground and Independence Hall in the distance. We actually wanted the Pavilion to be as invisible as possible so that one was aware only of the Liberty Bell. Viewing windows made it possible to approach within 20 feet of the bell and hear a recorded message even when the building was not open. This was a flexible building that would work well with the huge crowds of visitors expected during the bicentennial year and beyond.

Onsite construction of the Liberty Bell Pavilion commenced in early March 1975 and was to be completed by December 28, 1975. In addition to a late start, we had to overcome bad weather, a labor strike, and the acquisition of unusual materials, such as large sheets of inch-thick glass. We had to have the Liberty Bell ready for 1976.

While the construction of the Pavilion proceeded, we began to think about how best to safely move the Liberty Bell out of Independence Hall, across Chestnut Street and two-thirds of a block north to its new home. We had already determined that the bell would hang by its trunnions with the wooden yoke. But the cast iron Victorian supports were from another period, so we decided that at its new location the Liberty Bell would hang from two stainless steel posts. The posts would be stronger and much less intrusive than the cast iron supports.

We engaged the Franklin Institute Research Laboratories to tell us how to move the Liberty Bell so that it would not break en route. We were approached by the Eastman Kodak Company to X-ray the Liberty Bell to aid in the Franklin

Institute study. The X-raying, which was done free of charge, was accomplished at night and included the installation of lead sheets to protect anyone who might be walking by Independence Hall during the filming. It was the largest piece of X-ray film that Kodak had ever used.

Every year the park staff worked with the City of Philadelphia to produce events for Freedom Week and Independence Day activities. The person who did most of the work on these projects was Sylvia Kauders, the director of special events for the city. While we were working on planning the July 4, 1975, events, Sylvia expressed to me that she wished she had something special to plan for New Year's Eve to make a strong statement to the world that the bicentennial year of 1976 had begun. I suggested that we move the Liberty Bell at the stroke of midnight. Well, Sylvia is very imaginative and almost immediately had the entire event planned. She titled the event "The Bell Moves at Midnight." When the Centennial Bell in the tower struck midnight, a bright beam of light would climb the Penn Mutual Building behind Independence Hall. When the beam reached the top of the building, fireworks would explode into the air and the front doors of Independence Hall would open, and the Liberty Bell would travel across the street and down the block to its new home.

The funds to physically move the Liberty Bell had been used to build its Pavilion, so we asked the contractor who would move the bell, J.J. White, to undertake the job without cost to us. The move would include lifting the bell from its supports in Independence Hall and lowering it onto a cart specially designed by the Franklin Institute. J.J. White's workers would help push/pull the cart to its new building and then lift the bell onto its new supports. Although we paid J.J. White nothing for the move, he received a substantial amount of free publicity in return. His entire staff showed up in new white hard hats and coveralls with the company name in large letters on them. Nearly every picture taken of the move has the name "J.J. White" in it somewhere!

The local publicity for the event was so great that the media estimated that a million people would be on Independence Mall to witness the move. Parties were being planned for every office that had a window overlooking the mall. The Friends of Independence sponsored a dinner for dignitaries before the move and held a dance afterward at the nearby U.S. Mint. We requested that everyone bring a light or candle to illuminate the mall during the move. To insure the lighting effect that we desired, thousands of chemical candles were passed out during the evening. Local and national news media were ready for the event and the television networks were planning to broadcast live from the mall during their New Year's programming.

We had prepared for everything except the weather. It began to rain during the evening of December 31st, and every hour that passed, it rained harder. The temperature began dropping, and by midnight the rain had turned to snow and strong winds came with the snow. One could hardly imagine worse weather for the fragile and auspicious activities that we had planned. But the show must go on, as they say, and at midnight the front doors of Independence Hall opened and the procession began. In the lead were the fife and drummer of the U.S. Army's Old Guard, followed by the Liberty Bell on its specially built cart. Following the bell in

The Liberty Bell in the Liberty Bell Pavilion. Photo by Thomas L. Davies. *Image Courtesy of Independence National Historical Park*

the procession were Mayor Frank Rizzo, John Cardinal Krol, Secretary of the Army Martin Hoffman, Congressman William J. Green, William and Beth Lyons from the White House, Ron and Paula Coleman of the CIA, actor Lee J. Cobb, and a host of city government and local dignitaries. When my turn came to step out of Independence Hall as part of the procession, I heard one group of the crowd begin to sing "God Bless America"

and others join in, and finally the whole mall was singing as one. Despite the rain, it was estimated that 250,000 people were in attendance. The singing crowd, the lights, and the snow created one of the most emotional moments I have ever experienced.

A wooden ramp had been built over the steps in the front of Independence Hall for the bell to move on its cart, and smaller ramps had been constructed for both curbs of Chestnut Street. A metallurgist holding sensor cups attached to the bell accompanied it along the entire route to detect any further cracking or other damage. When the bell reached its Pavilion, the members of the procession waited in the chamber nearest Market Street while the workmen put the bell in place on its new steel supports.

A specially invited group from the procession then surrounded the Liberty Bell and Cardinal Krol offered a prayer. Lee J. Cobb read an appropriate poem and then we retired from the building. The doors to the Pavilion were then opened so that the public could visit the Liberty Bell in its new home. The Pavilion stayed open all night and through to closing time on New Year's Day.

Addie-Lou and I went to the dance at the U.S. Mint for a while and then came back to the Pavilion to watch the people streaming through the building. The landscaping outside the Pavilion had not been completed, so the ground in front was muddy from the rain and snow. I stood there outside the Pavilion for a few minutes and thought about all the effort of the past four years that made this moment possible. Then I sat down in the mud and cried.

In less than a year, the National Park Service had taken the Liberty Bell, which we didn't own, from Independence Hall, which we didn't own, moved it to a piece of land that we didn't own, and put the bell in a Pavilion for which there was no design or money to build it. I was weeping in the mud and yet the eventful, once-in-a-lifetime Bicentennial Year of 1976 was only a few hours old!

D. Franklin Court

Franklin Court is a combination of features related to Benjamin Franklin and a resource at which to tell the story of this man of unlimited dimensions. It is comprised of five Philadelphia row houses, 314-322 Market Street (although 314 and 320 were never owned by Franklin). Immediately behind 316 and 318 Market, Franklin had his print shop, and behind the print shop he built his house. From Market Street, the house was accessible by a tunnel or carriageway through 316-318 and through the print shop. So Franklin's house stood in the center of the block surrounded by Third, Fourth, Chestnut, and Market Streets.

In the 19th Century, long after Benjamin Franklin's death, the simple Market Street houses were given additions that encroached on Franklin Court. Franklin's house and print shop were demolished and the carriageway was extended from Market Street, over the basement ruins of the house, completely through to Chestnut Street. The new street, called Orianna, gave Franklin's heirs more street-front property, thus adding to the value of his estate.

Benjamin Franklin was a theme in the legislation that authorized Independence National Historical Park; therefore, the Franklin Court site was included in the Park's land acquisition from the beginning. Through the years, the National Park Service and contract archeologists dug the entirety of Franklin Court looking for any 18th-Century remains related to Franklin. They found that a portion of the basement of Franklin's house beneath Orianna Street was intact: anything outside the street right-of-way was lost when buildings with basements were erected. Beneath the 19th-Century addition to the Market Street houses they found the privies and wells of the 18th-Century houses. Very little remained from the print shop, but a significant amount of printer's type was found on the site.

How could we take this altered scene and tell the story of one of the greatest Americans? As badly as we wanted to rebuild the house, there was not enough known about it to do a reasonable job. There was a rumor of a drawing or painting of the house, but nothing ever materialized. However, the common walls of the Market Street houses were intact, and enough could be put together from historical, architectural, and archeological research to accurately restore these buildings.

Based on recommendations by the Park, the Philadelphia firm of Venturi and Rauch was selected to do the design work for Franklin Court. The firm was known for its innovative and creative work but had no experience with historical preservation, so their contract included a requirement for them to associate with a firm called National Heritage, owned by a former National Park Service historical architect, John Milner. The Venturi and Rauch contract also included exhibit design, which required them to associate with the New York firm of De Martin, Morona, Cranston and Downs. We told the designers that they could not rebuild the Franklin house, but it should be marked and its remains displayed. The interpretive message should center on telling about the multi-dimensional life of Benjamin Franklin.

In order to get the project started, we called together a panel of Franklin scholars which included Claude-Ann Lopez from the Franklin Papers at Yale, Whitfield J. Bell, Jr., of the American Philosophical Society, Lyman Butterfield from the Massachusetts Historical Society, Edwin Wolfe II of the Library Company, Robert Spiller of the University of Pennsylvania, author Catherine Drinker Bowen, Edgar Richardson of the Pennsylvania Academy of Fine Arts, and Charles Coleman Sellers, a Franklin scholar. The experts sat at a table in the middle of the Park conference room and the designers, interpreters, engineers, etc., engaged them and listened to them talk about Franklin for some three hours. I had to go to Washington to receive our first check from the Daughters of the American Revolution for furnishing the second floor of Independence Hall, so Assistant Superintendent Jim Sullivan presided and did a great job.

Venturi and Rauch, and everyone else, left the meeting and went to work. They came back in a month with a design concept and a model that was brilliant. The National Park Service loved it, as did the Advisory Committee and the Park staff. Even with a conceptual design, it was obviously going to cost more money than had been appropriated. The exhibits alone would be more complex than any others that the National Park Service had ever done. Chet Brooks and I felt from the beginning that we should support Venturi's plan, but the Chief Historian in Washington, Ernest Connally, swung the decision. He reasoned that others of the founding fathers had their memorials, such as Washington at Mount Vernon and Jefferson at Monticello, so Franklin Court would be Franklin's memorial and it must be of the highest quality.

While the design development went forward, we began to look for money. I went to Washington to visit with Senator Hugh Scott, who was in the midst of budget reconciliation with the House of Representatives. I talked to his assistant, Ken Davis, about Franklin Court funds, and he took the information to Senator Scott. Shortly after I got back to Philadelphia, Ken called to say that Senator Scott felt comfortable in adding $500,000 to the budget for Franklin Court.

We considered using one of the Market Street houses as an operating post office. This seemed appropriate since Franklin had been the Postmaster for the Colonies and the first Postmaster General for the United States. I went to see Philadelphia Postmaster Vincent Logan about a post office at 316 Market Street and he put me in touch with the appropriate officials in Washington. I thought that Eastern National Park and Monument Association might be willing to operate a contract post office, as they did at Jamestown, Virginia. Instead, the

Postal Service was interested in operating a post office and a postal museum and they were willing to contribute $250,000 to expedite our construction costs. We were delighted.

John Yeo, a friend from St. George's Methodist Church, was an officer and founder of the Philadelphia Rotary Club Foundation, and they were looking for a bicentennial project. The Foundation decided that they would undertake the construction of an 18th-Century printing press for 320 Market Street. Their $25,000 contribution not only paid for the press but also allowed us to purchase the type for the press. Philadelphia Newspapers, Inc., was willing to undertake the furnishing of the newspaper office of Benjamin Franklin Bache (Franklin's grandson) at 322 Market Street. Their contribution was $15,000. We requested that the Friends of Independence undertake a $38,000 donation to complete the architectural and archeological exhibit in 318 Market Street. They agreed!

We still had a shortfall, so we finally decided to eliminate $130,000 in exhibits about the Executive Branch from the First Bank of the United States, which we probably would not be able to complete by 1976 anyway. The large open space on the first floor of the First Bank served us so well as a multi-purpose venue for special exhibits, receptions, dinners, and other special programs that we have never since made an effort to do the executive branch exhibits.

When the Franklin Court project was bid, the construction award was made to the R. M. Shoemaker Company, and we could have hardly

done better. Its president, John Ball, who was also President of the Carpenters Company, was extremely agreeable and easy to work with. This was a very difficult and complex project. At one time we had archeologists working over a weekend

Franklin Court Site Prior to Construction Photo by E. M. Riley, April 13, 1950. *Image Courtesy of Independence National Historical Park*

so that the contractor could pour a concrete beam over the site on Monday morning. Another reason for the successful relationship was the quality of Venturi and Rauch's plans and specifications. Construction was underway by the summer of 1974, with plans to open Franklin Court in April 1976.

It was our desire that visitors could enter Franklin Court from both Market and Chestnut Streets. In order to enter from Chestnut Street, the visitor must traverse a 300-foot portion of Orianna Street, which was still an active street on the City Plan. Only an act of City Council could remove it from the Plan, and then the land would revert to the property owner on either side of the street. We wanted to own the street so that we could properly landscape it. I went to the Philadelphia Maritime Museum on the West side of the street and the Charles Kurz Shipping Company on the East, and after assuring them of access to parts of their buildings in emergencies, they each gave us the deed to their half of Orianna Street. I took the deeds to City Council, and the instant the street was removed from the Plan, its ownership passed to the National Park Service.

Thus in April 1976, Franklin Court was comprised of the following elements:

(1) The Court Yard – The ground level landscaped area includes the steel sculpture creating a three-dimension outline of Franklin's house, with viewing ports showing the archeological remains below the ground. The ground floor foundation wall of the house is lined with white stone and on the inside walls are written descriptions of the house carved into black slate. The print shop is also outlined with the same steel as the house. Among the garden plantings is a mulberry tree, like the one that Franklin planted.

(2) Underground Museum – A ramp from the courtyard leads visitors down to a museum at basement level. This museum covers the entire underground of the courtyard except that area where the archaeological remains of the house are located. The museum has a gallery of Franklin artifacts and family portraits. There are major exhibits on Franklin's civic contributions, Franklin the printer, Franklin the inventor, and Franklin on the world stage. The world stage exhibit features changing dioramas of Franklin arguing the repeal of the Stamp Act before the British Parliament, Franklin at Louis XVI's Court seeking French recognition for the United States, and Franklin at the Constitutional Convention. This $300,000 exhibit was the most expensive one ever undertaken by the National Park Service. There is also a telephone exchange where you can call any of 30 people throughout history who had given an opinion of Benjamin Franklin. Finally, there is a 130-seat theater that featured a 20-minute film about Franklin, who is portrayed by Howard DeSilva.

(3) The Market Street Houses – 314 Market Street is a bookstore and restrooms; 316 Market Street has a U.S. Post Office on the first floor and a Postal Museum on the second; 318 Market Street is a house built by Franklin which contains an archeological and architectural exhibit; 320 Market Street is the operating 18th-Century printing press; and 322 Market Street is the Benjamin Franklin Bache newspaper office.

The Post Office was called B Free Franklin because when Franklin was Postmaster for the Colonies, he had the privilege of free mail, so he wrote his name and the word "free" on the envelope; so today, B Free Franklin is used as a cancellation by this post office.

Franklin Court was so large and complex a project that it required total commitment and cooperation by all of those involved. The contractors, the designers, the resource specialists, and the managers worked together so well that we created the star of the Park's bicentennial development program. This hidden and little publicized project was as if one would open a modest jewel box and inside find the Hope Diamond. It was such a surprise and so well received. Through the years it has drawn the third largest number of visitors for Park attractions, just after Independence Hall and the Liberty Bell.

In 1984, the National Endowment for the Arts and the American Institute of Architects began issuing an annual Presidential Design Award for best in building design. The first of these awards went to Franklin Court. At a ceremony in the Indian Treaty Room in the Executive Office Building in Washington, a certificate was presented to Robert Venturi for the design and to me representing the client. The presentation was made by President Ronald Reagan.

E. Friends of Independence National Historical Park

Sometime in the spring of 1972, John Milley, Chief of Museum Operations, came to me and said that a self-portrait of Charles Willson Peale was to be auctioned. He asked if I had any ideas about where we might find funds to bid on it. Certainly there was nothing in our budget for the purchase of an expensive painting. The Park

portrait collection numbered some 200 portraits of political and military leaders associated with the founding of our nation, and Charles Willson Peale and members of his family had painted more than 80 of them. Milley asked if I would allow him to try to raise private funds to purchase the portrait. I encouraged him to proceed.

A few weeks later he told me that he had found someone willing to buy the portrait, but he had found them too late to participate in the auction. John was disappointed, but he suggested that the Park needed a support group like a "Friends" organization that we could depend upon to assist with projects such as this. Again, I encouraged him, and he talked it over with Ann Rowland, the person who had been interested in trying to secure the Peale portrait for us. Ann recruited her friend Susie Ashburner, and John went to some of our Junior League volunteer guides.

Beginning in 1963, Independence National Historical Park had worked with the Junior League of Philadelphia to provide volunteer tour guides for Independence Hall and Congress Hall. A new class of 25 Junior Leaguers was recruited each year to work for six months. In January they began their training with classes one day each week for six weeks. By March 1st, around the time when the spring school groups began to visit the Park in great numbers, each guide would work one day each week. This amounted to five trained guides each day Monday through Friday. This schedule lasted until mid-June, when seasonal rangers arrived and school groups diminished. Some of the volunteers came back year after year. My wife Addie-Lou, who was working at

Independence when I transferred there, began working in this program and actually worked as a volunteer for 27 years.

A number of preliminary meetings with a variety of people took place through the spring and summer. Of particular assistance was John B. O'Hara, a managing partner of Price Waterhouse. On September 17, 1972, in a ceremony on the second floor of Independence Hall, the Articles of Incorporation was signed and an agreement between the Friends of Independence National Historical Park and the National Park Service was executed. Deputy Regional Director George Palmer signed the agreement for the National Park Service. In a brief business meeting, officers were elected and Ann Rowland became the first chairman. Catherine Drinker Bowen, author of the book "Miracle at Philadelphia," addressed the gathering and suggested that there was no higher calling than to preserve buildings and objects that were part of the birth of the United States of America.

In all of the documents, the purpose of the Friends of Independence was "...to assist the National Park Service with the museum and interpretive programs of Independence National Historical Park." The Friends were provided an office space and a telephone within the administrative office of the Park. They could undertake no program that was not approved by the Park Superintendent.

The Friends got off to a modest start by conducting lectures, symposia, and classes about the Park's historical story or its collections. Sometimes basic publications came from these programs.

Each gathering usually included refreshments, which were always homemade. Perhaps you can imagine Mrs. Dorothy Haas (Rohm and Haas), her houseboy, and six volunteers in her kitchen making cheese straws for an evening lecture. After the meeting, they would wash the plastic cups in order to save money.

By 1973, Ann Rowland had declined another term as chairman and was replaced by Alice Lonsdorf, whose relationship to the Park began with the Junior League guiding program. Alice was a great leader and organizer who contributed to the Friends office operation and to increasing its membership. Meanwhile, John Milley received an Addingham Fellowship, and while studying in England he found portraits of James and Dolly Madison by James Sharples in the Bristol City Museum. The Park Portrait Collection included some twenty-four Sharples portraits, so these fit perfectly with our needs. The Bristol Museum had no use for them, so they agreed to sell the pastels for $20,000. The Friends raised the money and acquired them for us.

One of the Park's bicentennial projects was the restoration of the Second Bank of the United States, with the interior being adapted to display the Park's portrait collection. This magnificent Greek revival building would be restored and the exhibition in place by the fall of 1974. I went to the Friends and asked if they would help plan a proper opening. It was important that we do

something spectacular because this was the first of our bicentennial projects to be completed.

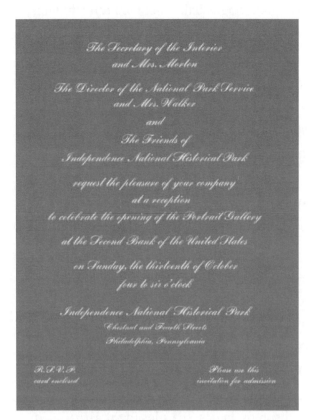

Invitation to the Opening of the Second Bank of the United States

Many committees worked diligently on this project for a year, and they produced the most fantastic opening you could imagine. Fifteen hundred people came to a reception in the Second Bank, followed by six-hundred-fifty for dinner in the partially completed visitor center. A host of dignitaries was on hand, including Director of the National Park Service Ron Walker and Secretary of the Interior Rogers C.B. Morton. This event undoubtedly propelled the Friends into the Philadelphia social whirl and convinced the public that there really was going to be a bicentennial. From this time forward, Philadelphia Inquirer columnist Ruth Seltzer always covered the Friends activities.

I went to Secretary Morton's hotel to pick him

up for the Second Bank reception and he asked me about myself. When I told him I was from Middlesboro, Kentucky, he stated that he was from Louisville and asked me if I knew the Hackney Jellico Grocery Company. He said that his family had flour mills, and as a salesman he had called on Hackney Jellico. I stayed close by his side during the evening in order to introduce him to people he encountered. He was very complimentary about the Gallery and the opening. His last words as he departed were "Congratulations, Independence National Historical Park is in good hands."

Bob Hope was the Independence Day speaker at Independence Hall in 1975. Just before it was time for him to speak, he took my arm and led me off the platform and asked where the restroom was located. The only thing close was the public restroom in the basement of the West Wing of

Secretary of the Interior Rogers C.B. Morton, Mary Carroll, and Hobie at the Opening of the Second Bank of the United States (October 14, 1974)

Independence Hall. Mr. Hope and I stood in line at the urinals in order to satisfy his needs. Several surprised visitors engaged him in entertaining conversation before he returned to the platform to deliver his speech. This experience convinced me that as we did more of these celebrations, we needed a place to gather the participants beforehand and to take care of needs that might arise during a program.

The Park had its security center on the second floor of the West Wing of Independence Hall, and this facility was about to move to a location in the new visitor center. I asked the Friends if they would consider furnishing a VIP Reception Room in this recently abandoned space. Alice Lonsdorf asked Sarah Leary to chair a committee to furnish the room. The committee turned out to be approximately eight of the wealthiest and best-known women in Philadelphia. They had either antiques, money, or taste that could put together such a room as we desired.

The first time I took them into the room, they were disappointed because nothing had been done. The room was just one large open space with institutional green walls. I showed them drawings of the work that our staff would accomplish. There would be two restrooms, a small kitchen, and the large reception area. The ladies got down to business when one said that she could provide the carpet, another had a table and a couch, and one said that she had nothing to provide, but would we take money? The women planned the wall

colors, the draperies, the carpet, and even the china and silver for the kitchen. The final product would equal the State Department Reception Rooms in Washington. Through the years the Independence

Nelson Rockefeller, Governor of New York, and Alice Lonsdorf (October 29, 1974); Creed Black, Addie-Lou Cawood, and Helen Rosenlund in the background)

Hall reception room has served hundreds of world leaders, and I always wished that Bob Hope would return so I could show him what his experience had created.

Other bicentennial projects for which the Friends assisted with the openings were Old City Hall, Franklin Court, the Visitor Center, and the premiere of the film "Independence." At Franklin Court, the Friends even contributed $36,000 to complete the archeological and architectural exhibition at 318 Market Street. When it came time to premiere the film "Independence," searchlights in front of the Visitor Center greeted guests. Three members of the cast were present, along with Gary Everhart, Director of the National Park Service. After a few remarks and a showing of the 26-minute film, the 350 guests crossed the street to the partially completed First Bank of the United States for a reception and dinner. After dinner, Fred Waring and his Pennsylvanians entertained us. A super evening, and again provided by the Friends of Independence.

Lo and behold! A second Charles Willson Peale self-portrait was offered at auction by Freeman's Auction House in Philadelphia. We could not let this one get away. The catalog of the auction carried its value at $60,000. The Friends were ready to back us up to $125,000. We called everyone we could think of who might be interested in the portrait and suggested that it should be in our collection. The Friends called many private collectors they knew. The National Portrait Gallery in Washington even agreed not to bid until we had exceeded our limit. John Milley even asked the auctioneer to identify John Milley as being from the Park. He would not do it until the estimated value was exceeded.

On the day of the auction, members of the Friends filled the auction room. John Milley bid for the Park, and after a few minutes it was down to him and a telephone bidder. Milley bid $60,000, the telephone bidder said $65,000, and John followed with $67,500. The auctioneer said that he had $67,500 from John Milley of Independence National Historical Park. The telephone bidder withdrew, and when the portrait was knocked down to the Park, the entire audience stood and applauded. The Friends came into existence because we had missed a self-portrait of Charles Willson Peale, and now they made sure that we had one. I met the telephone bidder a few years

later and he had really wanted that portrait but said it was best that it go to the Park.

As a service to Park visitors in the summer, the Friends operated a kiosk in the holly garden east of the Second Bank of the U.S. They sold soft drinks, a punch called squash, and ice cream. Of course, they also made a little money for their effort. Students were hired to operate the Tea Garden, as it was called, but any time you came by, there were members/volunteers there to help. Often the service was being provided by a prominent Philadelphian. Even Queen Elizabeth II stopped by the Tea Garden during her walk about the Park on July 6, 1976.

The Friends became well known and appreciated by the community, and this was important to me in building the Park's reputation. The first time I met Drew Lewis (Governor, Senator, and Republican Chairman), he said he felt as if he knew me because he had heard of me through his friends who were members of the Friends of Independence. Naturally, it was important that the Friends and the Park were constantly written about in the Philadelphia newspapers.

From time to time, I had the opportunity to channel projects through the Friends which not only increased their visibility but also made them more convenient to carry out. For example, one day I was talking to Isadore Scott about some research that our curatorial staff had just completed. They had finally been able to identify the design of the Senate Chamber carpet that had been used in Congress Hall.

The United States Senate had ordered an Axminster carpet from England in the 1790s for their Chamber in Congress Hall. It was a magnificent carpet that contained many symbolic elements. The carpet vanished when the government moved to Washington, D.C., in 1800. The only description of the carpet was a written newspaper account that referred to land trophies, sea trophies, and an eagle. After years of on-and-off research, we solved the mystery and wished to have the carpet reproduced. I told Scotty that we could have the carpet handmade in Spain for $25,000, and for another $10,000 we could produce a book about the project. At the time he was on the board of Glenmeade Trust, and he helped us secure a grant for $35,000. I asked that the grant be made through the Friends of Independence so that they could pay the bills without us having to go through government procurement regulations.

On another occasion, after Mellon Bank of Pittsburgh acquired Philadelphia's Girard Bank, the Mellon people approached me about a project that they might undertake to show the community that they cared about Philadelphia. I shared a number of ideas with them, but the one they liked best was the completion of the landscaping in the garden behind City Tavern. For $30,000 they could complete the fences, walkways and plant material in this high-profile space. I asked that they give the money to the Friends of Independence, but that the Park staff would provide the plans and specifications, as well as the project supervision. When the project was completed, the Friends arranged a reception and ceremony with the news media and many dignitaries present. Mellon and the Friends got the credit and we got a completed garden.

Our relationship with Mellon remained strong, especially with its Vice President Richard Torbert. I received a telephone call from Vince Gleason, the National Park Service Chief of Publications in Harpers Ferry, West Virginia, telling me that he had funds to do a poster for the Edgar Allan Poe National Historic site. (I was also responsible for the management of this Philadelphia site.) He wanted to use a Poe portrait by the famous artist Leonard Baskin. Unfortunately, he did not have the funds to buy the art. I went to Dick Torbert to see if Mellon was interested in sponsoring the project. Torbert said "Yes" immediately, not just because Mellon would have its name on a poster printed by the Government Printing Office, but also because as a young person he had acquired a Baskin print and had been a fan of the artist ever since. Mellon also gave a reception for the unveiling of the poster, which Leonard Baskin attended.

The Friends always had superior leadership, beginning with Ann Rowland, and then Alice Lonsdorf, who really built the organization into a force. Alice was followed by Mary Carroll, an aggressive bundle of energy who was responsible for major contributions to the Park's publications and interpretation programs. Mary actually helped write a popular Park guidebook, and the Friends also produced a coffee table book called *Treasures of Independence*. This book had beautiful pictures and was written by members of the Park curatorial staff.

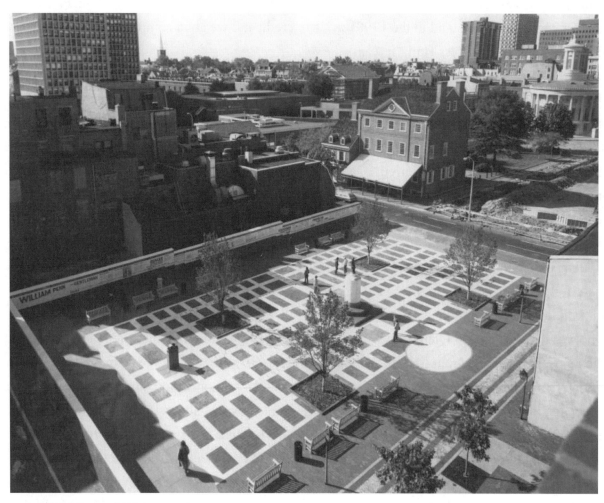

Aerial View of Welcome Park

Candlelight tours of the Park and its environs after normal closing hours were also a great success. The Park volunteers and the candle light tour guides were extremely well trained for their work. In fact, the training was equal to that given the Park Rangers. Our ranger staff included a significant number of entry level positions, and at one point, in order to give the rangers their NPS basic training course, we sent some 25 of them to Boston. For several weeks, volunteers from the Friends filled in for the trainees. They helped at the Liberty Bell and on Independence Square, but they operated the Second Bank Portrait Gallery

entirely by themselves.

Following Mary was another dynamo, Elizabeth "Libby" Browne. Libby's husband, Stanhope, was a Philadelphia lawyer and the Honorary French Consul General in Philadelphia. Besides an efficient operation, Libby was responsible for Welcome Park, one of the Park's most imaginative projects. Named for the ship that had brought William Penn to America, Welcome Park was designed by Robert Venturi, who had also designed Franklin Court. "Welcome" was also an appropriate name for another reason, since it was the first INHP site that was seen by visitors parking in the Second and Sansom Street parking garage. The surface of Welcome Park was a map of early Philadelphia showing the streets in white marble and the spaces in between in black slate. The four squares of the map were planters with Bradford Pear trees in them, and the center square (where Philadelphia City Hall now stands) was a stone obelisk with William Penn on top. Around the brick walls of the park were painted metal panels that told the story of the founding and early years of Philadelphia.

The first building on the site of Welcome Park had been William Penn's slate roof house (which no longer existed). Archeologists dug the site before the construction of the Park and found many artifacts dating back to the Penn era. The Friends purchased the land for $600,000, then spent an equal amount to develop it before giving it to the National Park Service. The owner of the land was James McCullough, who had hoped to utilize the old Keystone Telephone Building which was then on the site for some kind of development. After a rain-soaked wall of the building collapsed, the City of Philadelphia demolished it for safety reasons. McCullough was disappointed but then sold the land to the Friends for a "bargain price." When I was playing golf with Jim one day, he told me that those women I work with are tough. He said that they got his land for a bargain price and then solicited him for a $25,000 contribution. Jim made the contribution to the Welcome Park development. The two major contributors to the project were the Glenmeade Trust and the William Penn Foundation. When the Park was dedicated and given to the NPS, Ginny Thornburgh, the wife of the Governor of Pennsylvania, was there, as was Stan Hewitt, Associate Director of the National Park Service.

Tom McCallum, one of my best friends, followed Libby Browne as Chairman of the Friends. He came into office when we were beginning to plan the Bicentennial of the Constitution. The Friends were active in many aspects of this celebration, but their major commitment was the Second Bank of the United States exhibition called "Miracle at Philadelphia." Just as the Friends opening of the Portrait Gallery (1974) kicked off the Bicentennial of the Declaration of Independence, the "Miracle at Philadelphia" (1986) was a kickoff for the Bicentennial of the Constitution. This world-class exhibition is described in another part of this book.

One of the pre-celebration activities of the Constitution Bicentennial was the 200th anniversary of the Mount Vernon conference at George Washington's home in Virginia. Tom McCallum and I were invited to attend the two days of meetings at Mount Vernon. The Chief Justice of the Supreme Court, Warren E. Burger, had recently been appointed Chairman of the Federal Commission for the Bicentennial of the Constitution. Chief Justice Burger, or "the Chief," as his acquaintances called him, invited us to dinner at the Supreme Court. Tables and chairs were set up in the Main Hall of the building for some 200 guests and it was a memorable evening, with many national, historical and government figures chatting with us.

One of the people at our table was Raymond Smock, Historian for the House of Representatives. We talked to Ray about the

1985 NCAA basketball finals, which were being held while we were dining. He suggested that after dinner we go to his office in the Cannon House Office Building to see the end of the game. We were pleased with the result, as Villanova, a Philadelphia school, won the national championship. After the game, Ray invited us to visit the Capitol before we returned to our hotel. The three of us walked through the tunnel connecting the buildings and at midnight we were standing under the rotunda of the U.S. Capitol. What an experience! No one else was in sight; in fact, we had seen only a single guard on our way. This was a moment that Tom and I will never forget. There we were, looking up at the dome with the statues of America's greats surrounding us, and we had just come from a dinner where speakers discussed our government, The Constitution.

Tom had served as Chairman of the Friends for a longer period than usual, so when The Constitution celebration was complete, he retired and was replaced by Susie Montgomery. Susie was already on the Friends board, and she and her husband Ned came to Philadelphia from Pittsburgh as the local executive with Mellon Bank. They were supportive of the Friends from the beginning. Since they were very active socially, they kept the Friends name and reputation in front of the public. Later on, Susie helped work on my final bicentennial celebration: the 200th anniversary of the death of Benjamin Franklin in 1990. This means not that we celebrated his dying but that we celebrated his legacy.
The largest event in the 1990 Franklin celebration was the recreation of his funeral procession, which

in 1790 had included some 25,000 persons. In the 18th Century, groups that had a relationship with Dr. Franklin marched together in his funeral procession. Most of those groups still existed in the 20th Century, so we invited all of them to join us in a procession that started in Washington Square, then went by Independence Hall, Philosophical Hall, Library Hall, the Second Bank, Carpenters Hall, Franklin Court, Christ Church, and Franklin's grave, and concluded with speakers and a rally on the second block of Independence Mall. This was a great experience that honored the greatest of men.

Carter Ferguson replaced Susie as chairman of the Friends. It was during his tenure that I retired from the National Park Service, but the everyday good works of the Friends continued. From the day that they were founded until the day I retired in 1991, the Friends of Independence were important to the operation and development of Independence National Historical Park. Whether it was volunteer activities or fundraising or being an ambassador for the Park, the Friends made a difference. Today, many units of the National Park System have support groups that are invaluable to them, but during the heyday of the Friends there were very few, especially with the diversity and effectiveness of the Friends of Independence National Historical Park. They truly were pioneers.

F. Drama in the Park

I always thought that Independence National Historical Park had the best interpretive program in the National Park Service. Our visitors had the opportunity to enjoy history in innovative and creative ways. Whether it was audiovisual, exhibits, publications, or personal service by rangers and volunteers, we often taught history without the visitor realizing it.

Early in 1973, Franklin Roberts came to see me with the idea of using drama as an interpretive tool. He reasoned that we could tell elements of the Park story in a half-hour drama that could be performed several times each day somewhere in the Park. The buildings or gardens, inside or out, would become the set. Frank had owned an advertising and public relations agency, but he also had invested in New York shows such as *Applause*, *Fiddler on the Roof*, and *1776*. He had many contacts in the New York and Philadelphia drama world.

Roberts proposed going to Philadelphia corporations for sponsorship so that the Park performances would be free to the visitors. I had little experience on which to judge a proposal such as this, but it seemed to be worth a try, and I liked Frank. He convinced Bill Cashel, President of Bell of Pennsylvania, to sponsor the first show.

The first play was *It Happened Here, In John Dunlap's Philadelphia*, and was presented in Carpenters Court, a short cobblestone street with Carpenters Hall at the end and Pemberton House and New Hall on each side. The three buildings formed the outdoor set, so their windows, doorways, cellar doors, and steps were utilized. The story of John Dunlap was a half-hour presentation shown three times a day.

John Dunlap was an Irish immigrant who had worked hard and become the publisher of the newspaper Pennsylvania Packet. Through his eyes and experiences we followed the events of the

Outdoor Drama at Carpenter's Court

movement toward independence. He was not a reporter but a patriot, who served as a member of the First City Troop. On July 4, 1776, after the Declaration of Independence was approved, the document was taken to Dunlap to be printed and distributed to the States and the army in the field. This high moment was the show's conclusion.

Joe Leonardo directed the show and Neil Bierbower did the costumes; both men were in the theater department at Temple University. Jerry Breshin, Jude Ciccolella, and Jane Moore were the cast. Jude did several of our dramas, and I still see him frequently on television shows. The first time that I saw the show was at a dress rehearsal in Carpenters Court. I was blown away. What an effective way to tell a story. It ran daily from the last week in June until Labor Day in 1973. The word got around the National Park Service about this new and creative interpretative media. Roberts always had a playbill to give the audience which acknowledged the sponsors and gave them a souvenir to take home.

Independence spawned plays and musicals that Franklin Roberts created for Valley Forge, Gettysburg, Morristown, and Federal Hall. He also created touring musicals for the National Park Service, the Environmental Protection Agency (EPA), and the Ohio River Heritage Association. He even created *The Phantoms of the Capitol* for the U.S. Congress on its 200th birthday.

Here is a list of some of Robert's productions:

1973   *It Happened Here, In John Dunlap's*

Philadelphia

1974   *It Happened Here, The Daytime Ride of Paul Revere*
Revere brought the news of the blockade of Boston Harbor to Philadelphia. This had a great impact on the meeting of the First Continental Congress.

1975   *It Happened Here, Sails of Freedom*
The efforts to create a navy as seen through James Forten, a free black sail maker.

1976   *Dr. Rush: Rebel for Humanity*
The story of Benjamin Rush, an innovative medical doctor, founder of Pennsylvania Hospital, and a signer of the Declaration of Independence.

1976   *Spirits of 76*
The story of the drafting and debate about the Declaration of Independence.

1976   *The Case and Trial of John Peter Zenger*
The 1835 trial of a New York printer regarding freedom of the press.

1976   *We've Come Back for a Little Look Around*
-1977   Four historical personages come back to see what has happened to their country.

1978   *Song of the Old Bell*
A musical drama about the Liberty Bell.

1978   *When the Well's Dry*
An initiative for energy conservation by the National Park Service.

1986   *Four Little Pages*

-1987 A musical story of the creation of the U.S. Constitution

We've Come Back for a Little Look Around is based on a 1773 letter that Benjamin Franklin wrote to a fellow scientist about being able to come back in a hundred years to see what had become of the American spirit. He was in England and had received a bottle of wine from America, and when he poured the first glass, out came three houseflies. He scooped them out and laid them on the windowsill. The sun revived two of them and they flew off. Franklin contemplated being immersed in a barrel of Madeira with a few friends so they could come back like the flies and take a look around. In the drama, John Adams, Abraham Lincoln, and Mark Twain joined Franklin. This show played Independence Park, and a second company toured the Western national parks, being presented at campfire programs.

Another favorite was the musical *Spirits of 76*, the story of the Declaration of Independence, which was presented inside the First Bank of the United States.

At the climax of this story, the actors froze in a tableau that looked like one of the paintings of the signing of the Declaration. The set included a piece of green beige spread over a cabinet; at the conclusion, the cloth was removed to unveil a large museum case containing the Stone plate. This is a copper engraving plate, made by a man named William Stone, of the embossed copy of the Declaration of Independence; it was on loan to the Park from the National Archives.

The Stone plate had been made around 1825, by placing tissue paper on the Declaration of Independence and moistening it so that some of the original ink would fade onto the tissue. The tissue was then used to create an engraving on a copper plate that could be used to print other copies. A group of us took a million signatures, collected mostly by Sunoco stations and Wawa markets, to President Gerald Ford to ask for the loan of the original Declaration of Independence for the year 1976. We were received in the Oval Office, but we did not get the Declaration; instead, we got the Stone plate and a paper copy made from it. The plate was displayed in the First Bank and covered just before each performance of *Spirits of 76*. The uncovering brought a dramatic ending to the show.

My absolute favorite was the musical *Four Little Pages*. The title describes the length of the Constitution of the United States and the show tells the story of its creation. This show was presented in the park in 1986 and 1987. There was also a second company that toured the National Parks for seven weeks in 1987. The lyrics and music were spectacular, with the show-stopping finale being the Preamble of the Constitution sung like a hymn. You could look around the audience during the "We the People" number and many were mouthing the words along with actors. It was a stirring moment.

The shows were possible in the Park for so many years because of the generous sponsors, such as Bell of Pennsylvania, Colonial Penn Insurance Company, Girard Bank, Merck, Cigna, Knight Foundation, and the Friends of Independence.

G. Special Assignment – U.S.S.R.

In the spring of 1973, six National Park Service managers received a memorandum from the Director notifying them that they had been selected to go the Soviet Union. They would represent the NPS at an exhibition on outdoor recreation in America sponsored by the United States Information Agency (USIA). Since the exhibition featured the National Parks, they wished to have a uniformed ranger appear with it. During the course of a year, the exhibition would appear in six Soviet cities and, hopefully, would give Soviet citizens a better understanding of the Americans. This was the period called "detente" between the USSR and the USA.

The schedule called for the exhibition to open in Moscow; then it would go in order to Ufa, Irkutsk, Tbilisi, Kishenov, and Odessa. Each National Park Service person was assigned to be with the exhibition in one of the cities. My assignment was Kishenov, Moldavia (since the break up of the Soviet Union, the city is now called Chisinau and the country is called Moldova). In 1974, Moldovia was the second smallest of the Soviet Republics, bordered on three sides by the Ukraine and on the fourth by Romania. The Exhibition would be open to the public for four to five weeks in each city and would be torn down, moved, and reassembled in three weeks.

A USIA staff of about a half dozen stayed with the exhibition for the duration. There were two Soviets with the exhibition to help translate and expedite the needs of the staff, but probably their biggest job was to keep an eye on the Americans.

The "guides" for the exhibition were American students; most of them were at the graduate level and had majored in Russian studies, the Russian language, or in a related subject but could speak Russian. There were twenty guides who worked the first three venues and twenty different ones for the final three cities. Three specialists were also assigned to the exhibit at each location: A National Park Ranger, a U.S. Forest Service representative, and a person who could demonstrate outdoor skills such as fishing, hunting, camping, skiing, or ice skating. Besides talking with exhibition visitors and giving slide lectures and demonstrations, we would entertain visiting dignitaries and make field trips to their outdoor recreation facilities.

I was scheduled to be in Kishenov for three weeks in February and the first week of March 1974. About a month in advance, I went to Washington, D.C., to the studios of Voice of America to do a radio interview which would be broadcast over Eastern Europe and hopefully would promote attendance to the exhibition. The exhibition notwithstanding, we were the first Americans to visit Moldavia since 1941. I listened to some of the interviews and each answer would start with my voice and then the voice of the translator would take over.

I couldn't help but wonder who selected the people to participate in this program, because none of us had made application to be included. A couple of years later, Larry Haldley, the superintendent of Acadia National Park, told me that while he was working in Washington, the letter from the Director of the USIA to the Director of the

NPS requesting assistance came to him to be answered. Without consulting anyone, he selected six people who he thought would do a good job for the Service. Many years after the fact, I can only recall three others beside myself: Wayne Cone, Director of Training for the NPS; Granville (Granny) Lisle, Superintendent of the Blue Ridge Parkway; and Bob Barbee, Superintendent of Cape Hatteras National Seashore and future Superintendent of Yellowstone National Park. When Bob Barbee got back from Tbilisi, he called me and said that he had left me a box of supplies there, including a hot plate.

When plans for me to go to the USSR were first mentioned, my wife Shirley (my first wife, to whom I was married at the time) said that she would like to go also, but it would have to be at our expense. The only complication was that our son Stephen was in the first grade in Philadelphia. We decided to take him to Middlesboro, Kentucky, to stay with my parents, Eula and Pope Cawood, for the six weeks that we would be away. He could attend school there.

We went to Washington for a day of briefing, then flew overnight to London and, after a short layover, on to Moscow. We spent five days in Moscow before going on to Kishenov in order to adjust to the time and cultural changes. From this point on, Shirley and I were joined by Dan Williams of the National Forest Service and a man who was a hiking and camping specialist. He actually worked for the Federal Aviation Agency but he had written a book about hiking the Appalachian Trail and was a knowledgeable camper.

Upon arriving in Moscow, my first thought was that this country smells different. Not a bad smell, but different. Since we were traveling with our "official" U.S. Passport, the Russian authorities gave us a hard time. No one smiled. Dan Williams had a Bible, which was examined very closely. It was a modern printing of the Bible with color pictures which mystified them. Fortunately, the U.S. Embassy had sent someone to meet us and he did a good job of keeping us calm during our ordeal. He had a telegram for me from my brother George, telling me about the birth of his daughter Elisa on Ground Hog Day.

We were taken to the Metropole Hotel for a rest, then to the embassy for the first of our many briefings. It took place in a glass room inside a larger room. Even the furniture was glass, which insured that the room was not bugged. We were warned that we would be monitored in a variety of ways so we should not do anything that would get us into trouble. Above all, do not sell your jeans or any copies of Playboy that we might have. Both would bring a high price.

When we got back to the hotel, we knew that someone had gone through our luggage, because we found things from one suitcase in another and several other things were out of place. The airport interrogation, the embassy glass room, the baggage search, and our fatigue all contributed to our feeling of concern. Our embassy minder came by to take us to dinner at an upscale Moscow restaurant. When we entered the room, the smoky atmosphere, the dance floor, and the different-appearing people made it feel as if we were on the set of a spy movie, but it was real. As we were shown to our table, we passed the open door of a side room, and from the room came the music of Johnny Cash singing "Ring of Fire." This made us all feel better; we even forgot about the stares from the other patrons.

One evening in Moscow we secured tickets to a ballet at the Palace of Congress inside the Kremlin. It was a spectacular show, and I thought about how, with 5,500 people in the audience, we did not even have to speak the same language in order to follow the story. At intermission, everyone left the auditorium and went to a huge room for a snack. It was buffet style and I did not speak Russian, so I pointed to a plate of sliced meats. The server looked at me and said "cold cuts," and I said "Yes ma'am," and she handed them to me. In 20 minutes the entire audience was fed and went back to the performance.

After five days in Moscow, we were taken to the airport in order to fly a thousand miles to Kishenov. The only non-Soviets on the flight were four Americans and a Polish businessman. The foreigners were put on the plane first, and then it filled up with Soviets. The flight seemed unusually long, and after a rough landing in miserable weather, we were told to stay on the airplane while everyone else deplaned. After a half hour, someone boarded the plane who could speak English and told us that we were in Odessa and had been diverted from Kishenov because of bad weather. We were then taken into the terminal and locked in a poorly heated room. An hour later, someone who could speak better English came to our room and told us that the problem was that we only had visas for Moscow and Kishenov, so therefore we could not spend the night in Odessa.

I suggested that they allow us to rent a car and we could drive the 150 miles to Kishenov. I found out very quickly that my suggestion was not feasible.

For eight hours we were locked in a cold room with very little contact with anyone. Fortunately, I had a fifth of Jack Daniels Whiskey in my carry-on bag, which helped with the cold. At 8:00 p.m. we were told that they had been unable to make contact with the person who could approve a visa change, so we were not approved to stay in Odessa. We had to get back on the plane and fly to Kishenov, and it mattered little that we were going to make the trip in worse weather than had caused our earlier diversion. Four Americans and a Pole were put back on an airplane with a full crew, but no other passengers, and flown through a storm to a place where our visa said we could be. Our camping specialist worked for the Federal Aviation Agency and had flown large commercial airplanes and he was scared, so we were all scared, but we made it.

We left the plane and walked into the terminal, which was closed with the lights off because they were not expecting any flights. We finally found a group of Nigerian students who were stranded and sleeping on the floor in hopes of flying out the following day. One of them spoke English and Russian, so he translated to a maintenance man that we needed a ride into town. He arranged an old bus to take us to the Hotel Kishenov, where the exhibition team was staying. When we arrived at the hotel, the exhibition manager could not believe that we had made it. The embassy in Moscow had been trying without success to determine our location. We had a drink and were shown to our room. A technician examined Shirley's and my room and told us where the listening devices were located, and we went to bed.

I had a couple of days to get familiar with the exhibition before its grand opening. We also met Simeon Petroff, who was the specialist assigned to assist us with whatever needs we might have. We heard later that he was making a daily report on our activities. The exhibition was located in a large pavilion located a 20-minute bus ride from the hotel. When visitors entered the building, they were directed into a large room with a platform where Dan Williams and I would chat (through a translator) with visitors and give slide shows. From here they went into the main part of the exhibition, where they saw a variety of exhibits about outdoor recreation which included demonstrations on skiing, ice skating, fishing and camping. Skiers demonstrated equipment by skiing on a carpet that turned around rollers. Ice skaters performed on a small rink of floor tiles covered with silicone. We also had a lounge where we could get away from the crowds. When visitors exited, they were given a lapel badge as a souvenir, and Shirley volunteered to distribute them. This kept her busy because there was little she could have done on her own.

Bob Mathias, the Olympic decathlon champion and a Congressman from California, came to the grand opening. After a brief ceremony and a tour of the exhibition involving local dignitaries, we had a reception where we drank 23 toasts, some with vodka and some with bourbon. It was here that I first encountered the Soviet game, "drink the American under the table." The following day the exhibition opened to the public.

Every morning while we were riding in the bus to the exhibition, a staff member who had stayed up late and listened to BBC would give us a summary of the news. It was important for us to be well-informed because people were planted in the audience to ask questions that might embarrass us. By knowing what was coming, we could be ready. We were aware of "détente," but the Soviet officials did not seem to be. The Soviet people in general were grand and just eager to see and learn about Americans. English was the most popular language taught in school, so thousands of school children came to try out their English on us. Every day we hosted approximately 15,000 visitors, and the line to get into the building was usually several blocks long.

One day I was working on the platform in the specialist room when a man in a great coat yelled something as he entered the room. I asked my translator what he said: "You are an American, I would know the Americans anywhere. I fought with them on the Elbe." I told Boris, the translator, to have him come up on the platform. He was grizzled and smelled of cognac. He took off his overcoat, and on his lapel he was wearing a military decoration that identified him as a World War II hero. The crowd of over 200 was impressed. The man offered me a drink, which I did not take, and he said, "Americans are all big and good looking just like you and together we beat the Nazi." I told him he obviously was a great hero and that his country had given him an important medal to prove it. Now, on behalf of the American people, I would like for him to be recognized by the United States of America for his heroism. I took from my pocket an American flag pin and placed it on his lapel, and then I embraced him. The crowd went wild.

During my first week in Kishenov, when a young man and his wife were talking to me about my uniform, particularly my hat. he said that he would like to have my hat. He surmised that there were probably many hats like mine in America but that there were no hats like it in the USSR. So, if he had my hat he would be a big shot. I told him that I needed to have my hat to wear with my uniform for the remainder of the exhibition. He asked me if I liked his wife and I said that I thought she was very attractive. He then asked if I would like to trade my hat for his wife. I had to decline, but I should have asked him to come back in a month when the exhibition was concluded and we could negotiate further.

When I was on the platform talking about our National Parks, there were usually about 250 people in the audience. The conversation started with scenic parks, flora and fauna, and historic sites, but it often went on to what kind of car do I drive, how much money do I make, and all kinds of personal questions. One day we were chatting about religion and I said something about us having the freedom to worship or not to worship. During this exchange, I heard someone in the audience say "Oral Roberts." Two men and a woman who were dressed in black and identified themselves as Baptists had said it. They had heard my broadcast on Voice of America, so their congregations had sent them to see the Americans. Their clothes were ragged, and they said that it

had taken them two days to get to the exhibition. I became concerned that they would get into trouble with the Soviet crowd control officials who patrolled the building. Crowd control may have been part of their job, but another part was to keep an eye on us and even on their own citizens. Nevertheless, the crowd let the Baptists come up to the platform, and we had an open conversation about religion. They wanted to know if I was a believer and I told them that I was a Methodist, which didn't mean anything to them. Close examination proved that they were the poorest of the poor, and they said that their government persecuted them because of their belief. Eventually, one of the crowd controllers came into the room, and visitors began to push the Baptists toward the door to keep them out of trouble. That had been quite an experience for me and, I trust, for them. Later, when I went to lunch at the café in the Park, I opened the door and saw the Baptists sitting in the center of the room. Some members of our group were at tables beyond them. The Baptists were having tea, and as I passed their table, I placed three American flag pins into the folded hands of the lady. I did not speak or even look at them because I did not want to cause them trouble. After I joined my friends and ordered lunch, I looked back at their table and the lady nodded as if to say thank you. I would like to think that our conversation and those three American flags meant something special to those people and their congregation. It was very special to me.

When we entertained the Moldavian Commissar for the Environment and several of his staff at the exhibition, they wanted to show us some of their

Parks and Forests. We made a date, and they took Dan Williams, me, and our translator to a large natural area. We went to a Ranger's house, where they told us it was the custom to drink a glass of wine, take a pinch of bread, and eat some nuts before entering the house. We noticed that the Soviets did not drink all of their wine. The house was modest and clean, but as we walked through the living room, I noticed that the electrical cord on the television was still rolled up, as if new. We went to a large room with a table and chairs for all twelve of the party. Thus began a luncheon that lasted for five hours. We drank wine, vodka, and cognac and had many toasts. Our translator passed out for an hour and we did not miss him. We ate fish, pork, beef, wild boar, venison, and even bear, all fixed in every way you could imagine. The restroom was a hole in the floor that I was afraid I would fall into. I struggled to stay awake, because the reputation of my country depended on it. About 4:30 p.m., after kissing everyone goodbye, we departed. As soon as our driver turned on the heater, I passed out. I awoke back at the hotel, ran up to my room and regurgitated.

We worked six days each week and usually took an arranged tour on our day off. One of the trips was to a winery that had a trophy given by the U.S. Centennial Commission at Philadelphia in 1876 for excellence of product. The three specialists decided that we wanted to see Odessa, the Black Sea port. We had to apply for visa approval, and after a couple of weeks we were allowed to make the trip. A two-hour train ride got us there in time to take an Intourist guided tour of the city. The waterfront was beautiful, with many buildings in the western European style, apparently built by

shipping companies doing business in Odessa in the early 19th Century. Our hotel was wonderful and had real class. An Armenian bartender spoke English and could arrange for American cigarettes and whiskey. We figured that so many things came into the country through this Black Sea port, and it appeared that they took their 10 percent off of the top.

On the train back to Kishenov, an old woman and a boy were seated across the aisle. The boy seemed ill and the woman had a large heavy bundle that she was carrying. Our shadow was constantly with us, so we did not dare to assist them. When we left the train in Kishenov, without thinking, I turned to assist the lady with her bundles. Immediately, police surrounded us and the woman and boy were taken away. It was my fault that I called attention to her, and now she was in trouble. That really made me mad. The next day, a person who said that he was Armenian asked me to take a letter and mail it in America to someone in Fresno, California. I knew that it could be a trap but I agreed to take it. I kept it with me for a week and then, on debriefing at the Embassy, I turned it over to our people, who assured me that they would make sure it got to the addressee.

When we got back to Moscow, I went to the snack bar in the basement of the embassy and ordered a hamburger, French fries and a coke. Wow, was it good! Two days later we were back in Philadelphia with Steve, and Independence Hall never looked so good. A week later I went to Washington and did a final interview for Voice of America. It was a bright, sunny, spring day and

Washington looked great. My experience in the
USSR made me a better American citizen.

III.

THE CELEBRATION (1976)

A. First Continental Congress

By 1774 there was a great deal of unrest in the British North American colonies. The Boston Tea Party, the quartering of troops on private property, and taxation brought about a general protest from the colonies. There were public calls for an inter-colonial congress, and colonial legislatures appointed delegates to a meeting in Philadelphia to discuss their common grievances. This was the first time that the colonies worked together on an issue. This First Continental Congress met in Carpenters Hall from September 5th until October 26, 1774. There were 56 delegates from 12 colonies (Georgia did not come).

As a result of these deliberations, a number of complaints were identified and a report was sent to the British Crown. Basically, these were Englishmen requesting the rights of Englishmen. The Congress agreed to reassemble in Philadelphia the following spring to examine the results of their efforts.

For the Bicentennial of the First Continental Congress, the Commonwealth of Pennsylvania took the lead for planning the opening activities. The governors of the 13 states were invited to come to Carpenters Hall to consider issues of the 20th Century that were of interest to all. The meeting took place in the Park in Carpenters Hall on September 5–6, 1974. Their activities included a fife and drum procession, a tour of Independence Park, the official meeting, and a number of social activities. This time Georgia was represented by its Governor, Jimmy Carter.

For the closing activities on October 26th, a special delegation was appointed by the Congress of the United States, with Senator Hugh Scott of Pennsylvania taking the lead. Among the legislators attending was Lindy Boggs, a Congresswoman from Louisiana. This was the first of many bicentennial era activities for both of us. A ceremony was held on a platform at the south door of Carpenters Hall.

B. 1976

Daily Activities

After moving the Liberty Bell to its new Pavilion in the first moments of 1976, we were well aware that the bicentennial year had arrived. One problem that presented itself was the fact that the new fiscal year for the Federal Government began on October 1, 1975, but by January 1976, Congress still had not approved a budget. We had to operate on a continuing resolution that allowed us to spend on the same level as the previous fiscal year. During 1975 we had opened a major Visitor Center, Graff House, City Tavern, and Old City Hall, and had a new garden/landscaped area at Fourth and Walnut Streets where the Irvin Building once stood. In offices at the Visitor Center, we had installed a computerized security and detection system for all Park buildings. This system was to be monitored 24 hours a day and we had to have Rangers in the Park to respond to any alarms. After all, the buildings and their contents are some of our country's greatest historical resources. We were also planning to open the Kosciuszko House in February and Franklin Court in May.

Our staff and volunteers were stretched beyond belief, and our ability to even pay the utility bills for the new facilities was in doubt. The budget which had been recommended by the National Park Service had only a modest increase of some 18 new employees for Independence. I pleaded my case with my superiors, but they were unable to oppose the Office of Management and Budget. Putting 18 new employees in the budget was a major increase for a single unit of the National Park System.

One day in June 1975, I was entering the Bellevue-Stratford Hotel when I encountered Congressman Josh Eilberg, who asked me how things were going. Congressman Eilberg was not my Congressman, but I tried to maintain excellent relations with the six Congressmen from the Philadelphia area. When Eilberg asked the question, I quickly outlined my concern about being able to operate the new facilities that we were opening for the Bicentennial. As a member of the Executive Branch, I was not supposed to lobby the Legislative Branch, but when asked a question I must respond. The following day, he wrote me a letter, and after conferring with my Congressman, James Byrnes, I was invited to come to Washington to present my budget needs to the Philadelphia area legislative delegation. I went to Washington and made the case, but I would not know the results until the budget passed.

Finally, we got a budget in early February 1976 that included a substantial increase in funds and the allotment for over 50 new employees.

There were also significant funds for temporary employees to assist with the additional crowds expected in 1976. Fortunately, in January and February we received only modest visitor increases, but the floodgates opened over the Presidents Day weekend. The visitors began to overwhelm us. I yelled at Chief of Interpretation Kathy Dilonardo to get some people in uniform. She would not sacrifice numbers for quality and went about recruiting an outstanding interpretive staff, which included both permanent and seasonal personnel. By April we were in control of the situation. We made one mistake in hiring more employees and depending less on our volunteers. We made them feel as if they were not so important, and when we needed them later they were not there. Eventually, after we admitted our mistake, they came back.

Kathy organized her interpretive staff into four districts so that new permanent and seasonal personnel would learn their assigned district and not the details of the whole park story. District One was Independence Square (Independence Hall, Old City Hall, Congress Hall); District Two was the Second Bank Portrait Gallery and the Liberty Bell Pavilion; District Three was Franklin Court, Pemberton House, and New Hall; and District Four was the Visitor Center, Bishop White House, Todd House, and the Kosciuszko House. This efficient operation for 1976 was continued afterward, with personnel having the ability to transfer from district to district. Administrative Officer Howard La Rue reported that in mid-July 1976, Independence had a staff of 421 on the payroll.

Although 1976 was the Bicentennial year, and

all of our facilities were open, the period of special emphasis with many special activities was Memorial Day to Labor Day. All park buildings were open 8:00 a.m. to 8:00 p.m. The following summer events were available for our visitors:

SPECIAL INTEREST FOR CHILDREN:

Whimmy Diddles – A one-hour participation program featuring the life of a colonial child, ages 7 – 11, 5 times daily.
Boots for Dad – A half-hour puppet show about children whose father was at Valley Forge. Shows in the Rose Garden 4 times daily.
Story Time – Costumed Interpreters read colonial stories in the courtyard at Franklin Court.

LIVE DRAMA:

Spirits of 76 – Half-hour drama in the First Bank of the United States.
3 times daily, Tuesday – Sunday.
Dr. Rush, Rebel for Humanity – Half-hour drama outside the Second Bank of the U.S.
3 times daily, Saturday – Sunday.
The Carlisle Commission – Half-hour drama outside the Merchants Exchange.
3 times daily, except Tuesday.
1776 – The Broadway show, presented in the Independence Mall Theater Pavilion.
8:00 p.m., Tuesday, Wednesday, Thursday, Sunday; 5:00 p.m. and 9:30 p.m., Friday and Saturday. Tickets $3.00.
The First Hundred Years – Half-hour

presentation at the Arch Street Quaker Meeting House about William Penn. 4 shows daily.

SOUND AND LIGHT:

A Nation is Born – a 55-minute sound and light show on Independence Square. 9:00 p.m. nightly.

LIVING HISTORY DEMONSTRATIONS:

Print Shop and Binding – Typesetting, printing and bookbinding,
320 Market Street, Franklin Court.
18th-Century Military Life – Camp life, drills, musket use. Daily near Pemberton House.

FINE ARTS:

Artists In the Park – Students, graduates and faculty of the Pennsylvania Academy of Fine Arts and Philadelphia College of Arts demonstrate their skills. Visitors are encouraged to talk to the artists.

MUSIC:

Candlelight Concerts at Christ Church – Colonial period music by soloists, quartets, and ensembles playing the organ, harpsichord, and stringed instruments. Sundays at 6:00 p.m., Monday and Friday at 8:00 p.m.
Pop 76 Concert – Independence Mall Theater, Pop music at noon, Monday – Friday.

Fife and Drum Parades
– Throughout the Park, daily 11:00 a.m. –
4:00 p.m.
Mummers String Band
– South Portico of the Second Bank,
Friday evenings at 8:00 p.m.

Naturally, July 4, 1976 was our high point, with an estimate of a million people in the Park during the 24-hour period. The Philadelphia Inquirer carried a daily report on Park attendance, and it was not unusual for the Liberty Bell to exceed 25,000 visitors per day. On July 3rd-4th, the Liberty Bell Pavilion never closed. The annual head count for the Liberty Bell was 3,600,000 visitors. After the Legionnaires Disease scare in late July, the Liberty Bell figure dropped to about 15,000 per day.

When the year was over, many of us who had been involved in preparing for the Bicentennial of the Declaration of Independence were at a loss. Our focus for several years had been 1976, and now it had passed. We hired a psychologist to work with our staff, particularly the leadership. The result was that we accepted the fact that we were finished with 1976, but we were just at the beginning of the Bicentennial era. We would celebrate many future Bicentennial milestones at Independence National Historical Park, some modest, but at least one other that would rival 1976: The Constitution in 1987. We had a new vision and goal and could look forward with excitement.

VIP Visits

The Bicentennial year 1976 began on December 31, 1975, with the ceremony to move the Liberty Bell. Participating in the program were John Cardinal Krol, the Roman Catholic leader in Philadelphia; Martin Hoffman, Secretary of the Army; William Lyons, White House staff; Ron Coleman, CIA; Lee J. Cobb, actor; and 250,000 others who braved some of the worst weather that one can imagine, to come and spend their New Year's celebration watching the Liberty Bell being moved from Independence Hall across the street to its new pavilion. The move itself was of great historical significance and of unusual national news interest.

On January 13, 1976, the First Lady, Betty Ford, came to Philadelphia to see two new

First Lady Betty Ford at the Liberty Bell (January 13, 1976)

attractions: the sculpture by Louise Nevelson called *Bicentennial Dawn*, and the Liberty Bell Pavilion. Mrs. Ford went to the new Federal Court House to see the sculpture first, then came across the street to the Liberty Bell Pavilion. I was expecting to greet Mrs. Ford at curbside on Market

it. The modern design of the Liberty Bell Pavilion was somewhat controversial, but Mrs. Ford told the press that it was a great design and that it was appropriate for the Bell.

On January 17, Sir Peter Ramsbotham, British Ambassador to the United States, and Dennis

Yitzhak Rabin, Prime Minister of Israel, at the Liberty Bell (January 26, 1976)

Street, but security did not notify us that she would walk across the street. All at once someone yelled, "She's here," and I quickly ran to the other side of the Pavilion to greet her. We entered the pavilion and paused at the north end before advancing to the Bell. We spent approximately 20 minutes with my presentation to her and posing for pictures of the event. I concluded that my hair and sideburns were too long. That was the style but I overdid

Richards, British Consul-General, spent most of a day with me planning the visit of Queen Elizabeth II. A few days later, Prime Minister Yitzhak Rabin of Israel came for a visit to Independence Hall and the Liberty Bell. The Prime Minister was serious, even studious on this occasion. Governor of Pennsylvania Milton Schapp and Mayor of Philadelphia Frank Rizzo joined us for the tour.

This visit to the Bell and Independence Hall became a pattern that we called the "A" tour. The motorcade would drop the important visitor off at the Market Street curb, where I would meet them.. We would enter the Liberty Bell Pavilion, pausing at the north room to remove coats and adjust their appearance. Then we would walk to the Bell, where I would give a 10-12 minute presentation. When my talk was over, pre-positioned press would take photographs and tapes. The important visitor would often take a few questions from the press, and then we would exit the southeast door of the Pavilion and walk up the Mall to Chestnut Street. En route I would stop and talk about the three buildings on Independence Square: Old City Hall, Congress Hall, and Independence Hall. For a time during the last decade of the 18th Century these three buildings served as the home to four levels of government: City, County, State, and Federal.

The "A" tour proceeded across Chestnut Street and into Independence Hall. We would pause in the hallway facing the Pennsylvania Supreme Court Room, where I would talk about the construction of the building and the branches of Pennsylvania government that occupied the building. While I was talking about this, the press was admitted to a space inside the Assembly Room. I would watch for everything to be in place, and then I would escort the guest into the Assembly Room, the room where our nation was born. Only four or five members of the tour would be admitted inside the Bar, with the press and the

Count and Countess Philippe de Lafayette (January 26, 1976)

remainder of the party staying outside the Bar. I would make a 10-12 minute presentation, then the guest would ask questions as we looked at the tables, the Syng Inkstand and the Rising Sun Chair. Approximately fifty percent of our special visitors did not speak English and it usually took a little longer to work through a translator. There was plenty of time and opportunity for the photographers and reporters. We then went to the front door and down the steps to the limousine that was curbside on Chestnut Street. Total tour time was 1-1 ¼ hour. Often Mayor Rizzo and/or Governor Schapp were also in the tour and had an event for the important visitors before and after they visited the Park.

In the afternoon of the day of Rabin's visit, the Count and Countess Philippe de Lafayette visited the Park. I greeted them at the Liberty Bell, but Park Ranger John Tom Shivone gave them a tour of the Park in French. On January 28th, actor Henry Fonda visited Independence Hall, and two days later a group of Congressmen visited the Park. They were ably cared for by the staff.

In February 1976, a group of 150 diplomats from the United Nations came down from New York in buses. They were divided into smaller groups for tours of the Park. This was a special tribute to our country from most of the countries represented in the United Nations. In February we also dedicated

Carl XVI Gustav, King of Sweden, and Hobie at the Liberty Bell (April 6, 1976)

and opened the Kosciuszko House, which drew several well-known individuals and members of Congress. This was where I had the thrill of meeting Stan Musial.

In March, actress Sandy Dennis came on the 11th, and on the 19th we hosted Liam Cosgrove, the Prime Minister of Ireland. He came to Independence Hall first, followed by the Liberty Bell. Police Commissioner Joseph O'Neil was excited to be involved in a visit by a dignitary from Ireland.

As the weather improved, so did the number of VIPs. On April 6, Carl XVI Gustav, the King of Sweden, arrived. The Delaware Valley was first settled by Swedes, so the King visited a number of Swedish historic sites: a Church in Wilmington, the Swedish Museum in Philadelphia, Gloria Dei Church (Old Swedes) National Historic Site, and Independence National Historical Park. The King was young and unmarried, so all of the young ladies were interested in his visit. In fact, I think that he did get out for some evening entertainment while he was in town. Besides visiting Independence Hall and the Liberty Bell, he also visited Graff House, where Thomas Jefferson lived in 1776. His visit was good but not as smooth because he spoke very little English. Addie-Lou and I attended a reception and dinner for the King where I was able to use my toasting skills that were taught to me by my Swedish friend Hjalmar Wicander.

The Ambassador from Egypt came on April 14th, and on the 30th we received British royalty in the persons of the Marquis of Blenheim, the Duke of Marlborough, and the Duke of Argyll.

During the first week of May, Helmut Kohl, future Chancellor of West Germany, met Governor Milton Schapp of Pennsylvania in the west wing reception room, after which I gave Mr. Kohl a tour of Independence Hall. I discovered later that the subject of the meeting was to discuss the location of a Volkswagen assembly plant in Pennsylvania.

On April 20th, we held the dedication and opening of Franklin court. The program included Senator Richard Schweiker of Pennsylvania, Assistant Secretary of the Interior Nat Reed, Director of the NPS Gary Everhardt, Regional Director Chet Brooks, and myself. Six days later, Betty Ford came to see the Liberty Bell and Independence Hall, and she brought the Stone engraving plate of the Declaration of Independence that was loaned to the Park by the National Archives. I met Mrs. Ford on Chestnut Street and we walked into Franklin Court via Orianna Street. After we

talked about the "ghost structures" that outlined Franklin's house and I pointed out the Market Street houses, we went underground to the museum and theater. While we were waiting for the presentation to begin, we were just chatting, and I asked Mrs. Ford if she would do me a favor. My mother had passed away two years before, and within the past couple of days my father had remarried. I asked Mrs. Ford if she would consider sending the newlyweds a letter of congratulations. She said that she would be thrilled to do it, so I gave her assistant their names and address.

After the presentation, Mrs. Ford completed her visit by going into the B Free Franklin Post Office, where postmaster Al Fisher gave her several souvenir stamps. A couple of weeks later, my father, Pope Cawood, called and was excited to say that he and his wife Glenna had received a letter of congratulations from President and Mrs. Ford. I asked if it was from both of them or just from Mrs. Ford. He said that it was from both of them. A few months later, when I actually saw the letter, it was obvious that the letter had originated in Mrs. Ford's office and had been signed by her, but there at an angle below "Betty Ford" was "Jerry Ford." The President's signature looked as if it had been made by a ballpoint pen, leading us to believe that while Mrs. Ford was signing the letter, she turned to her husband for his signature as well.

The President of France, Valery Giscard d'Estaing, came on May 19th, and the details of his visit are included elsewhere. Following his visit was Harald, the Crown Prince of Norway, and his

Crown Prince Harald of Norway and Princess Sonia with Hobie (June 1976)

wife Sonja, who was very attractive. Harald later became King following the death of his father. Both Harald and Sonja had the look of outdoor people with tanned skin and rosy cheeks. They made a very attractive couple and seemed to enjoy their visit.

The Canadian Ambassador brought a horse troop of Royal Canadian Mounted Police to the Park around the First of July. They performed several riding shows on Independence Mall and were great crowd pleasers.

We celebrated Independence Day with President Ford and Queen Elizabeth. Then we had a few days to catch our breath before the July 17th visit of West German Chancellor Helmut Schmidt. Chancellor Schmidt spoke excellent English, so our "Tour A" was running a little ahead of schedule and I needed to kill some time. Schmidt had taken out his cigarette lighter and struck the Bell to see if it would ring. I quickly got his attention and told him that we had many visitors from his country who came to see the Liberty Bell.

For those who wished to learn about it in their language, we have brochures and an audiotape in German that we can play for them. I signaled Kathy Dilanardo to start the tape, and while Chancellor Schmidt was listening to it, I turned to Mayor Rizzo and whispered to him that we also had an Italian language tape but there were no words on it because Italians talk with their hands. I thought that was clever, but Rizzo did not. He looked sternly down at me and said, "Hob, I want you to know that the Italians made this town." Humor was not one of his characteristics.

I received a call one day in late July from City Councilman Jack Kelly, who told me that his sister and her family were in town, and he wondered if

Helmut Schmidt, Chancellor of Germany (July 17, 1976)

I could show them Franklin Court. His sister was Princess Grace of Monaco. A couple of days later, I met "Kell" with Prince Rainier, Princess Grace,

Princess Grace of Monaco (Grace Kelly) and Princess Stephanie with Hobie at Franklin Court (July 1976)

and their three children, Albert, Caroline, and Stephanie. They had been in the Park on a number of previous occasions, and this time they only wanted to see the recently opened Franklin Court. We spent approximately two hours seeing the film, using the telephone exchange, and even watching all three parts of the exhibit, "Franklin on the World Stage." Their visit was very low key, with no press, and a good time was had by all.

In late July, the outbreak of Legionnaires Disease occurred during an American Legion convention at the Bellevue-Stratford Hotel. Because it took so long to identify the cause of the disease, the daily attendance at the Park dropped by about a third. I am not sure if this impacted visits by VIPs or not, but August was quiet.

On September 9th, President William R. Tolbert, Jr., of Liberia came for a visit. The President and his wife were in West African dress and made a stunning appearance, as did the entire party. Addie-Lou and I were invited to a cocktail party

on November 13th at the home of J. Welles and Hannah Henderson in nearby Society Hill. The object of the party was to meet former First Lady Bird Johnson and her friend Betty Talmadge, wife of the Senator from Georgia. I was excited because I had worked with Mrs. Johnson on devising a master plan for the LBJ National Historic Site in 1968. At the party, Welles went around the room introducing his guests, and when he came to us he said, "This is Addie-Lou and Hobart Cawood, who is with the National Park Service." Mrs. Johnson backed up a step and said, "Hobie Cawood," and I said "Hi, Mrs. Johnson." She then gave me a big hug.

We spent most of the following day touring the Park and its environs and even had a light lunch in the West Wing Reception Room, courtesy of the

William R. Tolbert, Jr., President of Liberia, and Mrs. Tolbert. September 9, 1976. Photo by Martin Degen. *Image Courtesy of Independence National Historical Park*

Friends of Independence. Our tour group included Welles and Hannah Henderson, Ernesta Ballard,

President of the Pennsylvania Horticultural Society, and our special guests.

The remainder of the year continued to wind down with such groups as the wives of Presidents of the American Association of Universities. However, the visitors of all descriptions gave us an opportunity for a welcomed rest in December. It had been a hell-of-a-year.

Valery Giscard d'Estaing

May 19, 1976 was to be a special day at Independence National Historical Park, because the legislature of the Commonwealth of Pennsylvania was to meet in session beneath the pavilion on Independence Mall, and the Park was to host an official visit by Valery Giscard d'Estaing, the President of France. Under normal conditions, the planning for official visits by the leader of another country did not include the State, other than in a security capacity, but in this case, with the Commonwealth government coming to Philadelphia from Harrisburg, the two events should logically be planned together.

The French had talked to us nearly a year in advance about a proper bicentennial gift from them to the United States which could be presented on this occasion. They obviously asked others the same question, because they decided to present a number of gifts (one of the gifts was a sound and light program for Mount Vernon). We suggested that they consider giving two portraits that were part of our furnishings plan for Congress Hall.

In the 18th Century, the Congress of the United States had requested that the French provide portraits of Louis XVI and his queen, Marie Antoinette, so they could hang them in their halls of government and always remember the role the French played in securing our independence.

The French had portraits of Louis XVI and Marie Antoinette from the palace at Versailles copied and sent to America. During the time that Congress Hall was the capital, these paintings had hung in Committee Rooms adjacent to the Senate Chamber on the second floor. When the government moved to Washington, D.C., in 1800, the portraits disappeared and have never been heard of since. We asked the French to copy the portraits at Versailles a second time so that we could hang them again in Congress Hall. The French agreed, and President Giscard d'Estaing would present them during his visit on May 19, 1976.

In planning the visit, the French advance team determined that there was some tension between Pennsylvania Governor Milton Schapp and Philadelphia Mayor Frank Rizzo. In a ceremony presenting the portraits inside Independence Hall, they dare not ask the Governor to introduce the President of France because it might offend the Mayor, and vice versa. The obvious neutral person who could make the introduction was me, the Park Superintendent. I understand English and speak eastern Kentucky, but my French was nil. My wife rehearsed me, and after a sleepless night of practice, I was ready to give it a try. Secretary of the Interior Thomas Kleppe came to Philadelphia to represent the President of the United States and accept the portraits.

On the day of the visit, Secretary Kleppe and I met the President of France and his wife at curbside in front of Independence Hall. We went directly into the Assembly Room, where I shared with them the story of the beginning of our nation. While we were inside, a number of selected guests, including the Governor and the Mayor, entered the Pennsylvania Supreme Court Chamber across the hall from the Assembly Room. The portraits

to the center of the room and said, "Ladies and Gentlemen, I have the pleasure to introduce to you Valery Giscard d'Estaing, the President of France." He stood up. I was relieved.

The President of France spoke excellent English. After a brief talk, he presented the portraits to the people of the United States. He and Secretary Kleppe then unveiled them and they

Valery Giscard d'Estaing, President of France, Madame dÕEstaing, Interior Secretary Thomas Kleppe, and Hobie at the Liberty Bell (May 19, 1976)

were placed on easels and covered with cloth in the Supreme Court Chamber. After our tour, we crossed the hall and joined the group in the Supreme Court Chamber. When everyone was seated, I counted to ten and nervously walked

were breathtaking. Secretary Kleppe gratefully accepted the portraits on behalf of the people of the United States.
There were a few minutes for everyone to admire the portraits and for the introduction of guests to

the President. Then we moved toward the front door of Independence Hall. While the President and I were awaiting our cue to exit the building, I asked him if he had been to America before. He said that he had come to New York after graduation from university and had bought a motorcycle. He then rode it across the country to Los Angeles.

Members of the local Alliance Francaise met us at the bottom of the Independence Hall steps, and a small girl gave Madame Giscard d'Estaing a large bouquet of lilies. We continued across Chestnut Street to the Liberty Bell Pavilion, where I gave them a presentation about the Bell. After I finished, during the press photographic opportunity, Madam Giscard d'Estaing, on impulse, laid her bouquet on the floor beneath the Bell. It was a very touching moment and became part of many of the media stories.

The President and his wife were then escorted across Market Street to the Pavilion on the Mall to participate in a meeting of the Pennsylvania General Assembly. One of the items of business that day was to pass a resolution that said, in part, "...the General Assembly of the Commonwealth of Pennsylvania does express its appreciation to Hobart Cawood, Superintendent of Independence National Historical Park and his staff for their courtesy not only to the General Assembly but to all visitors to Philadelphia in 1976..." The French government gave me a medallion to remember the occasion.

I do not remember the exact date, but some eight years later I received a telephone call from Valery Giscard d'Estaing, who was by then the former President of France. He told me that he was in Philadelphia to speak to the World Affairs Council and he was hopeful that I would have some time to escort him around the Park. Because of the crowds and security, he had not been able to enjoy it in 1976. Naturally, I had the time and asked if I could send a car for him. That was not necessary because he was staying just two blocks from my office, and I could meet him there. Libby Browne, President of the Friends of Independence, joined us for the tour. She had met Valery Giscard d'Estaing the night before; her husband Stanhope was the Honorary French Consul in Philadelphia.

He had no security with him, and when I notified our Park Rangers, I told them not to be conspicuous. For about two hours, the former President of France, Mrs. Browne, and I went in and out of Park buildings. We saw the portraits of Lafayette and Conrad Alexander Gerard (the first French Ambassador) in the Second Bank of the United States. We went to Congress Hall to see the portraits of Louis XVI and Marie Antoinette that he had delivered in 1976. We toured Independence Hall, and finally, at the Liberty Bell, someone recognized him. He posed for photographs. I walked him back to his hotel, and another exciting but unofficial visit had concluded.

July 4, 1976

The Independence Day Program, under normal conditions, was produced by the City of Philadelphia with the cooperation of the National Park Service. During this special year there was an additional partner, Philadelphia 76, Inc., which was taking the lead. This was not a problem with the NPS, but Al Guadiosi, who had replaced Harry Bellinger as City Representative, tried to keep Philadelphia 76 out of it. The Mayor and Richard Bond, Chairman of Philadelphia 76, finally resolved the conflict by including all parties in the planning and execution of the program.

We had known for some time that President Gerald Ford would be the principal speaker for the 1976 program. When his advance team arrived, we found out that his schedule for the day was to

President Gerald Ford, Charlton Heston, and Pennsylvania Governor Milton Shapp at Independence Hall (July 4, 1976)

begin at Fort McHenry in Baltimore, and then he would go to Valley Forge to visit the Bicentennial Wagon Train that had crossed the country and was encamped at Valley Forge. He was to then come to Philadelphia for the Independence Day Program and stay for the Philadelphia 76 luncheon, and

finally go to New York for the tall ships.

A few days before July 4th, Frank Fitzgerald of the Franklin Mint showed me a commemorative coin they were doing for the Bicentennial, which would be released on Independence Day. One side of the coin showed the likeness of a historical painting of the signing of the Declaration of Independence and the date "1776." The other side showed President Ford signing a paper on a table with candlesticks and an inkstand and was dated "1976." Their problem was that there was no picture showing President Ford signing something on a table that looked like that. Frank wanted me to set up the table and get President Ford to sign something. By photographing the signing, they could prove that such an event had taken place. I told him that I could set up the table, but the President's advance team would decide if he would participate in a project like they were proposing. I was surprised that they agreed to do it. As soon as the program in front of Independence Hall was over, I was to lead the President to the table where he would sign our VIP Room guest book. The White House photographer would take the picture.

Around July 1st, Lita Solis-Cohen, a close friend

of Addie-Lou and an antiques columnist for *The Philadelphia Inquirer*, called to introduce me to a man by the name of Set Momjian. Mr. Momjian worked for Philco Ford Company and was a collector of almost everything collectible. He called me later in the day and said that he had acquired a number of pieces of metal from the Liberty Bell. We knew that these fragments existed and came from the 1846 drilling on the crack in the bell in an effort to make it ring again. Set Momjian had an affidavit which proved the authenticity of the metal pieces. Mr. Momjian had the fragments made into six tiny thimble size likenesses of the Liberty Bell. He wanted to present one of these bells to President Ford when he came to Independence Hall on July 4, 1976. I told him that I could not make that decision, but if he would meet me at Independence Hall at 4:00 p.m., I would introduce him to the leader of the President's advance team. When he told him the story, the advance team was skeptical of the idea until Mr. Momjian showed them the bell in a beautiful red leather box with President Ford's name on it. They then told me that after the President signs the guest book for the Franklin Mint, I should introduce him to Set Momjian for his presentation. The actual day of July 4th started off hot and muggy. Because of fog, the President's helicopter had a difficult time landing and taking off from Valley Forge, but he finally arrived in downtown Philadelphia in time for the 10:00 a.m. ceremony. I met him and his daughter Susan at the back

door of Independence Hall. We went almost immediately to the platform after pausing in the Assembly Room to contemplate what had happened two hundred years before. Besides the President, the program included actor Charlton Heston reading excerpts from the Declaration of Independence. With special music and a parade

Friends of Independence National Historical Park Certificate Stating That You Were at INHP on July 4, 1976; Cost $1.00

of State flags, the program lasted an hour and ten minutes. At the conclusion, I escorted President Ford back inside, where he signed the guest book and met Set Momjian.

I joined Regional Director Chet Brooks and National Park Service Director Gary Everhardt at the Bellevue-Stratford Hotel ballroom for lunch. President Ford left after the luncheon and went to New York. I went back to the Park, which was filled with people shoulder-to-shoulder. Rich O'Guinn was very concerned with the crowd between Independence Hall and the Liberty Bell. They were climbing on the platform used in the morning program. Most of the streets in the historic district were closed to traffic. The Friends of Independence were selling a certificate for one dollar which certified that you were in Independence National Historical Park on the Bicentennial of the Declaration of Independence. When I saw Addie-Lou, she had just presented one of these certificates to Charlton Heston.

At about 3:30 p.m. we went to a cookout, where I saw a very thrilled Set Momjian. He was so pleased at President Ford's reaction to the small bell that he said now he would like to present one to Queen Elizabeth II when she came on July 6th. I did not think that there was a chance that it could happen, but I told him to meet me the next day and I would introduce him to British Ambassador Sir Peter Ramsbotham. Sir Peter was impressed with the gift, but he indicated that Her Majesty did not normally accept gifts. Since the Queen and her party had already left Bermuda on HMS *Britannia*, he would get in touch with them to see if she would accept Mr. Momjian's gift. Ambassador Rambotham called me that evening to say that the Queen would be pleased to have the gift. He asked me to have Mr. Momjian at the Liberty Bell during her visit there. After my presentation and pictures by the press, I should introduce Set Momjian to Her Majesty and he could make the presentation. This went off without a hitch.

About 4:00 p.m. on July 4th, Chief Ranger O'Guinn became so concerned with the crowd in front of Independence Hall that he was thinking of closing both Independence Hall and the Liberty Bell Pavilion. He spoke to Philadelphia Police Commissioner O'Neil, who got his men to disperse the crowd. That was followed by a heavy summer thundershower which further dispersed the crowd.

Any problems that we had with the million plus crowd on July 3rd-4th were simply a few hot spots of mostly young people who had too much to drink. In their enthusiasm to celebrate, they got out of control. I feel that the spirit of the crowd was that of patriotism and celebration, and it was not a volatile crowd. Our Rangers and the Special Events Team that was sent to assist us did a great job of patrolling the crowd and ensuring that hot spots did not turn into major problems.

An example of the spirit of the crowd happened during the fireworks show that night. The fireworks originated from the top of the Penn Mutual Building behind Independence Hall, and every square inch of the Park and adjacent streets was covered with people. I was in the garden near the corner of Fourth and Walnut Streets. During the show, a young man climbed upon one of the columns that were part of the brick wall of the garden. He was singing and waving his arms, and I was concerned that he might break his neck or damage the column. I asked him to come down but he was reluctant to do so. I was not in uniform, so he was not interested in my plea, but I demanded that he get down. He finally did climb down and I thought I might have a fight on my hands. He looked at me and smiled and said, "God Bless America."

One other story helps illustrate the spirit that we

all felt over the July 4th weekend. On July 3rd, an old hand-painted van with California license tags parked in a legal space on Fourth Street right in front of a neighbor's house. The windows were covered, and it reminded us of something that looked like a "hippie" car from a few years before. I talked to my neighbor Bill Spahn about it, and he was concerned that people might be using drugs or sleeping in the van. He finally saw two young men at the van, but most of the time it just sat there empty. It was there on the 4th, 5th, and 6th. After the visit by Queen Elizabeth II, the two young men who were in the van knocked on Spahn's front door and told him that they were California college students who had taken a year off from their studies in order to see America during the bicentennial year. They said that the three days they had spent in Philadelphia was the highlight of their lives. They hoped that it was not a problem for them to be parked in front of his house, and gave Bill a bottle of wine to express their appreciation.

Queen Elizabeth II

Early in January 1976, I received a telephone call from British Consul General Dennis Richards informing me that Sir Peter Ramsbotham, the British Ambassador to the United States, was coming to Philadelphia and would like to visit with me. We arranged to meet in the Reception Room in the west wing of Independence Hall on a very cold January 17th. Sir Peter informed me that Her Majesty Queen Elizabeth II was coming to Philadelphia later in the year to pay her respects to our bicentennial celebration and to present the

Bicentennial Bell, a gift of the people of Great Britain to the people of the United States.

Sir Peter had an audience with the Queen scheduled for the near future, so he wished to tour the Park in order that he might recommend an itinerary for her visit. I told him that the security people often decide where one goes on official visits. He said that in this case the Queen would tell them where she wished to go and what she wished to visit. So we spent the entire day going in and out of buildings; we even took time to watch the kite-flying contest on Independence Mall that was part of Benjamin Franklin's birthday activities. At the end of the day, I provided him with maps and photographs of the buildings and their interiors.

Over the next couple of months, I provided Dennis Richards with additional information as requested. In April a British security team, the U.S. Secret Service, the Philadelphia Police Department, the British Embassy, and the Park met to discuss the details of Her Majesty's visit to Philadelphia, scheduled for July 6, 1976. My only uneasiness about the date was that it was two days after the 200th Independence Day celebration, which would be huge. Nevertheless, I knew that we would do whatever was necessary to handle her visit. During the next three months there were many meetings; sometime the larger group was involved, but at other times, smaller groups worked out the details. When security matters were the issue, usually Chief of Protection and Interpretation Clyde Lockwood and/or Chief Ranger Rich O'Guinn represented the Park. Assistant Superintendent Douglas Warnock and I were involved as required. It must be kept in mind that in 1976 we were hosting a foreign dignitary every three or four weeks.

The plan was for Queen Elizabeth II and Prince Phillip to leave Bermuda on the yacht HMS *Britannia* on July 5th and arrive at Penn's Landing in Philadelphia early in the morning of July 6th. Since this was the point of entry into the United States for Her Majesty, President Ford sent Interior Secretary Thomas Kleppe to Philadelphia to represent him. The President would host the Queen at the White House a few days later. Kleppe was a proper choice, since the National Park Service is part of the Department of the Interior.

The Interior Secretary would arrive in Philadelphia only one hour before Her Majesty, so we had to devise a system that would allow him to introduce the Queen to several people during the course of the day. I wrote every name and title on a 3x5 card and put them in my hip pocket in the order that they would be needed. Just before an introduction, I would slip the next card to the Secretary. He would glance at the card, and as we neared the person to be introduced, I would step forward and gesture toward the person and the Secretary would say, "Your Majesty, I would like for you to meet…," whoever it was. As was the case with most foreign dignitaries, approximately a week before the official visit, I would receive a notebook from the State Department briefing me on protocol, such as what you do and, more important, what you do not do during the visit. There was also such information as how to address the person, dietary restrictions and cultural

preferences. Usually the notebook would have photographs of everyone in the entourage.

On July 4, 1976, we had a million people in Independence National Historical Park, and in preparation we had received Rangers from other Parks across the Country. They were there mostly for security reasons and they did an excellent job. Another group of Rangers had been sent to Fort McHenry National Monument in Baltimore because President Ford also visited there on July 4th. Our Regional Office suggested that the Baltimore Park Rangers might come to Philadelphia to help us with the Queen's visit before returning to their own Park. I agreed, not because they were needed so much as thinking the additional National Park Service uniform presence would be a good thing.

When the Fort McHenry group arrived on July 5th, and they found out that their uniform for the Queen's visit included a necktie and that they were not to wear their side arms, they rebelled. Their position was that they were commissioned law enforcement officers and that they wore guns and did not wear ties in carrying out their duties. The necktie was an everyday part of the NPS uniform at Independence, and for this occasion it seemed particularly appropriate. As far as firearms were concerned, I felt that Park Rangers should be friendly helper types and in the daytime should not appear as armed law enforcement officers. In a city such as Philadelphia, particularly at night, we must have the ability to protect our visitors and the Park resources. It was our policy that Park Rangers involved in protection and security activities, and with a Federal Law Enforcement

Commission, were to wear their guns only at night. Also at night we used two K-9 dogs. If the situation called for additional firepower, I would have allowed the guns, but without intelligence of a threat, I did not want the image of the National Park Ranger to be that of a gun toter.

I talked to Regional Director Brooks, who was supportive of my position, and early the next morning we met with the disgruntled Rangers. They expressed their opinion. I told them that when I visit their Park, I expect to abide by the rules and policies established by their Superintendent, and while at Independence I expect them to abide by our policies and decisions. I also said that earlier I had talked to British security and to the Secret Service and they saw no need for our Rangers to wear side arms. If there is anyone who cannot respect the decision of the Independence Park Superintendent, then we will be pleased to secure them transportation to the airport. If you stay, I would like to see you in a necktie like our staff, and if you did not bring one with you, please see Clyde Lockwood, who has a sufficient supply. Two men were given rides to the airport.

This whole issue came about as a result of a transition that was taking place both within the National Park Service and with other Federal Agencies. Because of the changing times and some specific incidents, it became obvious that Park Rangers involved mostly in law enforcement were going to have to become more professional in order to handle the crime that was beginning to take place in National Parks. In earlier years, law enforcement was a minor part of a Ranger's

job, but the needs had changed and some Rangers became entirely involved in law enforcement. They were required to attend an eight-week training course at the Federal Law Enforcement Training Center at Brunswick, Georgia. Some of us who preferred a lower profile for law enforcement would try to "de-fang" the Rangers when they returned from training.

On July 6th, Queen Elizabeth II left HMS *Britannia* in order to be at Philadelphia City Hall to meet Mayor Frank Rizzo at 10:00 a.m. This was about the time that Interior Secretary and Mrs. Kleppe arrived at Independence Hall. We discussed the schedule for the day and then went to the Liberty Bell Pavilion to await the Queen's arrival. We were both nervous, and while we were pacing the sidewalk waiting, Secretary Kleppe asked if I had ever imagined that he, a farm boy from North Dakota, and I, a hillbilly from Kentucky, would be standing on a curb in Philadelphia awaiting the arrival of the Queen of England. We were both excited about the day.

When the Queen arrived, William Codus, Assistant U.S. Chief of Protocol, introduced us both to her, and we went into the Liberty Bell Pavilion. According to our instructions from the State Department, when you first meet the Queen you refer to her as "Your Royal Majesty." From then on, you address her as "Your Majesty" or "Ma'am." The chamber where the Liberty Bell is displayed was filled with media photographers. I had told them of our plans just before the Queen arrived, and if they did not interfere, I would try to make sure that they received the coverage they needed.

Queen Elizabeth II and Prince Philip at the Liberty Bell with Secretary of the Interior Thomas Kleppe and Hobie (July 6, 1976)

When we arrived at the Bell, I gave a 3-4 minute talk about its significance, and the Queen actually touched it. After the presentation and questions from her and Prince Philip, we positioned ourselves so that the photographers had a good view of the Queen with the Bell. I moved out of the way, and in another minute, Interior Secretary Kleppe stepped back. We were right on time, so everyone was happy. We escorted the Queen back to her car and she was driven to the Penn Mutual Building observation deck, where she had a great view of the entire historic district of Philadelphia. From there she returned to *Britannia* for lunch.

After the Queen's visit to the Liberty Bell, I took Secretary and Mrs. Kleppe to the Independence

Hall Reception Room and reviewed the event. The Queen was elegant in her black and white wavy, vertical stripped dress, a modest white hat, and a white purse. My presentation at the Bell and the photo session for the press had gone very well. Our conversation drifted to the Queen's hat and purse, and we wondered that with an entourage that included ladies-in-waiting, what could Her Majesty be carrying in her purse.

The Kleppes then joined the Queen on HMS *Britannia* for lunch. During that time, I was making sure that everything was in place for the dedication and the ringing of the Bicentennial Bell.

The Bell was made by Whitechapel Foundry, the same foundry that originally cast the Liberty Bell, and had arrived a few weeks before. It had been installed in the tower at the Park Visitor Center. The Bell weighed 12,446 pounds, nearly four and a half times as much as the Liberty Bell, and it carried the inscription "Let Freedom Ring". Also on the face of the Bell were the words: "FOR THE PEOPLE OF THE UNITED STATES FROM THE PEOPLE OF GREAT BRITAIN 4 JULY 1976". It was to be a ceremonial bell and would peal in celebration on national holidays. It would toll on national days of mourning with a muted hammer. For the enjoyment of Park visitors, it would ring every day at 11:00 a.m. and 3:00 p.m.

The guests for the presentation of the Bell by Queen Elizabeth II were invited to arrive at 2:30 p.m., with the ceremony beginning at 3 p.m. To entertain the guests before the ceremony, the Liberty High School Band from Bethlehem, Pennsylvania, was assembled on the steps of the First Bank of the United States across Third Street from the Visitor Center. In between the First Bank and the Visitor Center were as many chairs as could be fitted into the space. This band was recommended to me by Dennis Richards, British Consul-General, who had seen them before and was impressed by their music and by the fact that they wore a costume similar to one that Her Majesty wore as a young schoolgirl. They were a great hit.

Beginning with my high school and college football days, I have from time to time enjoyed chewing tobacco. A highlight of my life was a day when my grandfather, father, brother George, and myself sat under a mulberry tree at Pappie's

house and chewed tobacco. I kept a supply in my office, and on this particular day, to calm myself I took a small amount of tobacco and hid it in my jaw. It was hardly noticeable and it was only necessary to spit occasionally, when no one was looking. When the caravan with Her Majesty arrived at the visitor center, I was to open the door so that she could exit the limousine. As I took the door handle in my right hand, I remembered the chewing tobacco in my mouth. I took it out with my left hand and, as I opened the door, I flung it away. With my last glance in that direction, I saw a cud of chewing tobacco coming apart as it sailed over the crowd that was cheering the Queen.

Everyone went into the visitor center, where I briefed them on the sequence of events for the ceremony and the walk about to follow. We had a few minutes to wait before the program was to begin, and while we were standing there, Secretary Kleppe whispered to me that he knew what the Queen had in her purse.

As the President's representative, the Secretary had been seated next to the Queen at lunch. When Her Majesty sat down at the table, she opened her purse and removed a "C" clamp that she attached to the table. She hung her purse on the clamp. When the luncheon was over she removed her purse, unscrewed the clamp, and returned it to her purse. She was ready to continue her visit to Philadelphia.

A platform was erected near the front door of the Visitor Center and adjacent to the tower where the Bell was installed. On the platform were four seats (Queen Elizabeth II, Prince Philip, Secretary

Kleppe, and Mrs. Kleppe) and a lectern. Beside the lectern was a column with a button on top that would activate the ringing of the Bell. The actual control was in the security center on the second floor of the Visitor Center. To run a wire from the platform to the controls would have been complicated, so we ran the wire from the platform, through a door, and it disappeared but was not connected to the controls. I was in a position to see the button, and when it was pushed, I would gesture to a Ranger who would radio to the security room and tell them to ring the bell. When I briefed Secretary Kleppe and the Queen, I told them that the bell would not ring immediately because it would take several seconds for the swinging bell to attain enough momentum so that the clapper would strike the sides of the bell.

The Queen came onto the platform accompanied by proper fanfare from the band. With the four people on the platform, the crowd gave them a wonderful greeting. All but Secretary Kleppe were seated, and he welcomed all in attendance and introduced the Queen. During quiet moments you could occasionally hear a disturbance in the distance. There was a demonstration taking place led by Reverend Carl McIntire, a fundamentalist minister from nearby New Jersey, protesting the fact that the

Bicentennial Bell did not have "GOD" in its inscription. We saw Reverend McIntire frequently at Independence National Historical Park protesting one cause or another.

The Queen made an address to the American people which was brief but brilliant. Part of what she said was that the British should celebrate

Hobie and bell ringer Harry Shuttleworth at the Bicentennial Bell before it was hung in the New Visitor Center Tower (June 15, 1976)

July 4th in Britain as we do in America, not in taking pleasure in the separation of the American Colonies from Britain but because you taught us a very valuable lesson, that there is a time to yield. Out of that lesson we lost an Empire but gained a Commonwealth.

Walter Annenberg, former American Ambassador to Great Britain and Philadelphia philanthropist, rushed up to me after the ceremony and excitedly suggested that we should put the text of the speech on the wall of the bell tower so that future visitors might enjoy it. A year later to the day, we unveiled the speech and a likeness of Queen Elizabeth II in bronze at the base of the tower. This was accomplished through a generous gift from Ambassador Annenberg.

Upon completion of the speech, Secretary Kleppe joined the Queen at the podium and he invited her to press the button to ring the Bell. She pushed, I nodded, the Ranger radioed the security office, and the dispatcher activated the Bell. One could hear the motors one hundred feet above us as they began to move the Bell, but after about twenty seconds or so Her Majesty got a concerned look on her face. Finally the Bell began to ring in the key of G below middle C, and we were all relieved. Apparently one of our Rangers was near panic as well, because someone told me later that they heard a radio transmission that said, "Dammit, Hobie said to ring the Bell."

Following the dedication and ringing of the Bicentennial Bell, we began a walk about that would go from the Visitor Center to Independence Hall, some two and a half blocks away. We would be traveling through a 25-foot-wide barricaded route with stops at Carpenters Hall, the Second Bank of the United States, and Independence Hall. I kept up a running commentary along the way.

The Royal Party included:

Her Majesty Queen Elizabeth II
His Royal Highness Prince Philip, Duke of
    Edinburgh
The Right Honorable Anthony Crossland,
Secretary of State for Foreign and
    Commonwealth Affairs
Mrs. Crossland
The Honorable Sir Peter Ramsbotham
British Ambassador to the U.S.
Lady Ramsbotham
The Duchess of Grafton, Lady-in-Waiting
The Honorable Mary Mavnison, Lady-in-Waiting
The Right Honorable Sir Martin Chanteris,
    Secretary to the Queen
Mr. Philip Moore, Assistant Secretary
Mr. Dennis Richards, British Consul General in
    Philadelphia
Mrs. Richards
Mr. John Moreton, Charge d'Affaires, British
    Embassy

The American Party included:

The Honorable Henry Catto, U. S. Chief of
    Protocol
Mrs. Catto
The Honorable Anne Armstrong, U.S.
    Ambassador to Great Britain
Mr. Tolin Armstrong
Mr. William Codus, Assistant Chief of Protocol
Mrs. Codus
The Honorable Thomas Kleppe, Secretary of the
    Interior
Mrs. Kleppe
The Honorable Milton Shapp, Governor of

Pennsylvania
Mrs. Shapp
The Honorable Frank L. Rizzo, Mayor of
  Philadelphia
Mrs. Rizzo

After we examined a map of the Park in front of the Visitor Center, we crossed Third Street, where the Queen greeted the band and its director. Our order of movement was the Queen in the center with Secretary Kleppe on her left and me on her right. A few feet behind us were Prince Philip with Mrs. Kleppe on his left and Assistant Park Superintendent Douglas Warnock on his right. Doug and I did most of the talking, for obvious reasons. The rest of both parties followed. Her Majesty and Prince Philip chatted with people along the way.

As we passed the First Bank of the U.S., I pulled the first card from my hip pocket and passed it to the Secretary. It had the name of John Gane, President of the Carpenters Company, whom he would introduce to the Queen. Doug Warnock told me later that it was around this time that a woman photographer with a huge lens on her camera pointed it at Prince Philip from a few feet away, and he said, "Madam, what part of my anatomy do you propose to take with that camera?"

As we neared the front of Carpenters Hall, I walked a few steps ahead and gestured toward John Gane and then, glancing at his card, the Secretary introduced him to the Queen. He in turn introduced the officers of the Company and we all went into the Hall, where the members were assembled. In a brief ceremony with remarks by Architectural Historian Charles E. Peterson, the Queen was given copies of the books *Preservation in America* and *The Carpenters Company Rule Book* (reprint). While the Queen was at the front for the ceremony, I was standing by Prince Philip, who asked Dr. Ernest Harding, Rector of Christ Church, Philadelphia, if he was a carpenter. Ernest, who was wearing his clerical garb, was surprised, and after a pause he said that he was not, but that he was the chaplain for the Company. Prince Philip responded, "That's good, after all your boss was a carpenter."

After we left Carpenters Hall, I pointed out Pemberton House (Army-Navy Museum) and New Hall (Marine Corps Museum) and we followed the route to Fourth Street. There were people five or six deep lining the route and the Queen would stop and talk to people along the way. We heard a voice with an accent that I assumed was British. The Queen went to the barricade and spoke to the gentleman, and when she turned back to me she said quietly, "My God, He's from Sydney [Australia]. You can hardly go anywhere in the world that you do not see someone from Sydney."

We turned to the right just before reaching the Second Bank and went through the Holly Garden. The Queen spoke to the students who were working in the Friends of Independence Tea Garden, and then we went to the front of the Bank and up onto the landing. We paused, and there were people crowded together for a whole block in either direction on Chestnut Street. Everyone was waving a white handkerchief, and it reminded me of the news reel scenes of World War II when the

Royal Family would visit London neighborhoods that had suffered from the bombing. The Queen waved back and we could tell that she was pleased. At the top of the steps, the Secretary introduced her to John Milley, Park Chief of Museums, who gave her a tour of the Portrait Gallery.

Inside the Second Bank I gave Secretary Kleppe the next card, which was Dr. Gloria Scott, Chairman of the Girl Scouts of America. A special area on the lawn behind the Second Bank had been reserved for two Girl Scouts from each State. Beside the Girl Scout area was an enclosure for the press, and we were to pause halfway down the rear steps of this beautiful Greek revival building for a photographic opportunity. When I had prepared the card for Secretary Kleppe, I

was not sure what the proper designation was for Dr. Scott. I selected "chairperson." So while the three of us were posing for photographs on the steps, Secretary Kleppe said to the Queen that the next person she would meet was Dr. Gloria Scott, Chairperson of the Girl Scouts of America. Her Majesty looked at him in mock surprise and with a smile said, "Chairperson? Have we come to that?" The Secretary blushed, but a few minutes later, when he introduced Dr. Scott, he called her "Chairman." We walked along Library Street, crossed Fifth Street and onto Independence Square.

On Independence Square we stopped near the statue of Commodore John Barry and I pointed out Philosophical Hall, Old City Hall, and

Queen Elizabeth II in the Assembly Room with Hobie (July 6, 1976)

Congress Hall before we entered the rear door of Independence Hall. This was the part of the tour that I had been dreading. I was going to tell the Queen of England the story of our efforts to gain independence from her ancestor, King George III. Her speech at the Bicentennial Bell certainly made it much easier, but still I did not want to say something that would be offensive. I should not have worried because both the Queen and Prince Philip were attentive and asked well-informed questions. They had been well-prepared. While they were moving about the Assembly Room, Sir Peter Ramsbotham asked if Doug Warnock and I could come to HMS *Britannia* at 5:00 p.m. The Queen wished to personally thank us for our efforts on her behalf. Naturally, I said yes.

The limousine that would take Her Majesty back to *Britannia* was at curbside on Chestnut Street in front of Independence Hall. When we came out the door, the applause was deafening. Again, the Queen waved to the crowd. We escorted her and Prince Philip to the limo and they drove six blocks to Penns Landing, where her yacht was docked.

A half-hour later, Doug Warnock and I went to Britannia for an audience with Queen Elizabeth II. There were four of us who had worked on the visit for a period of months. Besides Doug and myself, there were Chief Inspector Wolfinger of the Philadelphia Police Department and Special Agent in Charge DeMilio of the Philadelphia Office of the Secret Service. One at a time we went into the ship's salon and had an audience of several minutes with Her Majesty and Prince Philip. When my time came, they invited me to be seated and asked my assessment of the day. I talked

about the enthusiasm of the crowd and mentioned the white handkerchiefs. After chatting for a few minutes, they presented me with a leather framed and autographed photograph of them both. Before I got up to leave, the Queen said, "Mr. Cawood, my sister Margaret wished to be remembered to you." She obviously was referring to the visit to the Park by Princess Margaret in 1974. After all, they are sisters and apparently talk to each other. As Doug and I left the ship, the Royal photographer took our picture, another souvenir that was sent to us later.

On my way back to my office, a Ranger told me that my office was calling to see if I could join in a reporters' round-up of the day's activities at KYW Radio. The station is on Independence Mall, so I sat in with the reporters, and a question arose as to whether or not the Queen had touched the Liberty Bell. Some said that she did touch it, and since they were reporting live from the Liberty Bell Pavilion, they could play their tapes and prove it. I do not know why it mattered, but she had touched the Liberty Bell.

I rushed home from the radio station to get ready for a black tie dinner in honor of the Queen at the Philadelphia Museum of Art. A committee chaired by Mrs. Walter Annenberg had planned a gala evening that included the commission of a special set of china just for the occasion. One could purchase pieces of the china after the dinner, and this would offset some of the expenses of the evening. We purchased one dinner plate as a souvenir.

When Addie-Lou and I arrived for the pre-dinner

reception, one of the first people we met was John Wayne. Addie-Lou shook his hand and did not let go immediately, and when he tried to disengage, she told him that she had waited too long to meet him and did not wish it to be over too quickly. He got a chuckle out of her.

We sat one table removed from Her Majesty at dinner, and as badly as Addie-Lou wanted to meet her, I did not think it appropriate to approach her table. Although Mayor Rizzo, who was seated next to her, did some table-hopping, according to my State Department materials this would not be the thing to do.

After dinner we adjourned to the Great Stair Hall for champagne, and when the Queen descended the stairway in her peach gown and diamond tiara with the statue of Diana in the background, it was a moment to remember. People rushed forward to try to see her up close or to meet her, and since I had been with her during the day, I held back. We were talking to Isadore and Joannie Scott when I felt someone touch my elbow. I turned around and it was Her Majesty. She said, "You look quite different tonight" (I was wearing a tuxedo rather than my NPS uniform), and I said rather clumsily, "Your Majesty, you sure do look good." Then I presented Addie-Lou, and the Queen told her how pleasant it was to meet her. The Scotts were also introduced to her.

A few minutes later, everyone walked out to the front plaza of the Art Museum with its beautiful view of downtown Philadelphia, and from the Benjamin Franklin Parkway we saw a magnificent fireworks performance.

What a day it was!

Afterward – The Shock

By October 1976, the bicentennial celebration began to wind down. We were no longer in the newspapers and on television every day. The kings, queens, presidents, chancellors, and prime ministers were not coming to the Park any longer, and even though visitor use was significant, they no longer came in the numbers that came earlier in the year. By years' end our visitor count was nearly six million for 1976. Our staff had numbered 421 during the peak of the celebration, but now the seasonal personnel were gone. Because we had resources unlike we ever had before, we did not utilize our volunteers during the peak, and now they were no longer available.

I think that most of our permanent staff felt empty. Everyday we were reminded of how important we were to the bicentennial celebration and how we rose to the challenge. For five years I had daily been involved in preparing the Park or planning and executing the celebration, and we had met all of our goals. We spent more than 30 million dollars in five years and we came in on time and on budget. All projects were completed and in use and would serve visitors for years into the future.

One thing that had not changed was that I continued to be on the speakers circuit, although now I was reporting on the results of the bicentennial celebration rather than on what would happen in 1976. Every organization and group that invited me to speak usually gave me some kind of award or certificate, which was their way of participating in the bicentennial.

But the question was, "What are we going to do next?" We consulted a psychologist, who was helpful, but our staff, particularly the interpreters, began to talk and meet about the future. By the spring of 1977, we had developed a plan to celebrate a Bicentennial Era, 1774-1800, that mirrored Philadelphia's role in the founding of our nation. There would obviously be two huge celebrations: the Bicentennial of the Declaration of Independence (1776) and the Bicentennial of the Constitution of the United States (1787). But, there would be many smaller commemorations and celebrations which we would appropriately observe.

Some of the bicentennials that we anticipated were: Rochambeau's French Army passing through Philadelphia, French Recognition of the U.S.A., Battle of Yorktown, Return of the captured British Flags, Ratification of the Articles of Confederation, Treaty of Paris, Mount Vernon Conference, Annapolis Conference, Ratification of the Constitution by each State, death of Benjamin Franklin, Washington's Second Inaugural, Adam's First Inaugural, and selected landmark actions of Congress and the Supreme Court, 1790-1800, while Philadelphia was the capital. One date that I looked forward to was my home state of Kentucky being admitted to the Union (1792).

We had a plan.

Waiting for the Other Shoe to Drop

The year after the bicentennial celebrations of America's Declaration of Independence, I was informed by the Pennsylvania College of Podiatric Medicine that they wished to bestow upon me a Doctor of Humane Letters. Nineteen seventy-six had been an eventful year of national commemoration, with many of the festivities taking place front and center at Independence National Historical Park, where I served as park superintendent. Important leaders and public figures from around the world came to Philadelphia throughout that bicentennial year to mark the anniversary, and as park superintendent it was my job to be their host. History and the National Park Service had put my staff and myself at the center of the world's stage, and we had performed flawlessly. Still, I was puzzled by the College of Podiatric Medicine's intentions in their honorary degree.

I was not being asked to deliver the commencement address. I was not in the financial position to make a significant monetary gift to the college. Certainly the college would not enhance its reputation by granting a degree to me. The school's president, Dr. James Bates, and his wife were active members of the Friends of Independence National Historical Park, but that did not seem to be a sufficient reason for the honor. Why did they want to confer a degree on me?

A little hesitant, I accepted their offer. Keeping my eyes and ears open for clues to their intent, I looked forward to the ceremony. When I was introduced at the commencement, mention was made about my management of Independence National Historical Park, the bicentennial celebration, my relationship to the community, and my being an all-around good guy. Even after the hooding, I kept waiting for the other shoe to drop. My suspicions of concealed motives were justified when I was approached a short time after commencement; however, I was caught a bit off guard when they inquired about the possibility of donating my National Park Service uniform shoes to the College of Podiatric Medicine's Shoe Museum. It was during the explanation for the museum's request that I came to realize that my shoes were quite well-heeled in international circles. They had met presidents, kings, queens, chancellors, prime ministers, and a host of other dignitaries from around the world during the bicentennial year.

I was honored and a bit tickled by the college's petition and suggested that I continue to wear the shoes as long as I was the park superintendent. In this manner I could keep adding names that would make an even more impressive list of people that the shoes had met. There was no danger that I would wear the shoes out, because I only wore my uniform when it was important for me to be identified as the park superintendent. On average workdays I wore civilian clothes. In fact, the Shoe Museum had reasoned that over time, all other parts of my uniform would have been replaced, but not the shoes. Trousers, shirts, even belts would wear out much faster than the shoes. I was even told that over a period of seven years, every cell in the human body is replaced with new, so it could be reasoned that I was not even the same

person as the one who met all those people. The only constant in hosting twenty years of dignitaries would be my shoes!

So that is how it came to be that on my last day at work for the National Park Service, in April 1991, I took my uniform shoes and a multi-page list of the noteworthy public figures that the shoes had met over to the Shoe Museum at the Pennsylvania College of Podiatric Medicine, where they remain today.

IV.

THE BETWEEN YEARS (1977-1985)

...h Recognition

...gn country to give
...o the United States
...t 6, 1778, the
...ander Gerard, presented
...ican Congress at
Independence Hall. At that point in time, the
Second Continental Congress was our ad hoc
government, and they received the French
delegation.

The ceremony took place in the Assembly Room of Independence Hall, with the furniture arranged so that the chairs would be placed in a horseshoe shape around the wall. The President of the Congress, Henry Laurens of South Carolina, was located in the center, with the Congressmen filling in the remaining chairs. Ambassador Gerard, his aide, and a French admiral represented the French and stood at the open end of the horseshoe and faced the President.

After the Congress gathered in Independence Hall, two of their members, Richard Henry Lee and Samuel Adams, were sent in a carriage to collect the French Ambassador and his staff. Upon returning to Independence Hall, they entered the Assembly Room, and in a half-hour ceremony, their credentials were presented and accepted. After a few brief speeches, the Congressmen and the French retired to City Tavern for a proper reception, during which 21 toasts were made. Each toast was accompanied by artillery fire.

Well, this is a bicentennial event that we just could not miss. Our historical staff provided the materials necessary to our old friend and drama advisor Franklin Roberts, who scripted and produced a re-enactment of the event. Roberts worked with the Opera Company of Philadelphia to find the costumes and props that were required. We enlisted the following persons to play a role in the re-enactment:

Bernard Hughes, distinguished actor
  Benjamin Franklin
G. de la Villesbrunne, current French Consul-
  General in New York

Gerard de la Villesbrunne, French Consul-General in New York. August 6, 1978. Photo by T. Cohen. *Image Courtesy of Independence National Historical Park*

French Ambassador
John Fawcette, French Consul in Philadelphia
  General's Aide
Tom McCallum President FINHP
  French Admiral
Lawrence Coughlin, Member of Congress
  Henry Laurens
Raymond Lederer, Member of Congress
  Member of Congress
Joshua Ellberg, Member of Congress
  Member of Congress
John McCullough, Editor, *Philadelphia Bulletin*
  Member of Congress
Edwin Guthman, Editor, *Philadelphia Inquirer*
  Member of Congress
David Boldt, Columnist, *Philadelphia Inquirer*
  Member of Congress
Richard Lonsdorf, FINHP
  Member of Congress
Set Momjian, FINHP
  Member of Congress
Arthur Kaufman, Independence Hall Association
  Member of Congress

The tables were removed from the Assembly Room and the chairs arranged as historically appropriate. Our problem was that to do the re-enactment in the proper space, we would be unable to share it with the general public. So we decided that we would do the ceremony twice: once inside Independence Hall for the press and National Public Radio, and once outside on a platform of the same dimensions as the Assembly Room, so thousands could see the ceremony re-enacted.

Roberts felt that we needed someone to give a running commentary so that everyone would

understand what was transpiring. Who better than Benjamin Franklin to host something in Philadelphia. Even though, historically, Franklin was in France representing the States, Bernard Hughes, who had just won a Golden Globe for

Archbishop of Cyprus (May 30, 1979)

his performance in *DA*, did an outstanding job of portraying him as "the spirit of Franklin."

After the ceremony, as in the 18th Century, everyone retired to City Tavern for a reception. The Friends of Independence National Historical Park sponsored the reception by subscription so anyone who wished could attend. There ended up some 300 people in the City Tavern garden sipping champagne.

We borrowed two cannons from Valley Forge

National Historical Park and placed them a safe distance from the crowd. Each congressman stepped out on the City Tavern balcony overlooking the garden and delivered the toast we had prepared for him. I would then raise my handkerchief and our artillery crew would touch off a cannon. This went on for 21 toasts. Black powder, smoke, and champagne is a heady mixture, so a good time was had by all.

Bicentennial of the Articles of Confederation (March 1, 1981)

When the Second Continental Congress voted for independence on July 2, 1776, it did not create a new government; it merely said that the colonies wished to be free and independent. Richard Henry Lee's resolution that led to the independence vote also proposed the establishment of a Confederation of Thirteen States. Until a government could be created and approved, the Second Continental Congress became the temporary government until a permanent government could be framed.

A committee was formed to draw up a plan of union that was to be called the Articles of Confederation. A draft was quickly prepared, but because of disagreement over representation in Congress and the pressing issue of war, the matter was delayed.

A draft of the Articles of Confederation was completed on November 15, 1777. It referred to the thirteen sovereign States as the United States of America. The draft showed their distrust of a strong central authority by creating a Congress

of Confederation as the basic government. In the Congress, each State would have a single vote, and the delegates retained for the States all powers not specifically granted to the central government.

The Congress could declare war and peace, manage foreign relations, control Indian affairs, issue and borrow money, and establish an army and navy. It could not regulate trade, levy taxes, nor interfere with a State or its citizens.

One of the weaknesses of the Articles was obvious from the beginning: all decisions had to be unanimous. Twelve of the States approved the new government very quickly, but Maryland balked. Maryland objected to the western lands claimed by many of the States, and this issue held up the unanimous approval until March 1, 1781. The States finally agreed to cede their western land claims to the central government, so on that date Maryland ratified the Articles of Confederation.

Any knowledge of the Articles of Confederation by the American public is unusual; however, it is part of the evolution of our government that has brought us to this point in time. From the beginning of the bicentennial celebration, we were interested in celebrating a bicentennial era, so it was important that we not let this date go unnoticed.

Again we asked our neighbor and drama producer, Franklin Roberts, to work with the Park staff historian, Marty Yoelson, to create a half-hour radio script about the Articles of Confederation. WHYY, the Philadelphia National Public Radio Station, was interested in broadcasting such a program, and they would share it with the entire National Public Radio (NPR) network. The broadcast would take place from the Assembly Room of Independence Hall at 11:00 a.m. on March 1, 1981.

Roberts prepared a script that included three voices, and we were able to cast the following: Arlen Specter, U.S. Senator from Pennsylvania; Sheldon Hackney, President of the University of Pennsylvania, a historian, and the future Director of the National Endowment of the Humanities (NEH); and Emlyn Williams, a noted actor, playwright, and platform speaker. Mr. Williams was in Philadelphia doing a one-person Charles Dickens show at the Walnut Street Theater.

The broadcast went well, with only a handful of staff and friends being on hand for the event. Hopefully there were thousands of people in the radio audience who gained a new understanding of the Articles of Confederation.

As a conclusion to the celebration, we invited those who had been involved, along with the officers of the Friends of Independence National Historical Park, to a luncheon at City Tavern following the broadcast. Several people made brief remarks at the luncheon, and I presented Emlyn Williams with a bundle of leeks all tied up with a blue ribbon. The leek is an emblem of Wales. Mr. Williams was delighted because he is Welsh and March 1st is St. David's Day, the patron saint of Wales. The leeks were the only remuneration that any members of the cast received for their performance.

My friend Barbara Tiffany remarked, "We have just witnessed the successful completion of another of Hobie's non-events."

Treaty of Paris

Although the fighting in the American Revolution was mostly concluded in the Fall of 1781 at the Battle of Yorktown, it took nearly two years to officially end the war by the signing of the Treaty of Paris. Peace talks began in April 1782 in Paris, with Richard Oswald representing the British and Benjamin Franklin being the only commissioner of five appointed by the Americans who was present. By September, the Americans John Jay and Henry Laurens arrived and formal negotiations began. John Adams arrived next, but Thomas Jefferson, also appointed by the Congress, did not serve.

The negotiations went back and forth until, by November 30, 1784, a preliminary treaty was ready to send to the respective governments. The treaty decided the following issues: (1) The British would recognize the independence of the United States of America. (2) Boundaries were established for the United States: the St. Croix River dividing Maine and Nova Scotia; the St. Lawrence watershed divide; the 45th parallel through the Great Lakes; a line from Lake Superior to the Mississippi River; the middle of the Mississippi River south to Spanish Louisiana, the 31st parallel; then eastward to the St. Mary's River and on to the Atlantic Ocean. (3) The U.S. was given the right to fish the grounds off Newfoundland and Nova Scotia. (4) All debts due creditors were validated. (5) Congress would recommend to the States that all property belonging to Loyalists and seized during the war be returned. (6) Hostilities would stop and all British land and sea forces would be removed as soon as possible.

The treaty was sent to America and ratified by Congress and sent back to Paris, where it was signed by all parties on September 3, 1783. The signatories were the British, Americans, French, Spanish, and Dutch (Netherlands). The United States of America was recognized throughout the world as a sovereign nation.

To properly mark this landmark event in 1983, the Congress created a committee to plan and execute an appropriate celebration. The real worker on the committee was Dr. Joan Challinor of Washington, DC. Joan was a wonderful lady who worked tirelessly to have this important moment in American history remembered.

On September 3, 1983, at Independence National Historical Park, we had a day of celebrations, starting with a ceremony at Independence Hall. The U.S. Army Band provided music. The program went as follows:

-Welcome
Hobart Cawood, Supt. INHP

-Remarks and Master of Ceremonies
Faith Whittlesey, Special Assistant to the President

-National Anthem of Great Britain
U.S. Army Band

-Remarks

Michael Marshall, Deputy Consul General of Great Britain in New York
-National Anthem of France
 U.S. Army Band
-Remarks
Bernar Morbieu, Deputy Consul General of France in New York

-National Anthem of The Netherlands
U.S. Army Band

-Remarks
Herman J. duMarchie Sarvaas, Minister and Charge 'dAffairs, Embassy of the Royal Netherlands

-National Anthem of Spain
U.S. Army Band

-Remarks
Gabriel Manneco, Spanish Ambassador to the United States

-Issuance of a Postal Stamp
E. Herbert Dawes, Regional Postmaster General

After the ceremony, all of the participants sat at a long table and signed stamp caches for the first day of issue. During my 20 years at Independence, we had several first day of issue ceremonies for postage stamps. Stamp collectors and dealers flock to these programs in great numbers to get a specially printed envelope with the new stamp on it, and the "first day of issue" cancellation is special. What makes it even more special is to get the autographs of those participating in the program. We had a small luncheon at City Tavern

Willi Brandt, Former Chancellor of Germany. Fall 1983. *Image Courtesy of Independence National Historical Park*

for the participants following the signing session.

Throughout the afternoon a "Treaty of Paris" hot air balloon was tethered behind the Second Bank for people to see. The National Park Service has a regulation against the take-off and landing of aircraft in units of the National Park System. By having this balloon tethered by a long rope, we didn't feel that we were taking off and landing. One time before on Independence Mall, at a program which included a hot air balloon, we let them prepare the take off in the Park but required them to walk the balloon out onto Market Street to launch it.

Also in the afternoon, the U.S. Army Band performed a wonderful concert in Independence Square. This band, called "Pershing's Own," is one of the greatest musical groups in the United States. We were fortunate to have this band and other ceremonial bands from the U.S. Army

participate in many programs at Independence National Historical Park. Colonel Eugene W. Allen, the musical director, always arranged a great show. Mark Murray, who scheduled the ceremonial groups for the army, was a good friend and very helpful, and I do not think it was because his wife was a Cawood.

Another important and appropriate bicentennial program had been executed.

B. Other Activities

Opera Performances

The Bicentennial of 1976 had proven to the cultural institutions of Philadelphia that there was value in working together for the benefit of all. As a result, the Cultural Affairs Council was created to continue the cooperation. I served on its board. One day I was riding on a bus with the manager of the Opera Company of Philadelphia, on our way to a meeting. I confessed to him that I had never seen a live opera performance. He told me that the best way to see my first opera was to be in it. When I asked him what he meant, he said that there are people on stage in an opera who are part of the action but do not sing. However, they must learn the music because it cues their movement on stage. These extras or "spear carriers" are officially known as supernumeries. Michael wondered if Addie-Lou and I would be interested in performing in an opera. I said "Yes."

Approximately a month later, the chief

supernumerary called to ask if we would be interested in performing in Mozart's *Così Fan Tutti*. I would be a lackey and Addie-Lou would be a serving wench. There would be eight rehearsals and two performances and we would not be permitted to miss a single one. The reason was that only the principals and the "supers" would be on stage. The chorus was to be off stage and not seen. Also, the "supers" would change the set between scenes, so their complete knowledge of the music and the set was critical. We could make the schedule, so we agreed to participate. Our friend Franklin Roberts was a supernumerary also.

During rehearsals, Jane Nesmith, the opera company publicist, asked if we would allow her to try to get an article in *The Philadelphia Inquirer* about our being in the opera. She thought that our participation would be good publicity for the Opera Company of Philadelphia. The newspaper sent a photographer to our dress rehearsal, and the article even described where we would be standing. They felt that was necessary because with costumes and makeup, it would be difficult to tell who we were on stage.

We had so much fun with the costumes, makeup, and music that we continued whenever our schedule would permit. We received pay for the operas that were filmed for television: three dollars for each rehearsal and three dollars per performance. I performed with Luciano Pavarotti three times, in *La Bohéme*, *L'Elisir D'Amore*, and *Un Ballo in Maschera*. Addie-Lou worked with Pavarotti only twice because there were no female roles in *L'Elisir D'Amore*. Gian Carlo Menotti directed us twice. Our friends Tom and Jeanne

McCallum also became "supers," so we really enjoyed it.

Other than the problems with *Cosi Fan Tutte*, my greatest moment was when I played the "notaio" who performed the marriage ceremony in L'Elisir D'Amore. Addie-Lou's would be when she was the Empress of Russia in *The Queen of Spades*. She wore a special wig and gown worthy of an empress and entered the ballroom down a long flight of steps. There were two young men escorting her entry and then one danced her across the floor and they exited on the opposite side of the stage. Her entire performance was approximately 90 seconds. However, it was such an elegant scene that National Public Television used it to promote the showing of the opera on television. One day we were in Anchorage, Alaska, on vacation and in late afternoon we went to our hotel to rest. We switched on the television and, just before drifting off in a nap, we heard the music and looked at the television and there was Addie-Lou, the Empress of Russia. It was a promo for the opera, which would be shown on television the next week.

Demonstrations

Independence National Historical Park has always been a place where individuals and groups wish to gather to make their position known on any number of issues. It has always been the desire of the National Park Service to cooperate so long as the demonstrators conform to the permit system set forth in Title 36, Uniform Code of Federal Regulations, and so long as they do not infringe on the ability of visitors to enjoy the Park.

There were any number of places in the Park that were appropriate for these special uses, depending on the size and nature of the event. A good many of the demonstrators wanted to hold their events in the shadow of Independence Hall or at the Liberty Bell. Certainly, we were willing to coach them with what would work and what would not be appropriate. Larger groups, such as on Israeli and Greek Independence Days, Von Steuben Day, and Puerto Rican Day, used the Judge Lewis Quadrangle on the second block of Independence Mall.

The permit system was rather simple, and as long as name, address, organization, purpose of the event, and number expected were included, the permit was usually issued. At Independence we had so many requests that we created our own special use permit form. The information was usually taken by a ranger (public affairs) who would process the permit and review it with me for signature. Maria Burk, Dan Sharpe, and Susan Davenport managed the permits and the events.

The events varied greatly, from something as simple as wedding photographs in a garden or a high school choir performing on Independence Square to a major demonstration by the Klu Klux Klan. Events of a more serious nature required considerable planning and assistance from the Philadelphia Police Department. The police unit that we worked with on demonstrations was Civil Disobedience, commanded by George Fencl, one of the best in his field.

When I first came to Independence, we were having a number of demonstrations for and against the war in Vietnam. The Gay and Lesbian Task Force also frequently applied for a permit. There were 300-400 applications for a permit each year, but in 1976 we hit our peak with more than 1,500. One of my favorites was a group of Ukrainian ladies and men who wanted to have a demonstration in support of Professor Moroz, who was imprisoned in the Soviet Union for his activities. We helped them have a successful event. After several years of demonstrations, Professor Moroz was freed in an exchange, and he came to Philadelphia to thank those who had supported him. I met him at the Liberty Bell and he told the ladies that he had been aware of their efforts and he believed that their support was an important factor in his freedom.

The planning with a group did not always work. I issued a permit to We the People-200 for the official opening ceremonies for The Bicentennial of the Constitution. The permit covered Independence Square and the First Block of Independence Mall. A platform was erected in front of Independence Hall, with the audience being in Chestnut Street and on the grass in front of the Liberty Bell. Vice President George Bush and 13 State Governors were at the ceremony, which made security a necessity. To enter, the audience had to pass through metal detectors.

A group of demonstrators asked for a permit to demonstrate against Vice President Bush for a reason that I cannot even remember. I do know that this group had a reputation for being rather physical and even had tossed animal blood on people they did not like. I told them that they could not come into the We The People-200 permit space but that I would provide them an alternate space. On the day of the event, some 200 of them marched in a group with banners and mega phones, but instead of going into their assigned space, they began to shove and push their way into the audience area for the bicentennial program. Park Rangers and Philadelphia Police arrested several of them. The program went forward and was a success, but the demonstrators took us to account for keeping them out of the audience area, and the Judge told us that we were wrong to stop them.

Even though they were a group, carrying signs and chanting slogans when they presented themselves at the entry to the event, they were individuals and we could not assume that they were there to demonstrate. If after they entered the secure area they created a demonstration, they could be arrested. It was described to me that even though it looked like a duck, had feathers like a duck, and walked like a duck, it could not be assumed to be a duck until it said "QUACK."

Adventures On-board Ships

As part of the tricentennial of the City of Philadelphia (1981), the great ocean liner *Queen Elizabeth II* (*QEII*) came to Philadelphia instead of sailing to its usual American terminus in New York. The ship came up the Delaware River and docked at a commercial terminal in South Philadelphia. After the passengers disembarked, the *QEII* remained in port for three days before sailing on its return trip to England. While the ship was in port, it hosted a number of social activities related to the tricentennial. By far the most popular and best attended was an evening gala which included drinks, dinner, and dancing.

A couple of weeks prior to the gala, Richard Doran, the City Representative and Director of Commerce for Philadelphia, called me to say that he had four extra tickets for the gala and he offered them to Addie-Lou and me, and anyone we would like to invite. We jumped at the opportunity and invited Tom McCallum, Chairman of the Friends of Independence, and his wife Jeanne.

On the night of the gala, Tom and Jeanne picked us up at our house and drove us to the docks where the *QEII* was located. The event was black tie and the ladies looked great. Addie-Lou wore a gown

Addie-Lou and Hobie Dancing on the QEII

with bare shoulders, and to add to the feeling of a gala, she wore long white gloves that came well above her elbows.

Despite having to run a gauntlet of Irish demonstrators, we were prepared for a great evening. Politicians, business people, and community leaders across the board were all there. We drank, we ate, we toured the ship, and we danced the night away. This was a night to remember, so you can imagine we were very late in getting to bed.

Our telephone rang at seven o'clock the following morning and awakened us from a deep sleep. It was our friend Alice Lonsdorf, who asked Addie-Lou if she had seen the front page of the Philadelphia Inquirer this morning. Addie-Lou told Alice that we were asleep when she called and that we had not seen it. Alice told her to get out of bed and get the paper. We were not having a paper delivered at that time, so I had to put my clothes on and walk two blocks to get a copy. On the lower half of the front page of the Philadelphia Inquirer was a large picture of Addie-Lou and me dancing at the gala on board the *QEII*. The picture was more of Addie-Lou and her long white gloves than of me. Usually when we were mentioned together in the newspaper we were listed as "Hobie Cawood, Superintendent of Independence National Historical Park, and his wife Addie-Lou," but in this case the caption read "Addie-Lou Cawood and her husband Hobie." We figured that it was the long white gloves.

HMS *Bulwark*

One day at the office I received a telephone call from Captain Carl Josephson, Chief of Staff at the Philadelphia Naval Base, inviting Addie-Lou and me to dinner at his house on Saturday night. The British aircraft carrier HMS *Bulwark* was in port in Philadelphia and had suffered a fire on board. British Admiral John Cox was in charge of the Fleet to which *Bulwark* was attached and had come to Philadelphia to investigate the fire and supervise the repairs. Carl had invited the Admiral to dinner, and he wanted to include some local people in the dinner party.

When we arrived at Carl's house on the Navy Base, we found that there were eight of us in addition to Admiral Cox, and we had a great time. The Admiral was a very personable man who told us that he was going to be in Philadelphia for a few days and that maybe we could come to the *Bulwark* some evening and join him in a "can of beans." We all agreed that it would be fun but no plans were made before the evening ended.

At seven o'clock on Sunday morning, our doorbell rang and I stumbled out of bed and answered it. On our front step stood a British Royal Marine, who saluted and handed me an envelope which enclosed an engraved invitation. The Admiral was inviting us to a black tie dinner (with medals and decorations) on board HMS *Bulwark* on Monday evening. I invited the Marine in while we prepared a written response to the invitation. When we gave him our affirmative answer, he asked if we would like for him to provide transportation and we told him that was not necessary, so he gave us a sheet of driving instructions that would take us to the *Bulwark* gangplank.

When Admiral Cox had first mentioned the "can of beans," we thought we would be visiting a ship that had suffered from a fire and that we would have a modest dinner, but now, with the black tie and an engraved invitation delivered by a Royal Marine, well, we didn't know what to expect. Monday was a rainy, windy day, and when we drove up to the gangplank a seaman was there with umbrellas. The Captain of the *Bulwark* met us at the top of the gangplank and asked Addie-Lou if she would like to visit a room where she could fix her hair. We were then led to a reception room where we saw our friends from the Josephson's party and met the senior staff of the *Bulwark*. The drink of the night was the traditional "Horse's neck" of the British Navy. I think that it is a mixture of brandy and ginger ale.

The *Bulwark*'s officers were in dress uniform and were most attentive to their guests. In fact, I got the impression that certain ones were assigned to individual guests in order to make sure that everyone had all of their needs fulfilled. Just before dinner was served, a seating chart mounted on a silver holder was shared with the guests so that we would be able to find the seat where we were to dine without confusion. As I recall, there were about 20 of us at a single table.

The meal was wonderful, with white bait and a white wine for the first course. The main course was lamb, roast potatoes, and green beans with a red wine. After dessert, the women were dismissed so that the men could talk and enjoy cigars and port. Afterward, when the women

returned, Addie-Lou and I offered to organize a tour through the Park and the adjacent historic district for them. They accepted and we agreed on a date.

What an evening! We had a great time, and over the course of two dinner parties and the tour we became good friends with Admiral Cox. He even invited us to visit his house in Hampshire, England, which we did on a future trip to the UK.

Other Nautical Adventures

On one occasion, three British guided missile ships were visiting Philadelphia and we attended a reception on the HMS *Alacrity*. During the evening, we were invited to sail with them the following day to Annapolis, Maryland. The Philadelphia Branch of the English Speaking Union arranged for return bus transportation for those of us who decided to go. This turned into a unique experience because we were able to visit the war room on the ship and see how they spot targets hundreds of miles away. It was also wonderful just to be on board as we went down the Delaware River, through the Chesapeake–Delaware Canal, and then into the Chesapeake Bay. We left the ship at the United States Naval Academy and returned to Philadelphia by bus.

On two occasions, Addie-Lou and I participated in cruises sponsored by the Friends of Independence National Historical Park. Joanne Buller, who arranged fundraising tours for the Friends, planned these. One cruise was from Vancouver up the Inland Passage to Alaska, and the other was from Montreal down the St. Lawrence River and back to Philadelphia. My passage was complementary because I would give talks and illustrated lectures on bicentennial activities during the cruise. Both were well-organized and enjoyable.

Japanese Crown Prince Akihito and his wife, Princess Michiko, came to Philadelphia to see two of his former tutors, Mrs. Elizabeth Gray Vining and Miss Esther Biddle Rhoads. Between the two of them, they had taught the Crown Prince for fourteen years. The morning after his reunion with his teachers, the royal couple came to the Park to see the Liberty Bell and Independence Hall.

I met the Prince and Princess at the Liberty Bell in the company of Mayor Frank Rizzo. The visit had been announced by the news media, so there was a large crowd lining both sides of the first block of Independence Mall, with the center being kept clear as the route for the tour. The future Emperor of Japan was dressed in a dark western-style suit and the Princess wore a white suit with a white hat. They were small in stature and spoke excellent English.

I gave them a presentation at the Liberty Bell, after which they quietly asked a few questions. The press asked them for pictures at the Bell and they modestly complied. After the photographs, we exited the Liberty Bell Pavilion and walked up the eastern walkway of the Independence Mall. Someone called out the Princess's name from outside the barricade and she ran to greet them. It was an old school mate of hers from college. After a brief pause, we continued to the front of Independence Hall, where I called their attention to Old City Hall and Congress Hall.

Crown Prince Akihito and Princess Michiko of Japan (June 26, 1978)

We entered Independence Hall and went straight into the Assembly Room, where a selected number of reporters and photographers were already in place. We walked to the center of the room, where I told them about the creation of the United States. They then posed for pictures at the Rising Sun Chair and Mayor Rizzo presented them with a Philadelphia Bowl (a Wedgewood small punch bowl decorated with 18th-Century drawings of famous Philadelphia buildings, a gift frequently given to visiting dignitaries).

While they were examining the furnishings, Prince Akihito looked out the window and asked what the crowd in Independence Square was doing. I told him that this was a naturalization ceremony and the people in the seats were becoming citizens of the United States. It was obvious that he noticed a significant number of Japanese in the group.

I walked them back to the front door, where they

expressed their appreciation for the tour and then entered their limousine on Chestnut Street. A very low-key but pleasant visit. In 1989, Akihito succeeded his father Hirohito to become Emperor of Japan.

Special Use Permits

Persons who would like to hold some sort of special program or activity in the units of the National Park System can make application and the Park Superintendent has the ability to issue or deny the request. There are Service-wide conditions for the issuing of a permit included in a publication called Title 36, Uniform Code of Federal Regulations. An applicant must give their name and address, identify any organizations that they might represent, and establish their relationship to them. The activity must not interfere with normal operations of the Park or the enjoyment of Park by its visitors. It is also important that applicants estimate the number of people who might attend their activity.

A Park could establish its own special requirements, and at Independence we had special rules for Independence Hall. The first floor would be used only for official activities of the National Park Service. This usually included

visits by Presidents of the United States, official visits by international leaders, and bicentennial activities. The second floor could be used for activities that had occurred there before 1800. This would be receptions, ceremonies, and social activities approved by the colonial governors of Pennsylvania. Exceptions could be made by the current Governor of Pennsylvania or the Secretary of the Interior. The other requirement was that anyone who held a special program or activity must leave the Park in the condition in which they found it.

The permit system was important to the NPS in maintaining control of what was being conducted on Park grounds. It was also important in keeping more than one party from using a given space. As you can imagine, two opposing parties in one space could lead to trouble.

When I first went to Independence Park, I was

Bishop Desmond Tutu with Hobie, Philadelphia Mayor Wilson Goode and Mrs. Goode (January 15, 1986)

caught up in the many requests for permits by groups protesting the war in Vietnam. This caused me to realize that there was no better way to make one's point-of-view known than in the shadow of Independence Hall or close to the Liberty Bell. Warren McCullough, who managed Independence Hall for the City of Philadelphia before it was turned over the National Park Service, managed the special use permits until he retired around 1974. Maria Burks replaced him in that position and we worked to simplify the special use permit system. Maria would accept applications, and every few days she would come to my office, where we would go over the permit requests and approve or reject them. Most were approved. If they were asking for something inappropriate, then Maria would work with them until their request was for something that we would approve. We wanted their demonstration or activity to take place and we would work with them to make it a success.

In the early 1970's I issued a permit to the Vietnam Veterans Against the War to hold a demonstration in the vicinity of the Commodore Barry Statue on Independence Square. One of their members, in his excitement, ran to the front of Independence Hall and hurled a vial of blood onto the steps. The demonstration was being covered live on the radio, so within an hour I had a telephone call from the Rev. Carl McIntire, a fundamentalist preacher from New Jersey. McIntire came often to the Park, and he wanted a permit to bring his followers to Independence Hall and wash the front steps. I approved it. The Veterans and the Fundamentalist were pleased and I had clean steps.

During the early 70's a man called Almighty Martin would show up almost daily carrying a sign for a variety of causes and beating his drum. We usually cooperated with him unless he became a nuisance to the visitors. Since the Park was some eight city blocks surrounded by the city, we usually coordinated our permits with the Civil Disobedience Squad of the Philadelphia Police Department. Its leader, George Fencl, worked with our Chief Ranger who was in charge of security for the Park. Charles Mason was in that position when I arrived in 1971, and he was followed by Clyde Lockwood, Rich O'Guinn, Randy Cooley, and Bob Burns. All were good people who knew law enforcement but could temper it with good judgment. If I was not available to approve a permit that needed an instant decision, I told them that they should make the decision. If there was a problem, we could deal with it later.

Once I issued a permit for a group that was called "Jews for Jesus," and the next time I saw George Fencl, he told me that I had made a big mistake. He said the group was unruly, impossible to manage, and would even completely undress in public. This story was reinforced by any of his officers that I saw in the next two weeks. I got up early on a Saturday morning and was standing in Independence Square when George Fencl marched in with the group. He saw me and just fell over laughing. His prank had worked because he had gotten me to come to work on my day off to see a harmless group of kids play the guitar and sing songs.

George Fencl was a great guy who was respected by all of the groups with which he worked. One day a protest group led by Milton Street, a brother to a future Mayor of Philadelphia, was having a protest about some Federal program at the Federal Office Building on Independence Mall. Their objective was to get the attention of the press, but that wasn't working, so they decided to march south two blocks to the Curtis Building to picket some Federal offices there. En route they passed Independence Hall. At about 3:00 p.m. I got a call that there were 60 demonstrators sitting on the floor of Independence Hall. Fortunately, our staff had quickly closed the doors of the Assembly Room to protect the historic furnishings there.

I called the U.S. Attorney, who suggested that we let them sit there until 5:00 p.m., when we close the building. I said that I would prefer to throw them out, but not give them the publicity of arresting them. Besides, visitors could not enter the building if they were there. I was always concerned that someone making a once in a lifetime visit would be denied their experience. The U.S. Attorney still said "No." A ranger inside the building then reported that someone had just lit a cigarette. I told the U.S. Attorney that we had a fire hazard and I was going to throw them out. Our rangers and Fencl's officers entered the building and began to carry them outside. George grabbed one arm of Milton Street and I grabbed the other and carried him out on the sidewalk and dropped him. We cleaned out the building in 15 minutes and restored visitation. The press never heard a word of it.

One group that we saw often was the Gay and Lesbian Task Force. Early in the gay movement, Mark Siegel would try to chain himself to the Liberty Bell, but we kept bolt cutters close by and would cut his chains before the media showed up. Rita Adessa of the Task Force was easy to work with; consequently, her activities were always successful.

In 1976, the Park issued over 1,500 special use permits. Maria Burks had two assistants, Dan Sharp and Susan Davenport, to assist with issuing and managing the permits. This system helped us manage the Park activities in a very busy year. Joanne Blacoe managed the permits during the Bicentennial of the Constitution.

In 1975, the three blocks of Independence Mall were turned over to the National Park Service by the State, and this caused us to get into the permit business in a big way. Larger groups could gather on the Judge Lewis Quadrangle, so we then became the site for annual programs such as Greek Independence Day, Israeli Independence Day, Von Steuben Day (German), and Puerto Rican Day. We were even the site for the baseball All-Star Game dinner and the conclusion of the parade given the Philadelphia Flyers when they won the Stanley Cup.

Without question, the two most difficult permits I issued were to the American Nazi Party and the Klu Klux Klan. Sometime early in February 1979, a skinny young man who identified himself as James Gutman came to my office and asked to see me. He said that he was a member of the American Nazi Party and he wanted to get a permit to have a demonstration on the Second Block of Independence Mall. I told him that he would have to fill out an application and that I would give him an answer in two days. When I asked for identification, he showed me a student card with his picture from City College of New York. The date requested for the demonstration was two weeks in the future.

Assistant Superintendent Bernie Goodman, Chief Ranger Bob Burns, and myself immediately called Interior Solicitor Roger Babb to see what grounds we might have to deny the permit. Roger said that unless there was an error on the application, there was little we could do but issue it. He agreed to fly down from Boston in order to assist us. I was hoping to keep the whole thing quiet for a while.

As soon as he left my office, Mr. Gutman went to several Jewish merchants near the park and bragged that the American Nazi Party was applying for a permit to have a demonstration. Well, all hell broke loose. The telephone began to ring off of the hook. I talked to the Jewish Community Relations Council and told them that I did not want to issue the permit but that I saw no alternative. I agreed to keep them informed as the event developed. Bob Burns called the Chief of Police in Skokie, Illinois, who had been through a demonstration like this, and he recommended that we issue the permit and get the demonstration over as soon as possible. By delaying, we would still have to issue the permit and we would just be extending the time that the issue was in the news.

Naturally, the media got the story and they got me at home, at work, and on the telephone. I began receiving threatening telephone calls. We sent our daughter Toni away until the crisis passed.

Addie-Lou and I had security with us day and night. Our house was periodically searched by bomb-detecting dogs. Rangers were positioned across the street in an apartment so they could watch our house and those who passed it. One day Addie-Lou came into the house on a cold, slushy winter day and, after leaving security at the door, removed her wet boots and skirt. The telephone rang and the caller said something about bombing the house. She dropped the phone and ran out the front door barefoot and in her slip. The rangers across the street rushed out to see what the problem was. Addie-Lou thought that the call was from them and they had told her she should leave the house. It was not from the rangers, and this episode scared her.

The Nazi permit nearly caused a problem with our performances with the Opera Company of Philadelphia. On another occasion, Addie-Lou went to have tea with a few local friends and a visitor from Paris. Her security, Ranger J.R. Tomasavic, was wearing a large NPS parka. When the ladies went to tea, Tomasavic sat at the next table, but he could not remove his coat because he was wearing a shoulder holster and pistol beneath it. Ranger Levi Rivers accompanied Addie-Lou and me to her February 22nd birthday dinner. He joined us because it was his birthday too.

I issued the Nazi permit and Mayor Rizzo said that he would not assist us with the demonstration. The mayor was running for re-election and did not wish to alienate the Jewish vote. George Fencl of the Civil Disobedience Squad told me that he and many of his men would take leave and assist us as volunteers. Meanwhile, we were working with

National Capital Police to bus a sizeable group to the Park on the day of the demonstration.

It was at times like this that reasonableness abandons everyone. I thought that the Jewish community would understand and accept everyone's right to demonstrate. After all, a permit is issued each year for Israeli Independence Day. Some of our Jewish friends suffered from others because they were friends of ours. If the public would just ignore the Nazis, the whole thing would have flopped. But this was not the case.

The Survivors of the Holocaust and the City of Philadelphia sued me in Federal Court to require me to withdraw the permit. On the day I was to appear, I called my father in Kentucky and told him what was happening. He thought for a moment and then said, "Son, The Constitution of the United States is a sacred thing." That was his way of telling me to suck it up and do the right thing. I also stopped by the Assembly Room in Independence Hall before opening time and thought about the Framers of the Constitution, and I knew it was up to me to defend their creation.

Federal Court was no fun. The lawyers from the Survivors of the Holocaust called witnesses to show their concentration camp tattoos and tell the horror stories of their torture. The City Attorney, Shelly Albert, got so close in my face that Judge Clifford Greene told him to back away. After a day and a half, Judge Greene said that from what he had heard, I had appropriately issued the permit. However, he had a question whether Mr. Gutman was who he said he was. This concern surfaced after Bob Burns called the American

Nazi Party headquarters and they denied filing an application for a permit. It was their opinion that someone was impersonating a party member.

Judge Greene asked me if he called Mr. Gutman forward to establish his identity, and he did not show up, would I withdraw the permit. I agreed, and the word went out that he had 24 hours to show up and establish his identity. Mr. Gutman did not show and I withdrew the permit. The City and the Jewish Community Relations Council said that I had done the right thing. The Survivors lawyer was critical. We requested that the FBI pursue Mr. Gutman to recover all expenses that had been incurred by the U.S. Government.

About a month later, an FBI agent came to my office with several photographs to find out if those of us who had seen James Gutman could identify him. We all picked the same one. His real name was Mordecai Levy from New York and he was an active member of the Jewish Defense League (JDL). Most Jews do not support the JDL, but that group was planning to send a fundraising letter to Jews in the Philadelphia area. They thought that an American Nazi Party scare would benefit their fundraising efforts. Most people never knew that the whole thing was a hoax.

Through the years, I issued and administered several thousand permits. My life was threatened three times and I was in Federal District Court several times, but this was far and away the most difficult experience I had with special use permits.

A few days after the permit was withdrawn, I received a letter from Richard Maloney, a reporter for KYW Radio, whose offices were on Independence Mall. Over the years, Dick had covered live many of the special activities in the Park. He wrote in part:

"I simply wanted to write to you and tell you of my great personal regard for your moral strength and fortitude in court… I've known and admired you for several years, both as a government official, and as a person. And I will tell you forthrightly, that I can't recall in my own experience an instance of moral courage on part of a middle level government official under such pressure.

Were I you, I would take a long and quiet walk with your wife and son through the empty chambers of Independence Hall and pause for a moment to accept the echoes of applause from the long-dead men who are standing in the shadows to honor your courageous defense of their ideals."

This event aside, the ones that I remember as being the most agonizing were the Roofers Union and the annual menorah lighting.

The newspaper *USA Today,* which built a printing plant just outside Philadelphia, wanted to have a reception for local leaders to show that they were a new presence in the community. We gave them a permit for the Judge Lewis Quadrangle, where they would erect a tent for the event. As the day approached, I was visited by men in three-piece suits from the Roofers Union. They wanted to demonstrate against the non-union newspaper and

requested a small space in the Park just off of the Quadrangle. They were so nice that I even went to *USA Today* officials and requested some space for them from the permit that I had already issued. They were dubious but agreed. On the day of the event, there were no suits to be seen; only goons with signs and megaphones. As people arrived at the reception, they were threatened and cursed. Some politicians saw them there and decided against attending the event. There was no way we could get them under control. I was embarrassed but the event went on, but with more than the newspaper to talk about.

The other controversial event happened during Hanukkah each year when Rabbi Shemtov of the Lubavitcher Center would request space on Independence Mall for a 15-foot-high menorah. The placement of a religious symbol on government property is always controversial, so you can imagine the calls and letters that I received. The menorah did not have a visual impact on Park buildings, and it was in no way associated with the NPS operation. People would call and wonder why there could be a menorah when we would not allow a manger scene. I would tell them that we would allow a manger scene adjacent to the menorah if they would only apply for permission. No one ever did. The main problem with Rabbi Shemtov was that he did not erect and remove the menorah when the permit indicated, and he would always damage the pavement, plantings, or park benches. He would never pay for the damages until we refused him the following year, and only then, in order to get another permit, he would come up with the money. The same pattern occurred year after year and it became painful to deal with.

The Rangers who had to administer the permits
always had the toughest job. Supervisor Bobby
Spears, Levi Rivers, and our two K-9 rangers,
Willie Durant and Roger Johnson, were critical for
maintaining control at each event.
The variety of activities and events which
took place in the Park during my 20 years as
Superintendent challenged our staff but also left
us with the feeling that we were America's Park.
We were important to our citizens as a place to
commemorate, celebrate and even to protest or
make some point of view known.

V.

GETTING READY FOR THE BICENTENNIAL OF THE CONSTITUTION (1984-1987)

A. History

When Independence was declared on July 4, 1776, this was only the beginning of the establishment of the United States of America. The Second Continental Congress became the ad hoc government until one could be created.

Richard Henry Lee's resolution which led to independence also included a proposal for a plan of confederation to be prepared and submitted to the states for their consideration. John Dickinson of Pennsylvania chaired the committee that on July 12, 1776, presented the "Articles of Confederation and Perpetual Union to the Congress." A year-long debate regarding the details of the government followed, and on November 15, 1777, the Articles were approved and sent to the states for ratification. Maryland delayed final approval because she would not ratify until the states claiming western lands ceded them to the United States. Finally, on March 1, 1781, our country, "The United States in Congress Assembled," was approved, and the old Congress became the new government.

French recognition by the American nation resulted in military assistance, and with the addition of Rochambeau's Army, the tide began to turn. The French and American Armies and the French Navy cornered the British at Yorktown, Virginia, resulting in the surrender of Lord Cornwallis's Army on October 18, 1781. British hopes of victory in America had ended and negotiations for a peace began. The Treaty of Paris that concluded the war was finally approved in the spring of 1783.

With the fighting of the American Revolution concluded, the Congress began the work of developing our nation. It quickly became obvious that the "Articles" was simply a confederation of sovereign states where each printed their own money, made their own treaties, and enforced their own tariffs. The central government was so weak that it had to depend on taxes that were voluntarily paid by the states.

In March 1785, commissioners from Virginia and Maryland met at Washington's home, Mount Vernon, to discuss problems related to navigation on the Chesapeake Bay and the Potomac River. They agreed on uniform commercial standards and a common currency, but they also agreed that it was a bigger issue than just the two states, so they wanted to include Pennsylvania and Delaware in a future meeting. Finally, at Madison's insistence, all states were invited to a conference in Annapolis, Maryland, which took place on September 11, 1786, to discuss commercial problems.

Nine states accepted the invitation to Annapolis, but delegates from four states arrived too late to participate. Those in attendance discussed mostly commercial matters, but the report drafted by Alexander Hamilton called upon all states to send commissioners to a new convention at Philadelphia in May 1787 to discuss not only commercial problems but to render the constitution of the Federal Government adequate. Congress considered this matter and finally agreed that the convention should consider revising the Articles of Confederation and report its recommendations back to them.

By May 25, 1787, a quorum of states had arrived and the Philadelphia convention began. Other delegates continued to arrive, with the last being New Hampshire in July. Rhode Island ignored the convention and sent no delegates. The final total of delegates from all states was fifty-five. George Washington was nominated to be president and was unanimously approved. From the beginning, it became obvious that this convention was not interested in making adequate the Articles of Confederation. They seemed to have ignored the charge by the Congress and went about creating a new government.

Four days after opening the convention, Edmund Randolph presented the Virginia Plan for a new government. Outstanding features included: a bicameral legislature with proportional representatives; an executive selected by the legislature; and a judiciary, including a supreme court, elected by the legislature. This idea was debated until June 13th. Opposition to the Virginia Plan came from the small states because they feared they would always be outvoted by the large states. Those states gave a counter-proposal set forth in the New Jersey Plan, which expressed retention of the Articles of Confederation, but with changes such as giving the central government the powers to tax and to regulate foreign trade and interstate commerce.

After a few days of debate, the delegates decided to work toward a new government as visualized in the Virginia Plan and not retain the Articles. On July 16th, the Connecticut Compromise was approved by the Convention. This resolved the disagreement between the states by having a bicameral legislature: a House of Representatives with proportional representation, and a Senate with equal representation. During the remainder of July, August, and early September, the details of government were hammered out. By early September, a Committee of Style was appointed, with Gouverneur Morris assigned to prepare the final draft. The draft was debated, and on September 17th the document was approved by each of the 12 state delegations. It was sent to the Congress, and the Constitutional Convention adjourned. The Constitution of the United States would take effect upon ratification by nine states.

B. We the People - 200

In the spring of 1983, I went to see Richard Doran, City Representative and Director of Commerce for Mayor William Green. I told him that in advance of 1976 there was a federal commission, the American Revolution Bicentennial Administration, and it did such a good job that every community had a bicentennial project or celebration in 1976. Even though Philadelphia was where the historical event took place, and was the center of the celebration, a substantial portion of the bicentennial activities were spread generally across the country. Afterward, Americans referred to "The Bicentennial" as having occurred in 1976 and did not realize that 1976 was only the beginning of the process that created our nation. Dick Doran, whose academic background was in history and political science, was very receptive to our opportunity. Since there did not appear to be any interest in 1987 by the Federal Government or anyone else, we could put together a celebration that either would be the only show or, at least, provide leadership for the Bicentennial of The Constitution in 1987.

Dick spoke to Mayor Bill Green, who agreed to appoint a committee if I would be chairman. He also offered to provide me with assistance in the person of Fred Stein, an events planner used frequently by the mayor's office. I agreed to serve so that the committee would be appointed and we could go forward with the planning. The committee of approximately twenty interested and talented individuals was appointed and a first meeting was scheduled. Working with Fred, we put together a name and a mission statement to be considered at the first meeting. It was decided that the board would be called "We the People-200, A National Celebration of the Bicentennial of the Constitution in Philadelphia." Craig Eisendrath, Director of the Pennsylvania Humanities Council, brought up the idea that something educational should remain as a permanent program after the celebration was concluded. I appointed Craig, Jeff Garson, a Philadelphia lawyer, and Stewart Feldman to form a committee to look into that matter.

Before there was a second meeting, Bill Green decided not to run for a second term as Mayor. This left us wondering what would happen to "We the People-200" in a new administration. As it happened, Green's lieutenant, Wilson Goode, became the Democratic nominee, and he supported WTP-200. Nevertheless, the committee remained in limbo during the 1983 election and into the following year when Goode took office. Fred Stein and I met with Mayor Goode early in

his administration and received his approval to continue with WTP-200. We began to think about serious matters such as office space, staffing, funding and programs. Since we planned to blend the Independence National Historical Park programs with those which would take place throughout the community, we began to canvass the organizations and institutions about their plans for 1987. Our thought was that we could put together a list of Park Programs, WTP-200 Programs, and Community Programs that could be shared with prospective sponsors. However, from the beginning, we warned every organization which might do a project or programs that they should expect to develop their own funding. It might be that WTP-200 could be helpful in getting the funds and the institutions together, but they should not depend entirely on WTP-200.

The job of WTP-200 was to review the programs for appropriateness and make them "official" programs of the celebration. Then WTP-200 would assist with coordination, scheduling and promoting the programs. Museums, school districts, patriotic organizations, churches, libraries, Independence National Historical Park, and even the Philadelphia Flower Show became part of the national celebrations of the Bicentennial of the Constitution in Philadelphia.

On May 23, 1985, a blueprint for WTP-200, a Bicentennial Celebration of The Constitution, was unveiled at Independence Hall. Mayor Wilson Goode called on all citizens to become partners in the 1987 year-long celebration. Hobie Cawood was identified as the chairman of the celebration committee and Fred Stein was the director of "We the People-200."

C. Mount Vernon and Annapolis Conferences

The Mount Vernon Conference (March 1985) was a two-day event that previously included session of scholars presenting papers on the 1786 conference and its importance in the process of creating the Constitution. I did not attend the first day of the conference, but Friends chairman Tom McCallum and I accepted the invitation of Chief Justice Warren E. Burger for dinner at the Supreme Court and then attended the conference on the following day. By this time the Friends were heavily involved in the Bicentennial, with their poster project and the creation of the exhibition "Miracle at Philadelphia." Again, one of the great values in attendance was the networking with people.

The Bicentennial of the Annapolis Convention (September 11-14, 1986) was a much more significant commemorative event, which was jointly produced by the Federal Commission, Maryland State Archives, Maryland Humanities Council, and the Department of Defense. The activities included the dedication of a new archives building, colonial encampments, a scholarly conference, and a military program at Fort Meade, which included a concert by the U.S. Army Band. The finale was a "Call to Philadelphia" delivered by a costumed horseman to Chief Justice Burger. Three days after the Annapolis Convention was adjourned, we opened our first bicentennial exhibition, "Miracle at Philadelphia."

D. Federal Commission

Although Public Law 98-101, "to establish a Commission to promote and coordinate activities to commemorate the bicentennial of the Constitution," was passed on September 29, 1983, a commission was not appointed until 21 months later. Those of us who had an interest in a Federal Commission thought precious time had been lost. Finally, on June 25, 1985, President Reagan officially appointed Warren E. Burger, Chief Justice of the Supreme Court, chairman of the Commission on the Bicentennial of the United States Constitution. Twenty-two commissioners were also named, with the individuals being recommended by the President, the President Pro Tempore of the Senate, the Chief Justice of the United States, and the Speaker of the House of Representatives. Membership was diverse but had a variety of experiences in law, scholarship, and public service. Two of the members who were personally known by me were: Ron Walker, former Director of the National Park Service, and Bill Green, former Congressman and former Mayor of Philadelphia. Before the celebration was over, I became acquainted with most of the commissioners. Mark Cannon became staff director following several years as the Administrative Assistant to the Chief Justice. A year later, Chief Justice Burger retired from the Supreme Court in order to devote full time to the Commission.

This all seemed to have been somewhat planned for some time, because Chief Justice Burger invited those involved in planning the bicentennial of the Mount Vernon Conference (March 1985) to dinner at the Supreme Court two months before the announcement of the Commission. Fred Stein and myself at first wondered if the Commission would be a benefit to our efforts in Philadelphia. We had been the only show before, and now the Commission had become the leadership in planning for the bicentennial of the Constitution.

Shortly after becoming chairman of the Commission, "The Chief" came to Philadelphia to learn about our plans and to visit Independence National Historical Park. Commissioner Bill Green, Mayor Goode, Dick Doran, Bernie Siegel (a close friend of Burger's), Fred Stein, and myself took the tour. All of the WTP-200 programs officially became programs endorsed by the Federal Commission.

The Commission on the Bicentennial of the Constitution was most effective in encouraging, sponsoring, and funding programs across the nation, which in turn created an awareness for the programs and activities of "We the People-200" in Philadelphia. They were most effective in responding to people who would say that we had celebrated our bicentennial in 1976. They reminded the nation that the creation of our nation was a long process and that in 1776 we had only declared our independence. It took us eleven more years to win a war, approve the Articles of Confederation, and write The Constitution of the United States. The activities of the Commission lasted through the ratification of the Constitution by the States and Washington's inaugural, and concluded with the approval of the Bill of Rights, the first ten amendments to the Constitution.

I was invited to attend two early meetings of the Commission on the Bicentennial of the Constitution of the United States. Since WTP-200, had started planning before the Federal Commission was established, and we were the historic site most obviously connected to the creation of the Constitution, they wanted to be up-to-date on our plans. My first meeting was in Salt Lake City and was hosted by O. C. Tanner, a member of the Commission. In addition to reporting in the business meetings, getting acquainted with the Commission members was important. At Salt Lake City, I felt that I got to know Fred Beibel, Judge Cornelia Kennedy, and Lynne Cheney. I renewed my acquaintance with Congresswoman Lindy Boggs and was pleased to see that Raymond Smock, a friend and the historian of the House of Representatives, always accompanied her. At my second meeting, I renewed my acquaintance with Secretary of the Army John Marsh. Secretary Marsh had also been planning in advance of the Commission and would eventually be the liaison for the Bicentennial of the Constitution for the entire Department of Defense.

In any case, by being interested in the activities and programs of the Commission, and joining them at every opportunity I was able to establish with everyone involved that We the People-200, Philadelphia, and Independence National Historical Park were players and would be an important part of the national celebration.

E. The Constitution: That Delicate Balance

I believe it was early in 1984 that I entered my office and saw two men sitting in my reception area awaiting my arrival. One I had previously met, Judge Arlen Adams, a Philadelphia lawyer who had served as a justice on the Third Appellate Circuit (Federal), and he introduced me to Fred Friendly. Fred had been a partner with Edward R. Murrow, and together they had been responsible for numerous television programs, such as "See It Now" and "CBS Reports." After serving as President of CBS News, Fred became a journalism professor at Columbia University, where he created Media and Society Seminars. Fred had the idea of doing 13 one-hour programs for public television, which he would call *The Constitution: That Delicate Balance*. A changing panel of experts would examine thirteen Constitutional issues in depth in the series, and its accompanying book would become an important tool in the study of Constitutional law. His panel for each show included leading scholars, lawyers, jurist, journalists, government officials, and even President Gerald Ford.

Fred Friendly's reasoning was, where better to film the thirteen programs than in the building where the Constitutions was written, Independence Hall. I told him that such a plan might be possible if he could film after visiting hours or at night, since I did not want to deprive any visitors who might be making a once in a lifetime visit to the place where their nation was born. He did not think that after hours filming was possible. He was very disappointed, so I asked Arlen and Fred to walk up to Independence Square with me. I suggested that instead of Independence Hall, we use the House of Representatives chamber in Congress Hall. This worthy historic building had been the Capitol of the United States (1790-1800) and the site of Washington's second inaugural and John Adam's first. Any time they were not shooting the programs, visitors would be able to file through the building behind the bar and get a glimpse of those involved in the filming. The moderators were Benno Schmidt, dean of Columbia Law School, Louis Kander of Columbia Law School, and Tyrone Brown, a prominent Washington lawyer. Justice Potter Stewart of the Supreme Court and Fred were the hosts.

The filming was carried out in three different sessions, with the participants arriving for a session on Friday evening for a reception and dinner. Shows were filmed Saturday morning, Saturday afternoon, Sunday morning, and Sunday afternoon. An extra show was filmed on Saturday during one of the weekends. Fred and Potter filmed their introduction and comments after hours in Independence Hall a few weeks later. Channel 13, the PBS station in New York did the filming. The subjects of the various sessions included: Freedom of Speech, Freedom of the Press, Free Exercise of Religion, the Death Penalty, the Insanity Plea, Affirmative Action, The Right of Privacy, States Rights or National Supremacy, and Power to Make War.

Each subject had a different panel comprised of experts from both sides of each subject. The moderator's job was to provoke the participants and keep the debate going. An audience filled the seats in the House Chamber behind the participants, so Addie-Lou and I sat through much of the filming.

Fred Friendly and Martha J. H. Elliott produced a book, also called *The Constitution, That Delicate Balance*, that complemented the show and could work as the text for a Constitutional law course. When the show aired in 1984-85, I got calls from many colleagues from around the country. It was possible to buy the series from Media and Society Seminars.

Much to my surprise, in May 1986 I was notified that one of the shows in the series had been presented an Emmy by the National Academy of Television Arts and Sciences. I was given a certificate saying that an Emmy had been awarded to me, and Fred Friendly said, "Cawood's vision of the long-term significance of the series on the Constitution and his perception of Congress Hall as the appropriate setting made him one of the very few special persons most responsible for the PBS series."

F. Miracle at Philadelphia

As we began to think about the Bicentennial of the Constitution, we made an inventory of the resources we had in Philadelphia that would illustrate the story of the creation of the Constitution. I talked to my colleagues Whitfield Bell at the American Philosophical Society, Edmund Wolfe II at the Library Company of Philadelphia, and James Mooney at the Historical Society of Pennsylvania about their collections and our treasures, which included the following:

1. Dunlap Broadside of the Declaration of Independence – Independence National Historical Park
2. Second draft of the Constitution with marginal notes by delegate Benjamin Franklin – American Philosophical Society
3. First and second drafts of the Constitution belonging to delegate James Wilson – Historical Society of Pennsylvania
4. Resolutions submitted by the Committee on Detail (26 July 1787) belonging to delegate James Wilson – Historical Society of Pennsylvania
5. Second Draft of the Constitution with notations by delegate John Dickinson – Library Company of Philadelphia

These documents are actual items from the Constitutional Convention and could form the core of an exhibition. Our discussion led us to believe that the impact of these original documents would be greater if they were displayed together. I made the suggestion that since Independence Hall was the site of the Convention, we should be the venue for the exhibition. Further, we would make the Second Bank building available to display our treasures and would raise the funds for the exhibition. Finally, with the exhibition location only a city block away from Independence Hall and the Liberty Bell, we could depend on a very large number of visitors. Everyone agreed that we should take the lead in the exhibition.

The use of the Second Bank was an obvious choice, since we had already decided that the Portrait Gallery in the building needed refurbishing and we could place the portraits in storage or loan them to others if they were not used in The Constitution exhibit. I asked the Friends of Independence to sponsor the exhibit. They agreed and provided Peggy Duckett as the project coordinator. Peggy and her husband John lived in Society Hill, close to the Park, and her background included teaching grant writing in Texas and Massachusetts. In 1983, Peggy wrote a $15,000 planning grant application to the National Endowment of the Humanities (NEH) on behalf of the Friends. The Friends could receive government grants while the Park could not. When the money was received, contacts were made with exhibit planners, and an advisory committee of professors advised on the subjects to be included in the exhibition.

A second grant, which totaled over 300 pages, was submitted to NEH in 1984 to plan and facilitate the exhibit, develop educational materials, create an audio-visual component, and devise a plan to publicize the exhibit. This was Peggy Duckett's masterpiece, and it was funded by NEH for $550,000 but required a $275,000 match. Peggy talked to another neighbor, Robert I. Smith, President of the Pew Charitable Trust, and they eventually provided the entire matching grant. Product sales, other Friends fundraisers, and private contributions came to $165,219, for a grand total of $965,219 raised for the exhibit.

With funds in hand, the Friends engaged Richard Rabinowitz of American History Workshop as the historical consultant. Nick Paffett of Krent/Paffett of Boston was engaged as the exhibit designer. The first thing that was agreed upon was the title, "Miracle at Philadelphia," after the book about the

Constitutional Convention by Catherine Drinker Bowen. As the planning moved along, an opening date of September 17, 1986, one year before the bicentennial of the signing of the Constitution, became the goal. We were also mindful that with the Friends' assistance in 1974, we had begun the Bicentennial Era celebrations by opening the Second Bank Portrait Gallery, and now we were kicking off the Bicentennial of the Constitution with the Friends opening of the exhibit, "Miracle at Philadelphia."

One of the rules of the May-September 1787 Convention was that the delegates would not share with the public the business that was being conducted inside Independence Hall. With the exception of a few personal letters to friends and family, the delegates maintained the secrecy. In the years afterward, a few remembrances surfaced, but we still would not know many of the details of the work of the Convention, were it not for the notes James Madison wrote in his daily journal. The Madison journal was at the Library of Congress under strict environmental protection, but these notes written during the Convention would be a great addition to "Miracle at Philadelphia."

I went to Washington and met with Jim Hutson, archivist at the Library of Congress, and asked about the loan of Madison's journal. Jim told me all of the reasons why the notes could not leave the Library of Congress, and I told him that we were prepared to meet any condition that he required. When I left the meeting I did not think that we had a chance of getting the manuscripts, even though Jim Hutson had been on Peggy Duckett's advisory committee for the exhibit. But Jim called a few days later and said we could have the journal, and he set the conditions, which related mostly to security and light levels. This was the final piece that would make "Miracle" a blockbuster.

Utilizing all of the rooms on the main floor of the Second Bank, the "Miracle in Philadelphia" exhibit began in the vestibule and moved clockwise through the building to tell the story. It began with the American Revolution and its conclusion, then showed the Articles of Confederation and their inadequacies, the conferences at Mount Vernon and Annapolis, which led to Philadelphia, the Convention, and ratification. Highlights of the exhibit included:

1. A full-size sculpture of James Madison standing by a table on which lay his journal, covered by a plexiglass box to filter out the harmful light rays. We were also required to maintain humidity records and switch the pages weekly so that no page of the journal was on display longer than seven days.
2. An audiovisual program runnning continuously that introduced the audience to all 55 delegates. Our staff did a magnificent job in finding a likeness of nearly all of them.
3. The William Rush carved wooden statue of George Washington, a man who took small part in the debate but who served as President of the Convention, and was important to its success.
4. The three drafts of the Constitution which had been written and printed in

secrecy, and used by the delegates during the debates.
5. In the area devoted to signing the Constitution was a display of the final document, with a space at the bottom for visitors to sign their name. The mechanism was a roll of paper that, when turned, gave a clean signing space. The Park agreed to keep those signatures, to be reexamined at some future date.
6. The story of ratification and the uniqueness of this short (four-page) document that has only been amended twenty-six times, but has served this diverse and complex nation for over two hundred years.

On the evening before the opening, the Friends of Independence sponsored a preview fundraiser that contributed $43,695 to the budget. Subscribers to the event could tour the exhibit in the Second Bank and exit onto the lawn behind the building to a tent where there was food and drink. It became know that Chief Justice Burger would be attending the preview, so Rita Adessa, Director of the Gay and Lesbian Task Force, wanted to stage a protest near him because of his position on cases that were of interest to them. I had already issued a National Park Service permit to the Friends for the entire city block in which the exhibit and the reception were being held. The Gay and Lesbian Task Force then asked the City for a permit to parade in the streets around the block. I did not object.

Chief Justice Burger arrived at the Second Bank in a limousine that was parked on the reconstructed 18th-Century Library Street behind the Second

Chief Justice Warren Burger, Tom McCallum, Chairman of Friends of Independence National Historical Park (FINHP), and Hobie at the opening of "Miracle at Philadelphia"

Bank, but near the reception. Peggy Duckett, Tom McCallum, and I toured the exhibition with "the Chief" and then went to the reception tent for refreshments and a brief program. Beside "the Chief" and several local dignitaries, actresses Carol Channing and Mary Martin, who were in Philadelphia doing a show, added to the excitement of the occasion. Of course, another bit of entertainment was the several hundred demonstrators of the Gay and Lesbian Task Force, with lavender and yellow balloons, marching and chanting as they circled the block. Everyone was aware of the demonstrators but their activities were not disruptive.

During the program at the reception, Chief Justice Burger made some remarks about our "outstanding" exhibition, and how important the Park and "We the People-200" were to the celebration of the Bicentennial of the Constitution.

Carol Channing and Burger had an interesting exchange of remarks when she referred to him as "my little ole Chief Justice." Tom McCallum then asked Burger to unveil the Ray Metzker poster, which was the second in a series of three that the Friends had commissioned for the Bicentennial of the Constitution. With his official duties completed, Burger did some hand shaking as he moved toward his limo. The demonstrators in the street sensed that the Chief Justice was about to leave and that his limousine would be coming out of Library Street onto Fifth Street, and perhaps they could block his route and get his attention. There then developed a race between the limo and the balloon-festooned demonstrators to see who would arrive at the intersection of Library and Fifth Streets first. The limo won but not by much.

The following morning, we held the official opening of the exhibition, with remarks by A.B.

136

Dick Howard, University of Virginia Law School and Chairman of the Virginia Bicentennial of the Constitution Commission, on the Chestnut Street steps of the Second Bank. The Old Guard of the U. S. Army provided music and period drill. We cut a ribbon and "Miracle at Philadelphia" was opened to the public. It remained open for 15 months.

A highlight of "Miracle at Philadelphia" was the collateral educational materials that were created and distributed or sold. Perhaps the most creative were the 55 delegate cards, which were much like baseball cards, with a portrait of a delegate on one side and a biography with his major contributions at the Convention on the reverse. The National Endowment of the Humanities was so impressed with these cards that they invited the Friends to apply for funds to print an additional 10,000 sets of the cards. There was also a three-dimensional 1787 map of historical Philadelphia with notations at specific sites relating to the Constitution, and a delegate poster utilizing the same portraits as were used on the delegate cards. A special newspaper was laid out in a modern format but contained 1787 news. There were also two booklets, *The Intellectual Heritage of the Constitutional Era – The Delegates Library* and *A Bicentennial Bookshelf – Historians Analyze the Constitutional Era,* compiled by Jack Greene of Johns Hopkins University; and a booklet of educational activities that could be done in concert with a visit to the exhibit.

Some 5,000 packets containing the above materials were mailed to school districts in the Philadelphia area, education leaders in the 50 States, and

through the United States Information Agency to U.S. bases throughout the world. Eastern National sold individual pieces at the exhibit bookstore in the Second Bank.

G. Promise of Permanency

In 1976, while visiting Boston, we saw a computerized exhibit that really impressed me. When you entered the exhibit, you were given a computer card and a soft lead pencil. At each panel of the exhibit, you answered a question by darkening a spot on the card that best reflected your answer. There were 20-25 questions. At the conclusion, you fed the card into a computer and it told you which Bostonian you would most think like on the eve of the Revolution. Addie-Lou thought most like the artist John Singleton Copley, a Tory. My answers showed I was most like Benjamin Franklin (born in Boston), who was slow to get involved in the independence movement but, when he became committed, gave his all. You can imagine just how effective an interactive exhibit such as this could be.

Around 1983, when we began serious thinking and planning for the Bicentennial of the Constitution, the idea of an interactive computerized exhibit surfaced. We had a great place for it: the large public spaces in the Visitor Center. Of course, there had been great advancement in computers since the 1976 Boston exhibit, especially at the 1984 Worlds Fair in New Orleans, which had showcased interactive exhibits utilizing computers.

I asked the Park's Chief of Interpretation, Kathy

137

Dilonando, to take the lead on this project and put together a package that we could try to fund. To get ideas and cost figures,, she talked to Albert Woods in New York, one of the few exhibit companies that had experience with computers. We were talking about a $2 million project. When we got the package together, we went to

President, Community Affairs, Bell of Pennsylvania, invited me to come to his office to discuss projects for the company. He liked the computer exhibit idea but wanted me to come back and make a presentation to Gil Wetzel, President of Bell. Kathy came back with me, and Gil was impressed, but he needed to look at his budget and

"Promise of Permanency" *Image Courtesy of Independence National Historical Park*

the headquarters of IBM in Armonk, New York, to talk to them about a sponsorship. When we left the meeting, Kathy and I felt that they would call us the next day with an affirmative answer. They did not call. I took our shopping list, including the computerized exhibit, to a variety of sources that were interested in Bicentennial of the Constitution projects. I even went back to IBM, but nothing happened.

One day late in 1985, Chuck Schalch, Vice

asked if we could come back the next day. We went back and were already in his office when Gil Wetzel came in wearing a Christmas tie; they were having the office Christmas party. He said that they would do the project at a $1.2 million level, which was $300,000 less than we had requested. We figured we could cut the cloth to fit the pattern. What a Christmas present! Afterward, when Kathy and I were walking down the street, I said that after months of trying to sell this project, now

138

we have to produce it.

Kathy went to work with Albert Woods in New York and was able to get Alan Tarr from Rutgers University, a Constitution scholar, as a subject matter consultant. As the work progressed, some staff at the IBM Educational Division in Atlanta came by Albert Woods's office, where they were working on our exhibit, and decided they wanted to be involved in it. We told them about our negative experience in Armonk and said that the exhibit belonged to Bell of Pennsylvania. They offered to give us the equipment and to maintain it over the life of the exhibit. After talking to Bell of PA, we agreed to accept their offer, but the IBM logos had to be removed from the equipment. This was so that no one would by inference give credit for the exhibit to anyone other than Bell. About 75 percent of the way through the development, Chuck Schalch rented a limousine and took two of his staff, Kathy and me, to New York to review the progress. I was amazed, and from this time forward I knew that we had a successful exhibit on the way.

The name of the exhibit came from a letter by Benjamin Franklin to a friend in France in 1788. He said, "…our Constitution is in place and shows a promise of permanency…". The remainder of the sentence is something that everyone knows, "…but nothing is certain in life except death and taxes." So the title of our exhibit about our 200-year-old Constitution became "A Promise of Permanency."

An article in *The Philadelphia Inquirer* by Janet

Anderson described the exhibit:

"As you enter the airy sky-lit Visitor Center you are greeted by a mass of images – huge photographs, video screens all working simultaneously – and the babble of many sound tracks. A sprawling mural of oversize photographs provide a backdrop for the display. This is a visual history of The Constitution from delegates in 18th-Century Philadelphia to Civil Rights marches to the Nixon impeachment hearings.
Scattered through the exhibit are curved space dividers containing video screens connected to a fancy interactive computer called 'Infowindow'. There is a semicircle of 26 marble-like tablets that give the changes in the wording of the Constitution by the year."

One of my favorite parts of the exhibit was where you picked a constitutional issue from a menu and the computer showed you the part of the Constitution that is used to decide that issue. This included such issues as integration, women's suffrage, affirmative action, abortion, and so forth.

Another favorite was several small booths which only one person at a time entered and saw a 30-second film about a constitutional issue, such as the death penalty. Then you had a chance to vote on it. After your vote, you were then informed how everyone who had entered the booth before you had voted.

The exhibition opened with a ceremony on May

13, 1987. A reception followed at the First Bank of the United States. We had assured Bell of Pennsylvania that the exhibit would run for three years, but it remained in place for more than ten. Millions of visitors saw it. Looking back at it, one realizes that "Promise of Permanency" was a groundbreaking exhibit utilizing technology that was on the cutting edge. I am proud of the project and of Kathy Dilonando's management of it.

One day in late September 1987, I received a call from someone who asked if I could meet the Chief Justice of the Supreme Court of Ireland and introduce him to the exhibit. When he came to my office, I took him over to the Visitor Center and left him with "Promise of Permanency." Two hours later, he came back to my office and said that he had learned more about the Constitution of the United States in a short time than he could have learned any other way. I knew that Chief Justice William Rehnquist and Justices Sandra

Day O'Connor, William J. Brennan, Jr., and Byron R. White of the U.S. Supreme Court were coming for a visit on October 2nd, so I called to see if the Irish Chief Justice could be included in a luncheon. He was able to attend and naturally was pleased at his good fortune.

H. Magna Carta

Judge Edward Becker, 3rd District, U.S. Court of Appeals, Stephen Harmelin, a prominent Philadelphia lawyer, and I met in Judge Becker's chambers to discuss the idea of bringing a copy of the Magna Carta to Philadelphia in 1987. It seemed to me as if this would be a great compliment to "Miracle at Philadelphia," an exhibit about the creation of the Constitution, and "Promise of Permanency," which was about the daily impact that the Constitution has on us. So why not bring to Philadelphia a copy of the Magna Carta, an ancestor of the Constitution of the United States.

The Magna Carta is a document authorized by King John in 1215 that guaranteed certain rights to the English Barons. It was renewed by successive kings and was a step toward a future constitutional government for England. Of course, the principles stated in the Magna Carta were brought to America with the English

"Promise of Permanency" *Image Courtesy of Independence National Historical Park*

settlers and are embodied in the Constitution of the United States.

Stephen Harmelin had recently talked to a lawyer associated with Ross Perot, who had acquired a copy of the Magna Carta. He agreed to pursue the idea of borrowing the document if we had an interest in displaying it during the Bicentennial of the Constitution.

I suggested that the Magna Carta could be shown on Independence Square by utilizing the vacant space on the second floor of Old City Hall. We would also need to do some planning for interpretation of the Magna Carta, particularly since it is written in Latin on sheepskin. Everyone has heard of the Magna Carta but very few know its strong significance. Harmelin and Becker agreed to pursue the funds that were needed to properly display the document if we could borrow it. Steve agreed to follow up with Perot's lawyer.

The project became considerably more complex when Steve found out that the Magna Carta is stored in a gas-filled sealed container which requires security and special arrangements in its movement. This added to the expense, but Ross Perot agreed to the loan, pending his approval of our exhibition plan.

The exhibit planning firm of Staples and Charles, from the Washington, DC, area was hired to work with us on this project. They developed a plan that would admit 50 visitors at a time to the second floor of Old City Hall. The group then entered a room that actually looked like a 13th-century tent, to create a feeling for King John's meeting with the English Barons at Runnymede. Inside the tent, visitors saw a six-minute film narrated by Bill Moyers which told the story of the creation and the reaffirmation of Magna Carta. The film concluded by telling how the English brought the principals of Magna Carta to the new world, and the impact the document had on the Constitution of the United States. The audience was then invited to leave by a doorway that led into the chamber where the document was displayed. As soon as the tent room emptied, another group of 50 was admitted.

The light in the room where the Magna Carta was displayed was kept at a low level, with the case containing the document highlighted. It was with an attitude of reverence that visitors approached the case for a close look at the one-sheet document. After viewing the Magna Carta, visitors would exit through a small room to the stairs. As they left, they were given a brochure about the Magna Carta and this exhibition. The planned opening for the exhibit was May 1, 1987. On the day before, Her Royal Highness Princess Alexandra of Great Britain, Queen Elizabeth's cousin, and her husband, Sir Angus Ogilvy, arrived in Philadelphia to participate in the opening. Addie-Lou and I gave them a 2-3 hour tour of Independence National Historical Park. They were extremely nice people, and the Princess told us that she had the best possible position in the Royal Family; she could go about without a great deal of security, but she still got invited to all of the swell parties. While we were touring the "Miracle at Philadelphia" exhibit at the Second Bank, Addie-Lou told her that she had a new great-niece who had been named "Alexandra," and asked the Princess if she would consider writing her a personal note. A lady-in-waiting later told Addie-Lou that members of the Royal Family do not do things like that. That night, at a ball given by several of the British heritage groups, the same lady-in-waiting brought to Addie-Lou a letter for baby Alexandra from the Princess. It was framed and placed above her crib.

The opening ceremonies were to take place in Independence Square adjacent to Old City Hall. Ross Perot came an hour early to see the exhibition. In fact, most of the participants gathered inside Old City Hall prior to the ceremony. Ed Becker had his picture taken between former Ambassador Walter Annenberg and Ross Perot and quietly let me know that, between the three of them, they controlled a great deal of wealth. I do not think that his absence from the photograph would have significantly altered the total.

Philadelphia's Academy Boys Choir entertained the audience from 10:00 a.m. until 10:45 a.m., when a processional of British heritage groups with their colors marched between the audience and the platform where all of the participants were seated. After the parade, the groups positioned themselves around the large audience. Remarks were given by me, Judge Becker, Steve Hamelin, and Mayor Goode, who presented Ross Perot with the Philadelphia Freedom Award. Perot responded, after which Walter Annenberg introduced the British Ambassador, who introduced Princess Alexandra. It was a beautiful sunny day and everything went like clockwork. When the ceremony ended, we went

to the Chestnut Street door of Old City Hall, cut a ribbon, did a walk-through of the exhibit, and then it was opened to the public.

Some 150 invited guests then went to a luncheon at the First Bank of the United States. Addie-Lou and I sat at the table with the Princess and several of the program participants. This was mostly a wrap-up luncheon, with very little in the way of a program. The only entertainment was by a Men's Chorus from Cornwall, England. A couple of months before, their leader had called and said he had been given my name to possibly let them perform in the Park as part of their tour of America. I told him that I would find them a venue in which to perform. I was thinking that it would be more of an outdoor public concert that our Park visitors would enjoy. As time for the opening of the Magna Carta exhibit drew near, I thought that I could use them in some way with those activities. Their performance was at the luncheon, and they were thrilled to be performing for such a prestigious group, including a member of the Royal family. They sang from the second floor rotunda, which sent their music from the dome down to the first floor diners.

The exhibit was in place for six months and its attendance was equal to its carrying capacity. A great success!

I. Friends Poster Project

During the Bicentennial celebration for the Declaration of Independence, the Park had three posters planned by the National Park Service publications office at Harpers Ferry,

West Virginia. The Posters were designed by well-known artists (Leonard Baskin and Ivan Chevyroff), printed by the Government Printing Office and sold nationwide. They called attention to the celebration and the Park. There is something to be said about someone taking something that relates to your Park or its story and displaying it in their home, or business, or classroom. As the Bicentennial of the Constitution neared, I asked Vince Gleason at the Publications Office of The National Park Service about posters for the Constitution celebration, but he said there were no funds to do posters for 1987.

By about 1984, at a Friends of Independence board meeting, the fact that there would be not Government Printing Office posters for 1987 was discussed. There was agreement that posters could help promote the celebration, so Chairman Tom McCallum appointed a very impressive committee to look into the idea and its feasibility:
Libby Browne
Former Chairman, Friends Involved
Philadelphia Museum of Art

Bonnie Wintersteen
Art Collector and Patron
Philadelphia Museum of Art

Peter Somlinson
President, University of the Arts

Ned Donahue
President, Lawyers for the Arts

Bebe Benoliel
Prominent Art Consultant

Margot Dolan
Art Consultant and Gallery owner
Sarah Leary
Friends and Museum of Art supporter

Bill Millhallen
Friends, Ad Agency Executive

Tom McCallum
Chairman, FINHP

Hobie Cawood
Park Superintendent

The committee quickly decided that a series of posters should be issued, one each year for three years. The first poster would be designed by a graphic artist, the second by a photographer, and the third by someone in the fine arts. The committee was looking for imagination because it could be difficult to portray the Constitution in an art form. They were also aware that after one selects an artist and has a familiarization session with them, they are on their own to create, and what they produce is what you have to use. They would request that the artists donate their works, but they would be paid for expenses including printing.

Peter Somlinson suggested Saul Bass, the Academy Award winner from California, as the graphic artist for the first poster. Mr. Bass quickly agreed and went to work. He produced a striking poster with a large splash of colors that appear to take the shape of a quill pen that has just written the words "We the People." Across the bottom, as with all of the posters, is "Commemorating

143

the Bicentennial of the U.S. Constitution 1787-1987." The poster was unveiled by William Penn Mott, Director of the National Park Service, at the 1985 annual meeting of the Friends. It was so impressive that the Department of State ordered a thousand of them to distribute to their embassies and consulates.

Ray Metzger, a renowned Philadelphia photographer, was selected for the second poster. After the assignment, Friends Chairman Tom McCallum called Metzger to check on his progress and was told not to worry, that he was going to Italy for three months, and when he returned he would have the poster. True to his word, he did. The Metzger poster was a black and white photograph of a portion of the American flag. The flag had an "arty" look about it, as if it were homemade. The poster looked as if it could be displayed vertically or horizontally. Metzger had a preference, but we saw it on television hanging on a courtroom wall in Florida during a famous trial and it was not hanging with the stripes vertical as the artist preferred. The second poster was unveiled on September 17, 1986 by Chief Justice Burger during the opening of the exhibition, "Miracle at Philadelphia."

Modern painter Larry Rivers was selected to do the third poster in the series. A manager represented Mr. Rivers, so there was little contact with the artist. His painting was a startling juxtaposition of George Washington and a bald eagle. It actually appears as if the eagle representing our nation is rising from the body of Washington. The work became a limited edition print, as well as a poster. The Museum of Modern Art in New York, by

agreement with the artist, received print number one. The poster was unveiled at the Historic Woodlands Mansion in Fairmount Park at a party for Philadelphia Open House in the spring of 1987.

The budget for all three of the posters was approximately $20,000. Eastern National Park and Monument Association primarily sold the posters through their National Park Service bookstores. The Friends of Independence retailed several posters at their special events until the supply was exhausted. The project was a great success and met the criteria of promoting the celebration, the Park, and the Friends.

J. Bicentennial Day Book

The Park's Research Historians, led by David Dutcher, had done considerable work in order to provide the historical details for the exhibits "Magna Carta," "Miracle at Philadelphia," and "A Promise of Permanency." With knowledge of the work that was being done, Deputy Regional Director George Palmer suggested that we might be able to put together a daily account of what was going on in the Constitutional Convention that we could share with the general public. We discussed the idea and concluded that we could produce something that we would call *Bicentennial Day Book*. This would be a diary of year 1787, and would include what was happening on a daily basis leading up to the Constitutional Convention, what was happening at the Convention, and what was happening afterward regarding ratification.

Work on this huge project began in 1984 and

lasted for two years, with David Dutcher as leader and David Kimball, Bob Sutton, and Coxie Toogood contributing a large amount of time to the project. Besides daily listings of what was happening in Philadelphia, in the remainder of America, and with the delegates, the team included an essay (each day) that would give the reader a better understanding of the facts. Dutcher recruited some two dozen people who had great knowledge of the subjects to be included to write them.

We had a daily log of the events related to the Constitutional Convention for the year 1787, which the general public would find fascinating, but how could we share it with everyone? Combined Books, a small publisher in the Philadelphia area, printed the Day Book, and the *St. Louis Times-Dispatch* sent copies to its Pulitzer Media partners, and we finally were able to get the Associated Press wire service interested in distributing it through their members. They would send it over the wire two weeks in advance, which included some 150 newspapers. Many newspapers carried a daily listing in 1987 of what was happening in America, in Philadelphia, and in the Convention, 200 years ago. Television and radio stations, scholars, and even ministers read it to prepare sermons and include facts in church bulletins.

The *Bicentennial Day Book* was one of the Park's bicentennial gifts to America.

K. Jack Marsh and The Department of Defense

Throughout the bicentennial era, Independence National Historical Park was always successful in being able to schedule ceremonial events from the U. S. military. Usually the events that they were invited to perform at were worthy of their participation. At other times, it was convenient for them to request a venue because they knew that we would promote the performance and they would draw a crowd. Of course, the Army-Navy Museum (Pemberton House) and Marine Corps Museum (New Hall) were part of the Park. One other reason for our excellent relationship with the military was that Mark Murray, who scheduled the events for the U. S. Army, was a friend.

In 1974, I became acquainted with John O. Marsh, a White House advisor to President Ford and former Congressman from Strasburg, Virginia. We met when President Ford visited Independence Hall during the bicentennial of the First Continental Congress. Marsh and I were out of touch until 1984, when he was Secretary of the Army and I began seeing him at Bicentennial of the Constitution activities. He was as excited as I was about the bicentennial and rightfully felt the Army should be part of it. Because of this interest, he was asked by the Secretary of Defense to coordinate the Bicentennial of the Constitution activities for the entire Department.

Secretary Marsh was a master at using the Army's ceremonial units to create a favorable public relations image for the Armed Forces. One of his successful annual programs was a pageant called *Spirit of America*, which he presented free for several days around the Fourth of July in the Washington, D.C., area. It included the U.S. Army Band, the Old Guard, an Army chorus, a drill team, the herald trumpeters, and a whole host of troops on special assignments. The pageant tells the story of the beginning of our country.

In 1986, Marsh called to invite Addie-Lou and me to see the show at the Capital Centre, just off of I-495 in Maryland. It was a spectacular show and we were treated like royalty, including being introduced to the capacity crowd as guests of Secretary Marsh. Mrs. Marsh was there and instantly became a good friend to Addie-Lou. At the conclusion of the show, the Secretary told me that he would like to do a "Constitution" version of the show in Philadelphia in 1987. I was delighted, but the only catch was that he would need to raise some money to make it happen and hoped that we could assist with $100,000. When I talked to the "We the People--200" board, we agreed that this was something which would add greatly to our celebration.

The Department of Defense, and particularly the U.S. Army, was probably more active in the bicentennial celebrations (1985 Mount Vernon Conference – 1991 the Bill of Rights) than any other organization, and it was directly related to the leadership of Jack Marsh. By 1986, Secretary Marsh had recruited Major-General Robert Arter to assist him with his bicentennial activities. They took a leadership role in the Annapolis Conference in 1986, undertook many publications, involved the military worldwide in the celebration, and assisted people like me with their activities. One

of his imaginative projects was to propagate an oak tree associated with George Washington and give small trees to appropriate sites around the country. We planted one in Independence National Historical Park.

The Philadelphia Newspapers, Inc., through The Knight Foundation, became the sponsors for the *Spirit of America*, which was presented at Convention Hall in the Philadelphia Civic Center, July 3-5, 1987. There was one performance on the first evening and then two performances per day for the next two days. The pageant was a patriotic spectacular that brought tears to your eyes and required a cast of 500. Every show played to a capacity audience.

Secretary Marsh came through again when he provided marching units from each branch of the Service and from the Service Academies for the Constitution Day Parade (The Grand Federal Procession). He was, without doubt, the most valuable asset that we had during the celebration.

In October 1987, Jack Marsh called and invited me to Washington on a particular date, but I could not go because Addie-Lou and I would be off on a vacation to Mexico. He then asked if I could comer down to Washington on the day after we returned. He was vague about the purpose, but I knew I should go.

Secretary Marsh was going to send a helicopter for me, but the day before, he called and said that there was a security problem at the Pentagon, so I told him I would take the Metroliner. When I arrived at Union Station in Washington, Bob Arter was there to meet me. I still did not know what was going on, but I was impressed that I was met by a Major General who had a major as a driver.

I was maneuvered through the Pentagon security, and when I arrived at the Secretary's outer office I was introduced to a Colonel who told me that I would be going into the Secretary's office for a personal visit but when Secretary Marsh stood up I was to proceed through a sliding doorway that the Secretary would open for me. I should move forward and stand by a row of flags and others would join us. He said that after the presentation I would have the opportunity to speak. I did not have the slightest idea what was happening. When I entered Secretary Marsh's office, Bill Mott, Director of the National Park Service, was there. I asked him why he was there and he said he would not have missed it. I still did not know what "it" was. Jack Marsh asked about Addie-Lou and said he thought that she might be with me. That further confused me.

After we chatted for a few minutes, just like the Colonel said, the Secretary got up from his desk and moved toward a wall that magically rolled back and opened into a larger room with a row of flags against the far wall. There were approximately 25 high-ranking military personnel in the room. I found out later that some of them were members of the Joint Chiefs of Staff. I went to the flags and stood by the Colonel. Secretary Marsh welcomed everyone, and the Colonel read a citation commending me for my years of work with the U. S. Army and particularly for giving them the opportunity to participate prominently in the Bicentennial Celebration of the Constitution in Philadelphia. The Secretary came forward and pinned a medal for Distinguished Civilian Service on my lapel. This is the highest award given to a civilian by the U. S. Army.

I was stunned, but now everything made sense. After saying some personal remarks that were very nice, the Secretary asked me if I wished to say anything. My head was spinning, and I told them how overwhelmed I was, first, because of this wonderful award, and second, because my military service had been as a PFC infantryman and I had never seen this much brass before. As it worked out, that was the right thing to say. I also talked at some length about my debt to Secretary Marsh for all the assistance he had provided the "We the People--200" celebration and said that I should be giving him a medal instead of receiving one from him.

After being congratulated by everyone, Bob Arter took Bill Mott and me to the Interior Building, where I visited until time for my Metroliner home. My only regret was that Addie-Lou was not with me at such a special time.

L. Funding the Celebration

By the fall of 1986, "We the People--200" had put together a plan for a celebration that would cost an estimated $17 million to fund. This was a tight number and it did not contain any contingencies for expansion or the addition of any events. The big-ticket items in the celebration budget were $6 million to stage the ceremonies and parade for September 17, 1987, and $2 million to construct a 4--½ story pavilion on the second block of Independence Mall. The pavilion would be a

Teflon-coated canvas structure which would be the centerpiece for the daily activities of the celebration. The remainder of the budget would fund the opening ceremonies, a visit by Congress, daily programs, some less expensive events, and the operation of the "We the People--200" staff. Mary Gregg was hired as director of development for WTP--200 and we were having some success in raising funds from local corporations and foundations, but by the end of 1986, we were not even halfway to our goal.

In mid-October, without consultation with the "We the People--200" board, Mayor Wilson Goode announced the formation of a private non-profit corporation called *We the People – 200, Incorporated*. The purpose of the new organization was to raise funds for the plans put forth for the "We the People--200."

Diane Semingson, the City Representative and Director of Commerce, planned to take a leave of absence from her job and become the President and CEO of the new non-profit. Philadelphia lawyer Ned Donahue became the chairman, and I agreed to serve on the board. This meant that I was chairman of "We the People--200" and a member of *We the People – 200, Inc.* fundraising board.

A couple of months later, after the Articles of incorporation for "We the People--200" was approved by the Commonwealth of Pennsylvania, we needed the Internal Revenue Service to approve its non-profit status. This process usually takes at least three months, and we needed that approval to assure donors of our non-profit status so their

contributions to "We the People--200" would be tax-deductible. I volunteered to try to speed up the approval and called my friend and neighbor, Jim Rideout, District Director of the Internal Revenue Service in Philadelphia, to see if he could help us. He agreed to review the application immediately, so I hand-carried the materials to his office and he assigned someone to review them. Within an hour, the review had been completed and Jim signed the approval. This certainly speeded up our fundraising.

Despite a conflict of interest issue raised by the media, Diane Semingson went to work as *We the People – 200, Inc.* President, and she sought a salary of $115,000 per year. I thought that the idea of a non-profit was probably the right thing to do, but I had two concerns about Diane becoming President and CEO. First, Diane was politically aligned, and up to this point, "We The People--200" had remained out of politics. Diane had worked in the 1976 Carter campaign and had been rewarded with a Schedule "C" appointment as the Regional Director of Housing and Urban Development in Philadelphia. After the Carter administration, Diane was active in the Democratic Party in Philadelphia and was appointed City Representative by Mayor Wilson Goode. My other concern was, what would Diane's appointment do to Fred Stein? Fred was a high energy, slightly disorganized but get a quality job done director of the daily activities of "We the People--200" staff. As President Abraham Lincoln once remarked, that he would like to have God on his side, but he must have Kentucky; I had to have Fred. He was a major contributor to the "We the People--200" plan, and I did not want to lose him.

During the summer of 1986, we began a number of efforts to raise funds for the "We the People--200" programs, one of which was the licensing of products. We would allow manufacturers to utilize the "We the People--200" logo on their products, and for this privilege they would pay us a royalty. We were able to sign up manufacturers of tote bags, clothing, souvenirs, and even wine, but it became obvious that the program would not raise big bucks. We also hired Richard Rovsek of Santa Barbara, California, who had successfully raised corporate funds for the Statue of Liberty and Ellis Island Foundation. After three months, there was little progress from Mr. Rovsek, so in December we encouraged him finally to get busy and helped him with some publicity.

On the eve of the Year of the Bicentennial of the Constitution, Walter Naedele of *The Philadelphia Inquirer* reported that "We the People--200" had raised only $7.4 million of the $17 million goal. Inadequate staffing, a shortage of funds, and running out of time made the Bicentennial of the Constitution appear to be floundering. I have always believed that it is darkest just before dawn, and even though we were struggling, some of our projects were moving forward. The big project which had to move forward immediately because of construction time was the Pavilion on Independence Mall that would shelter many of the events of the celebration, including a planned joint session of Congress. In late January, my friend Edward J. Piszek of Mrs. Paul's agreed to guarantee up to $2.5 million toward the construction of the Pavilion. This meant that we could get the Pavilion underway and raise the money later. Two weeks later, Ed withdrew his

guarantee because of a disagreement with "We the People--200" fundraisers. This jeopardized our schedule to have the Pavilion ready for the opening ceremonies on May 25th. Fortunately, the Pavilion contractor continued to work on the project despite the risk, and by February 20th, PSFS, a Philadelphia bank, extended a $2.1 million line of credit to "We the People--200" to resume the construction of the Pavilion. On February 27th, the *Philadelphia Daily News* wrote, "Philadelphia is planning a spectacular party this year – and President Reagan, the entire Congress, and up to 10 million tourists are expected. But from the looks of it, the City could be in big trouble when company comes." The problem was money. During the year, "We the People--200" was scheduled to have programming to handle 35 or so major events, while more than 150 others were to be produced by local organizations and museums.

The corporate fundraiser, Richard Rovsek, was not successful, and without consulting me, he was promising the use of Independence Hall to major sponsors for private functions. This was not acceptable. There was further turmoil when the media reported that Ms. Semingson had been holding executive committee meetings of *We the People – 200, Inc.* behind closed doors. The critical reaction to these conditions brought about the appointment of Willard G. Rouse III, a workaholic and prominent Philadelphia area developer, to lead *We the People – 200, Inc.* Diane Semingson resigned as President of the corporation and Bill Rouse pulled together a dynamic executive committee. This group included Ned Donahue (lawyer), Chuck Scalch

(Bell of PA), Moe Septees (entertainment producer), John Kaiser (ad agency), John Kalish (ad agency), Norman Tissian (ad agency), Sam Rogers (Convention and Visitors Bureau), and myself.

When Bill Rouse came on board, he asked the contractor for the Pavilion to stop work until he evaluated the situation. Within a couple of days, the Speaker of the House of Representatives, Jim Wright, and the Senate Majority Leader, Robert Byrd, decided that it was impossible to get the entire Congress to Philadelphia for a special session. They asked us to consider something less which would include 32 Senators and 105 Representatives. We talked to Congressional historians Richard Baker (Senate) and Ray Smock (House), and they came up with a plan for a meeting of 137 delegates in Congress Hall. The question now was, should we go forward with the Pavilion on the Mall if it was no longer going to be used for a joint session of Congress?

A few days later, Bill Rouse announced that work should resume on the Pavilion with or without a session of Congress. Besides the Congressional meeting, some 14 additional events were scheduled for the Pavilion, and many more were added during the year.

Meanwhile, we needed a public relations boost, and that came about on April 1, 1987, when President Ronald Reagan came to Philadelphia to visit the College of Physicians on its 200th anniversary. Since he was going to be in the neighborhood, the President agreed to come to Congress Hall and address a group of potential corporate and foundation sponsors about the importance of the Bicentennial of the Constitution. He also pledged that he would be back on September 17th for Constitution Day. Some of the potential sponsors had their photograph taken with the President in a Committee room on the second floor.

The plan worked, because on April 10th, Atlantic Financial Corporation of Bala Cynwyd announced they would give $250,000 to sponsor Maritime America weekend, which included boat races on the Delaware River, and the commissioning of the U.S. Navy Aegis Cruiser USS *Thomas S. Gates*. Next came Smith Kline Beckman Corp. with $250,000. Philadelphia Electric funded the lighting of the Benjamin Franklin Bridge, Colonial Penn sponsored the soapbox, and finally we had momentum. Two local foundations, William Penn Foundation and the J. Howard Pew Freedom Trust, sponsored a number of activities. The Knight Foundation undertook several projects, including the four-day pageant performed by the U. S. Army Band. Then the Commonwealth of Pennsylvania provided $5 million, which assured that we would reach our fundraising goal. The State grant was directly related to Bill Rouse and his relationship with Governor Robert P. Casey and the Pennsylvania legislature.

The fundraising cap came in July, when Chief Justice Burger's Federal Commission gave the National Park Service $600,000 for the September 17, 1987 activities. Our fundraising experience was a success, but one could only draw that conclusion at the end of the celebration. We seemed to get the money when we needed it and not before. Our attitude was always positive, and we had faith that if we planned and conducted a first class celebration, somehow the necessary funds would come.

Without question, Bill Rouse made the difference and was the hero of the "We the People--200" Celebration. Bill, with the help of his assistant, Madelyn Rankin, was still fundraising right up until September 17th. The final amount raised for the celebration was $21 million and people speculated as to what motivated Bill to work so hard on the celebration. Certainly he had no political ambitions, nor was there any profit, and he seemed to shrink from publicity. In my opinion, he undertook the job because it was important to his community and his reward was a successful celebration.

When it was over, we had a reception to honor Bill Rouse, who by then had already undertaken the job as Chairman of the Pennsylvania Convention Center Authority, a project to build a new convention center in Philadelphia. In an effort to say "thank you", "We the People--200" gave him two gifts: a glass sculpture of Independence Hall by Laura Lou Bates, and a Park Ranger hat.

M. The Constitution Pavilion

One of the most important assets that we had during the Bicentennial of the Declaration of Independence was the Pavilion on Independence Mall, where the musical *1776* was performed nightly and where special events were held daily without concern for the weather. The Teflon-coated canvas structure included a stage in the round with seating for several thousand. The facility overlooked the Liberty Bell and Independence Hall, so it was a prestigious venue for any activity. One of my special memories was a dinner the night before the Major League Baseball All-Star Game, where I was able to meet the most famous names in baseball.

The Pavilion served us well and even lasted through the winter and was used during the summer of 1977 for a less successful production of *1776*. By that fall, the canvas surface was beginning to look dirty, so according to agreement, we asked the City of Philadelphia to remove it. There was some discussion about cleaning it up, but during the winter a storm ripped the canvas and made its removal a fact.

When we were planning for 1987, we wished to involve numerous groups in hundreds of programs, and where better to do this than the Judge Lewis Quadrangle on the second block of Independence Mall. Of course, weather was a concern. Dare we erect another Pavilion for 1987?

"We the People--200" decided that we needed the facility for our programs in 1987, but we were interested in having a simpler structure which would only shield programs from the sun and rain. *WTP–200* asked an architectural firm, H2L2, to design something that would be functional and practical. They came up with a 55,000-square-feet open-ended structure resting on ten pillars. The roof would be Plexiglas supported by an aluminum and steel frame. The winning bid for construction was $2.5 million.

Constitution Pavilion. *Image Courtesy of Independence National Historical Park*

The plan was to have the Constitution Pavilion ready for the opening of "All Roads Lead to Philadelphia" in May, and it would be available for a joint meeting of Congress in July. Unfortunately, it was not completed in time for the May activities, and the Congress decided not to have a joint session in Philadelphia. The reasons for the construction delay were a late starting date, bad weather, and funding. The J. Howard Pew Freedom Trust and the William Penn Foundation provided half of the funds needed, but we were somewhat late in getting the remainder from PSFS.

The Constitution Pavilion was the venue for the Festival of States, a program running from June 7th to July 29th, where each State was assigned their Day in Philadelphia to be part of the celebration. Approximately 75 percent of the

States participated. Each State designed its own program.

Virginia Day happened on May 29th, before our Festival of States began, because that was the date during the Constitutional Convention on which James Madison presented the Virginia Plan. The Bicentennial Commission of Virginia chartered a train that began at Montpelier, Madison's home, then went to Richmond, Washington and Philadelphia, picking up members of the Commission and State legislatures along the way. Chairman A.B. Dick Howard, Lieutenant Governor Wilder, and Governor Gerald L. Baliles led a program on Independence Square. Afternoon tours and an evening dinner completed the event. The New Jersey Plan was presented on June 15th, so this became New Jersey Day. Connecticut Day was scheduled for July 16th, the date of the

Connecticut Compromise. The other days were scheduled at the convenience of the States.

Delaware Day was special because many of the participants came by water. They had a parade, led by Governor Mike Castle, from Penns Landing to the Constitution Pavilion, where they held a program and concert. Montana Day was July 9th and included a 78-piece band from Helena and a 63-voice choir from Kalispell. The next day was Minnesota, then South Carolina, Tennessee, etc.

Most of the States sent high school students who had worked to earn money for their trip. "We the People--200" asked performing groups to perform twice, at noon and at 6:00 p.m. The State days proved to be a special experience for many of the young people.

The Constitution Pavilion was the venue for the International Village Fair, July 25th–August 2nd. Since there were some 155 national constitutions in the world, and ours is the oldest, it seemed appropriate to have an international segment for our celebration. Over a thousand chefs, filmmakers, artisans, entertainers, dancers, speakers, and storytellers were part of programs. The schedule was as follows:

July 25	African and African-American
July 26	Latin America
July 27-28	Asian and Asian American
July 29-30	Western European
July 31	Eastern European
August 1	Appalachian, Canadian, English, Celtic
August 2	International Potpourri

Besides the workshops, there was a main stage for music and dance. Visitors could purchase food and watch cooking demonstrations from dozens of countries. The final day was billed as a National Day of Peace, with scores of children in costumes singing, and concluding with the release of a dove.

Constitution Day was the scene of a huge picnic at the Constitution Pavilion for sponsors, participants, and special guests. The ARA Corporation provided a picnic basket with food, drink, and utensils for everyone present. The picnic included approximately a thousand people and took place immediately after the Grand Federal Procession and President Reagan's speech. Our son Stephen was a sophomore at Wake Forest University and had just moved into an apartment with two roommates. One of the many needs they had in furnishing their apartment was eating utensils (knives, forks, spoons). Since we were supposed to keep the picnic basket and everything in it, we asked our friends around us for their flatware. Stephen was there and collected enough to take care of his needs.

The tables and chairs for the picnic were removed after lunch, and the Constitution Pavilion was set up for a meeting of the Pennsylvania General Assembly the following day. Former Chief Justice Burger publicly thanked them for their support and said some nice things about Bill Rouse and myself. The Legislature also passed a resolution expressing their appreciation for our efforts with the celebration.

Ten days after Constitution Day, my friend Tom Muldoon, President of the Philadelphia

Convention and Visitors Bureau, began a public relations effort to keep the Constitution Pavilion in place after the celebration was concluded. Muldoon made the point that the Pavilion had become an important physical symbol of the Bicentennial of the Constitution, and if it was removed, this would mean that the celebration was over. He did not want it to be over. Tom also thought that the Pavilion could be a permanent place for "banquets, concerts and theater – during visitors to America's most Historic Square Mile."

The National Park Service had only agreed to "We the People--200" placing the Pavilion on Park property if it would be removed it when the bicentennial was over. My opinion was that the Constitution Pavilion looked great when it was in use, but it was not as attractive when it was empty. It was used every day in 1987, but afterward it would only be used occasionally. I compared it to some of the buildings remaining in Knoxville, Tennessee, after the 1982 World's Fair was over. The buildings look like dinosaurs. Assistant Superintendent Bernie Goodman did some research and determined that it would take approximately $1.25 million to install a roof that could withstand winter weather and to update an electrical system. On top of that, some $250,000 would be required for annual operating costs. After conferring with my superiors, I decided that the Pavilion should be removed.

It is gone, but it served us well.

N. Park Fees

On December 17, 1986, I was in the shower, dreaming of a trip to England with Addie-Lou and Steve (Toni had to work) that we would take in three days. We were going to visit Elizabeth and Cedric Dickens and Pat and Michael Harwood for an old-fashioned English Christmas. This was to be my last break before we plunged into 1987, the year of the Bicentennial of the Constitution. Addie-Lou tapped on the shower door and said that a reporter was on the telephone and he had an urgent question to ask me. When I got to the telephone, wrapped in a towel, the radio reporter said he had just gotten a story from the wire service that the Department of the Interior was announcing that fees would be charged at Independence National Historical Park, beginning in 1987. What did I know about it?

I told him that I knew nothing of the plan; there had been some discussions about park fees several months before, but there was no specific plan for the Park that I knew about. In fact, considering the circumstances, I did not think it feasible to collect them. He asked me how I felt about the idea and I said, "To charge a fee at Independence Hall or the Liberty Bell would be like the money changers in the temple".

When I got to the office, I found that Interior had released a plan to increase fees at Parks where they were currently being collected and to add a whole host of new parks to the list, including Independence and Valley Forge National Historical Parks. They were hoping to make a deal with Congress that would allow the NPS to keep a portion of the fees that they collected. Obviously, they were looking at our attendance numbers and thinking this is a place where we can increase our income. The announcement was premature, because we had never talked to anyone about the feasibility of collecting fees.

My supervisor, Regional Director James W. Coleman, Jr., supported the fee idea presented by Interior, but despite my personal friendship with Jim since 1959, I said in the December 18, 1986 *Philadelphia Inquirer* that "I'm fighting it like the plague." I felt that I should stick my neck out and oppose the fees for a number of reasons:

1. We had worked hard at raising private money to create exhibitions, celebrations and programs for the Bicentennial of the U.S. Constitution, and our donors did not anticipate that the facilities would only be available to those paying a fee.

2. There was no consideration of how a fee would be collected, because the Park was some 40 buildings scattered over 8 city blocks. There certainly was no fence enclosing the Park. They did not include any new employees to collect the fees at approximately 23 buildings, so our interpretive staff would become ticket sellers or takers instead of assisting the visitors in understanding and enjoying the Park.

3. There had been no consultation with the owners of the buildings, because the NPS did not own several of the buildings and/or their contents; we managed them by agreement. The City of Philadelphia owned Independence Hall, Congress Hall, and Old City Hall, as well as most of the portraits in the Second Bank and the Liberty Bell. The American Philosophical Society owned Philosophical Hall and Library Hall. The Carpenters Company owned Carpenters Hall. Also, how would this impact Christ Church, Old St. George's United Methodist Church, Old St. Joseph's Catholic Church, and Mikveh Israel Cemetery, all part of the Park by legislation and agreement?

4. I immediately wrote a memorandum to the Director, William Penn Mott, through the Regional Director, Jim Coleman, stating my arguments and saying, "It would be disastrous to the Service to charge at Independence, especially in 1987, when we are the focal point of our own citizens and even the entire world."

By the following day (December 19th), Mayor Wilson Goode and Congressman Peter Kostmayer stated that the historic sites around Independence Hall should remain free to all visitors. Kostmayer was on the Interior Subcommittee on National Parks, and he called for hearings on the matter as soon as Congress returned on January 6, 1987. Kostmayer said of Interior, "They knew the cost of everything, but the value of nothing". The *Philadelphia Daily News* reported that Senator Arlen Specter, Congressman William H. Gray, III, Tom Muldoon, President of the Philadelphia Convention and Visitor Bureau, and Diane Semingson, President of We the People, were all against fees, and on the day we were leaving for England, *The Philadelphia Inquirer* printed an editorial, "Let's Keep Those Shrines of Freedom Free Forever." The editorial said, "Hobart G. Cawood, Superintendent of Independence National Historical Park, deserves strong public support and bipartisan backing in Congress for his firm stand against ending the free admission policy that has prevailed at the Park since its founding in 1951". And I was off to Merry Old England for Christmas.

We had a great Christmas in England and were back before the New Year so we could help ring in the year of the Bicentennial of the Constitution. As Congress went back to Washington on January 6th, George Wilson wrote an op ed column in the *Inquirer*, suggesting that charging fees at INHP was a bad idea. He cited the effort by Tom McCallum of the Friends to set them aside and said that the "plucky" Hobart G. Cawood stood up to be counted. McCallum actually wrote to the Philadelphia Congressional delegation and was successful in going to Washington for a meeting to oppose the fees.

On January 28, Peter Kostmayer said that the fees would be studied further and that the plan was dead for 1987. Congressman Bill Gray also said that the National Park Service informed him of the delay. He reportedly told Secretary of the Interior Donald P. Hodel that charging any fee at Independence was outlandish. Senators John Heinz and Arlen Specter met with Director Mott on January 30 in an effort to convince him that Independence was an urban park and should fit into a law that prohibited fees in outdoor recreational urban parks.

On February 3rd, Director Mott called me to Washington and I was "chastised" for publicly opposing fees at the Park. According to George Berklacy, the Director "confronted Cawood because he felt that Hobie's public criticism was not correct, constructive or productive." Berklacy said that "chastisement" is a good word to describe their meeting. He then said that "Cawood's opposition would not affect his standing in the National Park Service. I know for a fact that he (Hobie) is held in high esteem by Mott." When asked to comment on the meeting, I said, "I've said enough." Actually, I did not need to say more because everyone else had taken up the cause.

Next, Secretary Hodel issued a statement that their plan for fees at Independence would include only 10 of the 23 buildings open to the public. The exempted sites listed by Hodel were: Independence Hall, Congress Hall, Old City Hall, Liberty Bell Pavilion, City Tavern, Carpenters Hall, First Bank of the U.S., Second Bank of the U.S., Christ Church, Library Hall, Philosophical Hall, and two buildings in Franklin court. This was a plan that would be impossible to administer, plus it would cost more to collect the money than it would produce. An editorial in the *Inquirer* termed it "an unacceptable Park Fees plan".

On the following day, a *Philadelphia Daily News* editorial entitled, "Thanks Hobie", said "…10 of the 23 historic sites at the Park will be off limits if you aren't willing to shell out two bucks. This is unthinkable but we can't expect Hobie Cawood to carry the cudgels for us (I've said enough, he told reporters after Mott took him to the woodshed). If we want to reverse this abomination, we must maintain an insistent and unwavering clamor. Hobie can't do it all."

The Interior Subcommittee on National Parks of the House of Representatives decided that they would block fees in 22 Parks in urban areas, including Independence NHP. Another bill by my congressman, Tom Foglietta, and Congressman John Murtha of Central Pennsylvania, would accomplish the same thing but was not needed now. On March 26, 1987, Interior Secretary Hodel agreed to drop plans to charge fees at Independence National Historical Park.

For three and a half months, in one of the busiest years that Independence NHP would ever experience, I found it necessary to deal with this distraction. It was something that a simple meeting or a consultation with Park staff by the National Park Service and the Department of the Interior could have resolved.

Since we survived, the only negative was the result of my performance rating evaluation for the year 1987. I gave a great effort and helped produce a major national celebration, but because I had not followed the directions of my superiors regarding the fees, my supervisor, the Mid-Atlantic Regional Director, gave me the lowest performance evaluation that I received while serving as the Superintendent of Independence. When Jim Coleman talked to me about my rating, I told him that it was worth the price.

O. Flag Day, June 14, 1986

Every year on Flag Day, June 14th, the Philadelphia Flag Day Association presents a program at the Betsy Ross House on Arch Street. The house is one of the major visitor attractions in Philadelphia, and this program is popular and well attended. A stage is always erected in the center of the street and the program includes music, entertainment, and remarks by well-known speakers. The principal speech is made by someone who is presented the Philadelphia Flag Day Association Distinguished Service Award. A luncheon follows the ceremony. I was presented the award and made the speech in 1978.

The Director of the National Park Service, William Penn Mott, was selected to make the speech and receive the award on June 14, 1986. A few weeks in advance, Bill Mott called me and asked if I could pick him up at the airport at about 9:00 in the morning and show him around a bit until the program started at 11:30 a.m. June 14th was a Saturday, so I decided to go pick up the Director while wearing shorts and bring him to my house, where Addie-Lou would give him a cup of coffee while I changed clothes. We could then visit a couple of places in the Park and walk on over to the Flag Day program.

I knew his flight number and arrival time, so I went to the airport, parked the car, and walked to the gate to meet him. I was there just in time to meet the flight from Washington. Bill Mott was not on the flight. The airline personnel checked the airplane but he was not there. The airline's computers were down so they could not check to see if he was on the flight, but eventually they called Washington and found out that Director Mott had checked in at National Airport. I then went back to the baggage claim area but still no Bill Mott. Finally, I decided to go back home and he could call me if he still needed transportation. I got back home at about 9:45 a,.m. and Addie-Lou said that Bill Mott had called and was at the airport, and she told him that I would meet him at the baggage claim. I drove back to the airport and Bill Mott was not at curbside, so I asked a policeman for permission to leave the car and quickly check inside for the Director. I looked in the hallways, restrooms and even had him paged on the public address system, but no Bill Mott. I drove back home.

When I walked in the door, Addie-Lou said that Director Mott had called and said that he had decided to take a taxi because of time. He told her that when he gave the driver the address of the Betsy Ross House, he did not know where it was. When Bill told him that it was in Philadelphia near Independence Hall, the taxi driver informed him that he was in New York. Apparently what had happened was that small airplane shuttles from Washington were loading all of their flights through a single gate and Bill somehow had gotten on the wrong plane and ended up in New York. He asked Addie-Lou to tell me to substitute for him as the Flag Day speaker and to express his regrets for not being there.

I had approximately a half hour to get dressed and run to the Betsy Ross house, some five blocks away, but I made it. The first person I saw was my Regional Director, Jim Coleman, along with his wife Pat and his deputy, Don Castleberry, who all had come to hear Director Mott talk. I told them that they were going to have to listen to me. The Flag Day officials were disappointed but were pleased that I was ready to fill in for the Director.

With only a half hour to prepare, get dressed, and walk to the site, my remarks were completely extemporaneous. I began with the story of what had happened to Director Mott, and the honor for me to replace him. I then stumbled through how important the American Flag was as a symbol for our nation. I then told of a personal experience that illustrated its importance.

When I was in the Soviet Union with a U.S. Information exhibition in 1974, I spent five weeks in Kishenov, Moldavia. One morning through a translator I was talking to a group of some 200 visitors when someone asked me about Oral Roberts. I asked the two men and a woman, who were dressed in black and appeared to be very poor, to come to the front of the crowd. They said that they were Baptists and that they had heard my Voice of America broadcast, which I had made before I came to the USSR, and their congregation sent them to see the Americans. They had traveled several days to get to Kishenov. With the crowd listening, we talked about religious freedom and the way it works in our country. They wanted to know if I was religious. I said I was a Methodist and Boris our translator said that he was a Russian Orthodox. Suddenly, a group of Soviet officials entered the room and the crowd shielded the Baptists until they could leave the room. Having such a talk with these people who had made an unbelievable effort to see us had a great impact

on me. I hoped that what I had said in the few
minutes that we had together was significant.

An hour later I walked to a small café nearby to
join some of my colleagues for lunch. When I
opened the door I saw my group on the far side
of the room but in the center of the room sat
the Baptist having a cup of tea. I wanted to do
something for them but I couldn't draw attention
to them. I reached into my National Park Service
uniform pocked and found three small American
flag lapel pins. As I passed the Baptist table, I put
the flags into the hands of the woman and walked
on to the table of my friends. A few minutes later
I looked back to the Baptist and the woman gave
me an appreciative nod.

I do not know what happened to those three
symbols of America but I would like to think that
they were important to a group of badly oppressed
people.

I may have made one of the best speeches of my
career and I had no time to prepare it. We went to
the luncheon and I was given Bill Mott's award to
pass on to him, so all ended well.

VI.

THE CELEBRATION 1987

A. All Roads Lead to Philadelphia

The "We the People--200" events took place during the entire year of 1987; however, the period of emphasis for the celebration was the same period (May 25th – September 17th) as the meeting of the Constitutional Convention in 1787. The delegates to the 1787 meeting began arriving in early May, but because of adverse traveling conditions there were not enough delegates available for the targeted May 14th opening. It was necessary to wait until May 25th before a quorum was available.

It happened that May 25, 1987, was on Monday of a Memorial Day weekend, so the opening activities for the Constitution celebration were planned for four days, beginning on Friday. For the purpose of promoting the weekend, it was called "All Roads Lead to Philadelphia."

Prior to the weekend, on May 13th, the re-enactment of George Washington's arrival in Philadelphia was staged by the Delaware County and Philadelphia Bar Associations. The Delaware County ceremony took place at 8:30 a.m. in Chester, with the principal speaker being David Eisenhower, accompanied by his wife, Julie Nixon Eisenhower. Mr. Eisenhower, a historian and grandson of President Dwight D. Eisenhower, spoke about the importance of George Washington at the Constitutional Convention. The re-enactment party was shuttled to a National Guard Armory in Philadelphia, where Washington's carriage was accompanied by the horse-mounted First City Troop and began a parade down Chestnut Street to Independence

Hall. A ceremony involving Seymour Kirkland, Chancellor of the Philadelphia Bar Association, and National Park Service historian David Kimball took place on the steps of Independence Hall. Kimball spoke about the importance of Washington to the 1787 meeting. The Washington re-enactors continued on to Franklin Court to call on Dr. Franklin, as had happened in the 18th Century. Ralph Archibald, a Franklin impersonator, met them there.

The kick-off for the weekend began with a free concert at the Eakins Oval on the Benjamin Franklin Parkway on Friday, May 22nd. Grover Washington, Jr., and the pop group Chicago performed for an audience of 300,000. The concert was followed by fireworks from the Philadelphia Museum of Art. *The Philadelphia Inquirer* reported, "with mellow jazz, lively pop and crackling fireworks, the City of Philadelphia officially kicked off its 200th birthday bash for the nation's Constitution."

On Saturday, Independence Mall was the center for a 1787 festival, which featured re-enactors portraying life in the 18th Century. This activity continued each day during the weekend. The re-enactment of the arrival of delegates was presented by the American Morgan Horse Association. Centered on the Mall were the demonstration and sale of crafts, a restaurant festival, and music and dance performances. Members of the New Freedom Theater, the Royal Pickwickians, and the Theater Wing of the Philadelphia Bar Association presented historical skits. These activities also continued for the whole weekend.

May 23rd was also the beginning of the "Soapbox," a speakers platform and podium located on the Mall between Independence Hall and the Liberty Bell. Anyone could speak freely on any topic until asked by the crowd to step down. The first participant was Walter E. Fauntroy, who represented the District of Columbia in Congress, and he spoke about statehood for the District. The soapbox was in place every day until September 20th and was constantly in use. A group of entertainers was there to encourage the proper use. Provident Mutual Insurance Company sponsored this activity.

On May 23rd the fife and drum promenade began. The Old City Fife and Drum Corps paraded daily throughout the historic area and stopped at six selected locations for brief concerts. This activity continued daily until September 20th.

Since the delegates to the Constitutional Convention came from the States, "We the People--200" invited the Governors of the first thirteen states to a conference on May 24th to discuss issues that would be of common interest to the group. If the Governor could not come, we asked them to send a proper delegate. The meeting was to take place in the First Bank of the United States. Governors came from six states: William O'Neill of Connecticut, Michael Castle of Delaware, John Sununu of New Hampshire, Edward DiPrete of Rhode Island, Carroll Campbell of South Carolina, and Robert Casey of Pennsylvania. Some states were represented by former governors: Harry Hughes of Maryland, Brendon Byrne of New Jersey, Robert Scott of North Carolina, and

Charles Robb of Virginia. Other states were represented by the Secretary of State or another prominent State official.

After the business of the mid afternoon conference, there was a Governors Ball in a huge tent complex on the lawn behind the Second Bank of the United States. The event was underwritten by Fidelity Bank and its chairman, Harold Pote; Bill Rouse, Governor Casey, Mayor Goode, and myself were the Ball Chairmen. The 1400 attendees were encouraged to wear costumes or else black tie. The Governors arrived at the Ball via horse drawn carriages. Addie-Lou and I were in costume and came by carriage. There was a great meal, a brief program and dancing, including someone who instructed us in 18th-Century dancing. The highlight of the evening for me was an after-dinner toast to the Constitution using 18th-Century Madeira.

A few years before, I had spoken about the drinking of Madeira in 18th-Century America at a Madeira tasting party in Philadelphia. The President of the Madeira Wine Company was present to conduct the tasting. He seemed to enjoy my humorous stories about Madeira, so he gave me a cut glass decanter and a bottle of 1860 Madeira in a beautiful mahogany box. He also said that he had some old wines in the caves in Madeira and to let him know if he could ever help me. The Governor's Ball seemed like an event that would be worthy of a call to him. When I reached him, I asked if there was any possibility that he had wine made from grapes grown during the year that our Constitution was written. He said that he would check on it, and when he called back, he volunteered to donate enough 1787 wine so that we had 2 oz. per guest at the Governor's Ball. The toast was made to the Constitution with wine from the same year it was written. Everyone was impressed.

The Governor's Ball was by invitation only, so at 8:00 p.m. there was a waterfront concert at Penns Landing free to the public. The concert was given by the American Waterways Wind Orchestra and was followed by a spectacular fireworks display. The fireworks were produced by the Grucci family, choreographed to music of the '50s and '60s and narrated by George Plimpton. An estimated 400,000 people on both sides of the Delaware River saw the show.

The final day of "All Roads Lead to Philadelphia" started with a ceremony on the second block of Independence Mall to unveil the U. S. Postal Service's first Constitution commemorative post card. This first day of issue for the postcard created block long lines. George Washington, Ben Franklin, and David Stone, the postcard designer, were on hand to autograph the cards.

At 11:00 a.m. the first performance of *Four Little Pages*, a musical drama produced by Franklin Roberts ,was given at the First Bank of the U.S. This was the first of three performances every day through September 20th. The show was underwritten by *The Philadelphia Inquirer* and the *Philadelphia Daily News*. As a further contribution to the celebration, the *Inquirer* produced a souvenir color supplement that featured the celebration and even printed a sufficient number so we could distribute them to

visitors throughout the summer.

The official ceremony marking the 20th anniversary of the convening of the Constitutional Convention was held on a platform on Chestnut Street in front of Independence Hall at 2:00 p.m. Vice President George Bush was to be the principal speaker. I met him and Mrs. Bush at the rear door of Independence Hall at around 1:30 p.m. and escorted them inside to meet the other program participants. I had a few minutes to show the Vice President and Mrs. Bush the Assembly Room before we gathered for last minute instructions. At 2:00 p.m. the bell in the tower of Independence Hall rang 13 times, the door opened, and we walked outside onto the stage.

Chief Justice Warren E. Burger, Vice President Bush, Bill Rouse, and Mayor Goode sat to the left of the podium. James Earl Jones, Governor Casey, Mrs. Bush and myself sat on the right. The State governors and delegates were on the platform just behind us. The Constitution Bicentennial All-Star Marching Band, 300 high school students from 35 States, and the U. S. Army's Old Guard Fife and Drum Corps, had entertained the crowd prior to the program. After we were seated on the platform, the band played "God Bless America." Then clergy from the Presbyterian, Catholic, Jewish, and Islamic faiths delivered joint invocations. The Old Guard performed a 10-minute fife and drum marching drill, after which I went to the podium and welcomed everyone to this very special occasion. My remarks concluded with, "In our society we often preserve the home where great men were born" and I turned toward Independence Hall and said, "but in this house a nation was born." Then I introduced actor James Earl Jones as the master of ceremonies.

Jones made a few remarks and one by one introduced each Governor and state delegate. Each one stood beside the flag of his state and told a vignette about their delegation to the Constitutional Convention. At the end of the role call, a 30-foot high American flag, made of 30,000 red, white and blue balloons, was raised between the platform and Independence Hall. Mayor Goode and Governor Casey spoke briefly, then after some remarks, Chief Justice Burger introduced Vice President Bush, who spoke for six minutes. In conclusion, Broadway star Andrea McArdle sang the "We the People--200" theme song and the 30,000 balloons forming the American flag were released. We all left the stage and went back into Independence Hall. Vice President and Mrs. Bush said their goodbyes and I escorted them to their car behind Congress Hall.

Several days prior to the opening weekend, an organization that opposed American policy in Central America applied at our office for a permit to have a demonstration on the first block of Independence Mall on May 25th. Obviously, their target was Vice President George Bush. Fortunately, we had already issued a permit to "We the People--200" for that space as well as the Judge Lewis Quadrangle on the second block. These were the spaces that were being used for "We the People--200" during the entire weekend. We offered them the third block of Independence Mall, but they declined it because it was too far away from the Vice President, who would be near the front steps of Independence Hall. We worked

with the Philadelphia police and they accepted a permit to parade from City Hall east on Market Street to Penns Landing. That would bring their group down Market Street between the first and second blocks of Independence Mall, and they would probably pass through the area while our program was in progress, but hopefully it would not be disruptive.

During the program, long before the Vice President spoke, the group of about 100 demonstrators arrived at the Mall. They were a block away, blowing horns and carrying signs. They also had wreaths decorated with small plastic skulls, and police intelligence thought they even had a container of blood that they wanted to throw at the Vice President. The audience was aware of them but it was not disruptive to the program. When several of the group broke away from the parade and tried to enter the audience enclosure for the program, they were arrested, and some had to be physically removed. Even though City police, park rangers, and the Secret Service were all involved, since they were violating a City permit, the City made the arrests. Finally, the group passed on down Market Street and stopped in the 300 block, where they had their own rally. Since the police had already blocked Market Street, they just allowed the demonstrators to continue.

Chief Ranger Bob Byrne slipped up onto the platform and gave me a quick report on the demonstration. We continued to hear the demonstrators in the distance, and Mrs. Bush leaned over to me and asked, "What is going on?" I told her that it was a demonstration against the American policy in Central America. She said,

"George," and I replied, "Yes ma'am," and she said, "Oh!"

The following week, the demonstrators filed a suit in Federal District Court against the City of Philadelphia alleging that their civil rights had been violated by being arrested while attempting to enter a public gathering. The City said that they had arrived in a group with signs, horns and balloons, and were obviously involved in a demonstration that they attempted to take into an area for which they had no permit. Furthermore, they had violated the rules of the permit they had been issued. The judge ruled in favor of the demonstrators, saying that no matter how they presented themselves at a public event, they had the right to enter. If they were disruptive after they received entry, then they could be arrested. It was described as, "even though it looks like a duck, walks like a duck, and has feathers like a duck, it is not a duck until it says quack." The City could not prosecute the demonstrators and had to pay a token fine, but the bottom line was that they did not disrupt the event.

The finale of the weekend was a free concert called "Born in America," with Joseph Primavera conducting the Philadelphia Youth Orchestra. They performed the world premiere of Frederick Kaufman's "American Symphony #5." The performance was held on the Judge Lewis Quadrangle where the "We the People--200" Pavilion was nearly complete. The view across the top of the Liberty Bell Pavilion to the dramatically lighted Independence Hall was inspirational.

We had planned for three years, and now that we were underway, we wondered what the world would think of our kickoff. In part, the success of the remainder of the celebration depended on how we began. The response was over the top. An op-ed piece in *The Philadelphia Inquirer*, "On a Reflective Weekend, 1787's Spirit Lives Anew," was typical:

In a most unusual way, the spirit of "we the people" pervaded Philadelphia's observance of the start of the Constitutional Convention 200 years ago. It was everywhere....

The holiday weekend's events staged by We the People 200 went off without a hitch. The names of all the officials and volunteer workers who were responsible for that are too many too list in this space, but certainly deserving of special mention for their leadership are Willard G. Rouse 3d, head of We the People 200, Gov. Casey, Mayor Goode and Hobart G. Cawood, Superintendent of Independence National Historical Park. Kudos also should go to the Philadelphia police, National Park Service rangers and the Secret Service for the highly professional way they handled security and traffic and attended to people's needs and questions.

It was a grand beginning to Philadelphia's summer-long observations of the Constitutional Convention, giving promise of many more interesting pleasurable events honoring the men who met in Independence Hall in the summer of 1787.

USA Today called the Constitution Gala a "Button popper" and carried on its front page a color photograph of the flag made from 30,000 balloons. It also reported that 45,000 people were on hand at Independence Hall, more that 400,000 viewed the fireworks on the Delaware River, and 300,000 attended the opening concert by Chicago. The *New York Times* ran a front-page article and picture with the story continued inside with two more photographs. Also inside were excerpts from the speeches of Chief Justice Burger, Mayor Goode, and Vice President Bush.

"All Roads Lead to Philadelphia" created great momentum for the summer-long celebration for the Bicentennial of the Constitution. It also helped with fundraising and paved the way for the Independence Day activities, the visit by Congress, and Constitution Day.

B. The Momentum

By getting an early start on planning the bicentennial of the Constitution, "We the People--200" was a major influence on other organizations and institutions in the Philadelphia area. Even in the early days of planning, the news media was particularly good in publicizing the activities and progress of "We the People--200." Also, in the years leading up to the celebration, I was constantly on the "rubber chicken" circuit, talking about our plans and how others could be involved. This got to be a challenge for me because many people were members of several organizations, and I had to work to keep from delivering the same old talk to the same people.

In June 1985, when President Reagan appointed the Commission on the Bicentennial of the United States Constitution with Chief Justice of the United States Warren Burger as chairman, our creditability soared. We were now part of a national celebration. Before, we had labeled our efforts as being "a national celebration in Philadelphia," and now we were a significant part of a real national celebration.

Shortly after being named Chairman of the Commission, Chief Justice Burger came to Philadelphia to find out about our plans. During his visit, we toured Independence Hall and then Old City Hall, where the Supreme Court had heard its first case. Chief Justice Burger was obviously impressed at being in this historic setting, and he quietly said to City Representative Richard Doran and me, "Philadelphia will be a Mecca for freedom-loving people throughout the world in 1987." I looked at Dick and he winked because we both understood that we had just heard a wonderful quote from the Chairman of the Federal Commission. Boy, did we repeat that quote over the next two years.

There are some organizations, such as the American Philosophical Society, The Library Company, and the Historical Society of Pennsylvania, which would be obvious participants in the celebration. In fact, they had all contributed significant items, as well as their scholarship, to the Park exhibition "Miracle at Philadelphia." Nevertheless, they also did exhibitions and programs of their own. The Historical Society of Pennsylvania did a successful exhibit, "A More Perfect Union: The American People and their Constitution." Although The Library Company was a private library, they invited the delegates to the Constitution Convention to use their facilities, so their exhibition featured the volumes that were available to the delegates in 1787. This exhibit was called "The Delegate Library." Research for the project turned up the fact that Luther Martin of Maryland and Rufus King of Massachusetts borrowed books that they did not return. The American Philosophical Society did exhibits in its library about the city in 1787.

Raul Alfonsin, President of Argentina, June 19, 1987. Photo by Russel P. Smith. *Image Courtesy of Independence National Historical Park*

By the summer of 1987, most museums in the City of Philadelphia and its environs had an exhibition related to the Constitution. It took forever for us to get the Philadelphia Museum of Art involved, but finally curator Bea Garvin put together "Federal Philadelphia, 1785-1825," a magnificent exhibition of furniture, paintings, silver, costumes, and architectural elements of the Federal period. On the opposite end of the spectrum was the Please Touch Children's Museum, with its exhibit, "Red, White and Blue: Childhood and Citizenship." The Atwater Kent Museum did an archeology exhibition about historic Philadelphia. The Franklin Institute is a science museum but it produced a great show about Ben Franklin called "Born out of Time." It held this show in its rotunda, which itself is the Benjamin Franklin National Memorial. It would be impossible

to mention everyone, but needless to say, any institution that could in any way relate itself to the Convention or the Constitution did some kind of program calling attention to that relationship. A media survey in late summer 1987 established that all cultural institutions were having a significant increase in attendance.

One of the great events in Philadelphia each spring is the Philadelphia Flower Show, which is put on through the efforts of the Pennsylvania Horticultural Society. In 1987 they did an exhibition called "Tea at Grays Ferry," which is where famous 18th-century Philadelphia botanist John Bartram had a plant nursery. George Washington visited Bartram there about horticultural matters during a break in the Convention. The University of Pennsylvania Hospital Antiques Show was "A Federal

Procession: A Salute to the Constitution." The Pennsylvania Academy of Fine Arts did "Framing the Constitution: The Artist Record." Even the famed Mummers who strut up Broad Street on New Years Day titled their annual parade "We The People."

The surrounding counties of Bucks, Montgomery, Delaware, and Chester celebrated the bicentennial in a number of ways, from a soapbox for public speeches to banners, band concerts, and lectures. The Montgomery County Commissioners even held one of their meetings at Harriton House, the historic house of Charles Thomson, Secretary to the Congresses 1774-1789.

All of the area colleges and universities had programs, lectures, and exhibits during 1987. President Gerald Ford spoke about the Constitution at West Chester State University. The University of Pennsylvania had 10 signers of the Constitution associated with the school, so they did an exhibition entitled "The University of Pennsylvania and the Creation of the Constitution." I spoke at convocations at Thomas Jefferson University and Drexel University and received an honorary degree from both for my trouble. I went out-of-town to Knoxville, Tennessee, Fort Oglethorpe, Georgia, and Abington, Virginia, to make speeches.

In 1987 there were some 80,000 Federal employees in the Philadelphia area, so the Federal Executive Board held a three-hour celebration at the Constitution Pavilion on Independence Mall. This included a military band, a drill team, and exhibits about the many agencies involved. A unique collection of Federal Military and Civilian

Federal workers owe their job directly to the Constitution. Constance Horner, the Director of the Office of Personnel Management, and Federal Judge Ed Becker spoke. The United States Mint in Philadelphia minted Constitution Bicentennial coins, with the silver coin selling for $26 and the gold for $215. I was there to participate in the unveiling with Superintendent of the Mint Anthony Murray and Secretary of the Treasury James Baker.

Almost every church had some kind of commemorative program, including Mother Bethel AME Church, which hosted a tribute to 29 black families from Philadelphia. Some 120 members of families whose roots go back to 1787 participated and over 1500 came to the service. On September 15th, all Methodists were invited to my church, Old St. George's, for a brief service and a candlelight procession to Independence Mall for an interfaith service of 20 religious congregations from the old city area.

Most patriotic and hereditary groups used their annual meeting to have a Constitution themed program. They would usually have an after-dinner speaker who would talk about the Constitution or the celebration, and they would provide that person with some kind of award. I enjoyed these groups and actually spoke to many of them in 1987, and, of course, have a collection of plaques, certificates, and other awards as a result. According to my calendar, in 1987 I spoke to 85 gatherings where I was introduced as the principal speaker. My most unusual talk was on a cruise that Addie-Lou and I took from Montreal to Philadelphia. The five-day cruise on the Ocean Princess was organized by

Ann Pakradooni to benefit "We the People--200." My passage was free for delivering two lectures about the celebration during the trip. On the way we stopped at Newport, Rhode Island, where our friends Mary Will and Wells Darling sailed out to the ship and took us on a tour of the harbor. Mary Will was a roommate of Addie-Lou's at Bryn Mawr College.

CBS television news produced the series, *A Bicentennial Minute*, which showed every weeknight during the summer of 1987. It was a 60-second vignette about the Constitution delivered by renowned people, such as actors, sports figures, and politicians. There were some 50 of these *Minutes* produced. When the series began, Chief Justice Burger did the first one and I did the second. On the night after my minute was shown, I got a call from my cousin Connor Cawood in Lexington, Kentucky. Connor said that he was in a bar and had seen me on television. He told the people around him that I was his cousin and he asked me to speak to one of them to confirm our relationship. I assured the person on the telephone that Connor and I were first cousins; I assumed that he got a free drink out of the telephone call.

The celebration gained momentum as the year 1987 progressed; it seemed to gain a life of its own. There were activities that neither I nor the "We the People--200" office had any knowledge about. We had hoped to assist everyone with publicity and promotion for their events, but that was almost impossible. It was just a great feeling to know that I had helped create and plan celebrations in which hundreds of thousands were

participants and millions enjoyed as spectators.

C. The Congressional Pilgrimage - July 16, 1987

Barely four days after the Constitutional Convention convened in 1787, Edmund Randolph presented an outline of government (mostly James Madison's plan) to the delegates that is referred to as the Virginia Plan. The plan included a legislature whose membership would be based on proportional representation. That meant that the states with more population would have more delegates (votes) than the smaller states. The small states naturally opposed the Virginia Plan, preferring instead a legislature based upon equal representation for the states. William Patterson presented this concept, called the New Jersey Plan, to the Convention on June 15th. The Convention seemed deadlocked over the issue of the legislature until July 16th, when Roger Sherman of Connecticut presented a compromise of creating a legislature with two houses: the Senate, which would have equal representation; and the House of Representatives, which would have proportional representation. This Great Compromise or Connecticut Compromise was adopted, and at that moment that the Congress of the United States was conceived.

In 1985, Fred Stein of "We the People--200" and I had a meeting in my office with Dr. Richard Baker, historian of the United States Senate, and Raymond Smock, historian of the House of Representatives, in which we proposed the idea of a joint session of Congress in Philadelphia on July 16, 1987, the bicentennial of the conception of Congress. We agreed that we would work toward such an event, and we felt so comfortable with the idea that we included it in our plan for the celebration. We talked about it openly with everyone, including the Commission on the Bicentennial of the Constitution. Congresswoman Lindy Boggs was particularly supportive, but such a meeting would have to be authorized by a Congressional Resolution. In 1986, we had gained the support of Speaker Tip O'Neill and President Pro Tempore Robert Dole, but the 1986 elections brought a change, with Robert Byrd replacing Dole, and O'Neill retired, with Jim Wright becoming the new Speaker.

Ray Smock brought Jim Wright's Chief of Staff, Marshall Lynam, to Philadelphia to inspect the site and discuss the idea. He was followed by Dick Baker with Walter Stewart, Secretary of the Senate. Fred Stein, Mary Kimmett, Diane Semingson, and I made sure that they saw the Pavilion under construction, the House and Senate Chambers in Congress Hall, Independence Hall, and all of the open spaces in the Park. All of this was taken back to Washington for consideration. The Park staff, "We the Peoploe--200," and the Congressional historians became so close in working on this project that we referred to ourselves as charter members of the "Society of the Rising Sun," after the sun carved on Washington's chair in Independence Hall. Every time we met, we greeted each other with the fingers of both hands spread wide and placed beneath the chin.

Everyone had an opinion about what the Congress should do to celebrate their beginnings, and fortunately all ideas included sending a delegation to Philadelphia:

1. The whole Congress (525 members) should meet in a joint session beneath the Constitution Pavilion on Independence Mall.
2. Fifty-five members to match the number of delegates in 1787 would be appointed to participate in a ceremonial program in the Assembly Room of Independence Hall.
3. One hundred thirty-seven members of Congress, 32 Senators and 105 Representatives could assemble in the Senate and House Chambers in Congress Hall. The first five Congresses met here, 1790-1800.

In every case, it was envisioned that the Congressional visit would be one of ceremony and solemnity, as well as festivity and entertainment.

In May the House passed a resolution calling for an official delegation of 55 members – one member from each state, plus the Speaker of the House, and the minority and majority whips of both Houses. The resolution also bestowed a ceremonial role on the 25-person Pennsylvania delegation. The Senate passed a similar resolution, but their version required that 10 percent of the 55 delegates must be senators. Besides the official delegates, all members of Congress were invited to attend along with their family members. They planned to travel to Philadelphia by train on July 16th.

Senate Majority Leader Robert C. Byrd and Speaker of the House Jim Wright decided against sending all 535 members of Congress because of time, cost, and security. There was also a procedural problem with having a joint session outside of Washington. Some suggested that had Tip O'Neill and Bob Dole still been in leadership positions, the joint session would have taken place. We will never know.

As one might expect, a gathering of members of Congress outside of Washington was a magnet for groups that might wish to protest or demonstrate their message to the members. Rita Adessa, executive director of the Lesbian and Gay Task Force, made application to the Park to hold a demonstration on Independence Mall, between Independence Hall and the Liberty Bell. We normally did not grant permits for that space because it would interfere with the use of the Park by the normal park visitors. However, we had already issued a permit to "We the People--200" for Independence Square and the first two blocks of the mall. The Task Force had originally applied in April and filed a revised permit in June. The "We the People--200" permit had been in place since 1986.

We offered the Lesbian and Gay Task Force an alternate space behind the Second Bank of the United States and an opportunity to march from that location to Independence Mall after Congress had finished its session. This was not acceptable to them, so they filed a lawsuit in Federal District Court, and on July 14th, I was witness before U.S. District Judge John P. Fullam. After hearing both sides, Judge Fullam ruled that the Task Force had failed to prove that the National Park Service had abused their discretion by setting unreasonable

limits to the protest or that we had discriminated against the Task Force in any way because of its members' sexual orientation.

On July 16th, a chartered Amtrak train called the "We The People – 200 Special" arrived in Philadelphia at around 11:30 a.m. Some of the Philadelphia area Congressmen, Lawrence Coughlin, Peter Kostmayer, and William Gray, rode the train from Washington. Senators Arlen Specter and John Heinz and Congressmen Tom Foglietta and Robert Borski met the train at 30th Street Station in Philadelphia. Ray Smock reported that 220 members of Congress made reservations for the trip (189 Representatives and 31 Senators) and nearly 600, counting their guests, were on the train.

Congresswoman Lindy Boggs, who was so closely involved in the Congressional trip, got off of the train first and with a small group of friends quickly came to the West Wing Reception Room of Independence Hall. The groups was mostly female and included Barbara Kennelly (CT), Louise Slaughter (NY), Barbara Boxer (CA), Nancy Pelosi (CA), Mary Rose Oban (OH), Don Edwards (CA), and Ted Weiss (NY). She told us that the buses would arrive with everyone in about 20 minutes.

Independence Square behind Independence Hall had been secured and refreshments were made available to the members of Congress and their guests when they arrived. Of course, portable rest rooms were available. The program in front of Independence Hall was scheduled for 2:00 p.m., so for an hour the area between the Barry Statue and the rear door of Independence Hall was filled with Congressmen, Senators, and their guests. It was a great experience to mingle with them and to be introduced by members that I knew. Reporters moved throughout the group, collecting stories about the trip and the importance of the day. It was obvious that the members were impressed and honored to be there. Joseph McDade (R-PA) of Scranton, dean of the Pennsylvania delegation, said, "This is one of the most really exciting times that I've had in Congress. I went to Congress 25 years ago and never in my wildest dreams did I think I'd get to participate in something like this." McDade had been picked by the Pennsylvania delegation to represent them at the special session inside Independence Hall. Representative John Lewis (D-GA), a former civil rights activist, said, "I feel deeply moved and greatly blessed to be here." They were pleased to be in Philadelphia for this special occasion.

Just before 2:00 p.m., guests were notified that they would be escorted to seats in the audience on the opposite side of Independence Hall. We then assembled the members of Congress and marched them through Independence Hall and out to the platform on Chestnut Street, which accommodated them all.

Governor Casey welcomed the group to the Commonwealth and Mayor Goode did the same for the City. I welcomed them to the Park by pointing out the buildings on Independence Square: Independence Hall, Congress Hall, and Old City Hall. I said that Congress Hall is the place where the first five Congresses met, and they did many things for the first time that you as members of Congress do constantly in carrying out your duties. Then I said that when someone asks us where our home is, we usually refer to the place where we were born or where we spent our formative years, and with that in mind, it gives me great pleasure to welcome the 100th Congress back home. Pennsylvania Congressman Tom Foglietta recalled that his grandfather had shined shoes in the Bourse Building across the street, and today his grandson welcomes the Congress to the district that he represents. Congressman William H. Gray III concluded the welcoming program, and Fred Stein was kneeling near the platform to coordinate four U.S. Air Force planes in a fly-over that would coincide with the conclusion of Gray's speech. The timing was perfect and it provided a dramatic conclusion to the welcoming ceremony.

At 3:30 p.m., 55 delegates (one from each state plus the House and Senate leadership) gathered in the Assembly Room of Independence Hall. Lindy Boggs was elected chairman, and in her red dress she sat in the replica "rising sun chair" (Washington's Chair). Brief speeches were made by the leadership: Speaker Jim Wright, Senate Majority Leader Robert C. Byrd, Senate Minority Leader Robert Dole, and House Minority Leader Robert Michel. Then Majority Whip Tony Coelho presented a resolution that said in part:

"Resolved that the congressional delegates assembled in Independence Hall....do hereby recognize the bicentennial of the U.S. Constitution and the enduring contribution of the Framers of the Constitution in establishing the government structure that has served this nation for two centuries."

I stood in the Assembly Room behind the bar for a time to watch these events, but after they passed the resolution and all the delegates were waiting to sign it, I slipped out of the room. The only thing remaining was to pose for a photograph. A good many of the members of Congress had their own cameras and were recording the events for themselves.

When I went outside, the members of Congress who were not involved in the Independence Hall ceremony were beginning to file into Congress Hall: the Senate on the upper floor and the House on the ground floor. I was concerned about some of the Senators making it to the second floor because of the steepness of the stairs, but they all made it. Senator John Stennis (D-MS), President Pro Tempore, presided over the ceremony in the Senate Chamber, which produced several speeches about government and a resolution marking the occasion. Jim Wright presided in the House Chamber and had a similar program.

By 4:00 p.m., everyone was scattering to their hotels. I was having a pleasant conversation with Orrin Hatch (R-UT) about what was on the second floor of Independence Hall. I asked him if he would like to take a quick look, and perhaps even go up into the tower. He jumped at the chance, and in about 15 minutes we made the climb all the way to the Centennial Bell and had a grand view of the Park and the City nearby.

Just before dark, most of the Congressional delegation and their guests began arriving for cocktails and a dinner/dance beneath the Constitution Pavilion. Ridgewells was the caterer. Despite some delays because of security searches, this was a gala evening of dining and dancing.

Congressional Pilgrimage, Congress Hall. *Image Courtesy of Independence National Historical Park*

It seemed to us that even with 1200 people in attendance, everyone was especially nice to Addie-Lou and me. After dinner there were cigars and liqueurs, and entertainment starring Ben Vereen and Connie Stevens. The project manager for Ridgewells said that it was like "…staging a huge wedding, a formal dinner and a Broadway show all at once."

After the official evening ended, Ray Smock, Dick Baker, Mary Kimmett, Fred Stein, and David and Joan Dutcher came to my house at 410 Locust Street to have one more drink and to review the twists and turns of the day. These people were the original planners of the event that had been conceived in my office four years before. We were the "Society of the Rising Sun." Without doubt, this was one of the great moments in the celebration of the Bicentennial of the Constitution.

The Congressional celebration of the Constitution was concluded and some of the members of Congress returned to Washington that night or early the following morning, but many of them spent the weekend touring the Park and Philadelphia. The Philadelphia Chamber of Commerce arranged the city tours. *The Philadelphia Inquirer* reported, "Congress came home to Philadelphia yesterday on what turned out to be a great day…It was a superb spectacle…"

D. Maritime American & the *USS Thomas S. Gates*

In 1986 we were still putting together the "We the People-200" celebration when Captain Robert Sutton came to Philadelphia to investigate the possibility of commissioning a new ship for the U. S. Navy. Captain Sutton was to be the skipper of a new Aegis Cruiser that would be called the U.S.S. *Thomas S. Gates*, after a Philadelphian who had served in several high government posts including Secretary of the Navy (1957-1959) and Secretary of Defense (1959-1961). The fact that Secretary Gates was from Philadelphia and that we were having a major celebration in 1987, brought the Navy to the conclusion that Philadelphia might be a good place to commission the ship. We told Captain Sutton that we were planning a maritime themed weekend during August, and the commissioning of the ship could become a major element in what we were calling Maritime America.

The 567-foot, $990 million ship was then under construction at Bath Iron Works in Bath, Maine. The ship was a Ticonderoga class missile cruiser with an Aegis weapons system. The Aegis system is a series of electronically interlocking radars, missiles, guns, torpedoes, and anti-submarine helicopters. At any one time, the Aegis system can simultaneously track and attack scores of enemy air and sea targets.

Captain Sutton was stationed at Norfolk, Virginia, but came to Philadelphia periodically to meet with his committee (the Plank Holders). The Navy has a pattern that it follows when ships are commissioned that includes dinners, special events, receptions, and ship tours. Several of these activities cost money that they needed to raise. The U.S. Naval Academy Alumni Association and RCA became the principal sponsors, the latter being appropriate since RCA, across the Delaware River in New Jersey, had provided all of the electronics on the ship. On the day of the commissioning, the Philadelphia Contributorship, America's oldest insurance company, provided brunch for the Navy brass, including the Secretary of the Navy and the widow of Secretary Gates. They undertook this event because Thomas S. Gates had at one time served on their board of directors.

Maritime America began on Friday evening, August 21st, at 5:00 p.m. at Penns Landing. Two stages were set up at each end of the waterfront, with restaurant food booths lining the landing in between. Entertainment lasted until 10:00 p.m. and included performances of sea chanteys, story telling, folk musicians, dance groups, jazz and pop bands, and even a liars contest.

On Saturday, the U.S.S. *Thomas S. Gates* was commissioned at noon and the entertainment lasted until 8:30 p.m., when Pennsylvania and New Jersey orchestras performed on their respective waterfronts. The performance of Handel's "Concerto for Two Bands and Strings," "Water Music," and "Music for Royal Fireworks" was performed simultaneously by the two orchestras. The latter piece was coordinated with a fireworks display from a barge in the center of the Delaware River.

Sunday was much the same until 5:00 p.m., with the exception that all local yachtsmen were requested to be on the river adjacent to Penns Landing. With this mix of watercraft was a regatta of 16 ships from the 19th Century.

The Gates Commissioning began with a brunch for the VIP's at the Contributionship. Bleachers and a stage were set up at Penns Landing adjacent to the ship. A program involving the Secretary of the Navy, Mrs. Gates, Mayor Goode, and Captain Sutton lasted for about 45 minutes. All of the seamen who would serve on this ship were lined up in formation at dockside, and Captain Sutton gave the order to "bring the ship alive." The sailors sprinted to the gangplanks and everyone took their proper positions. In a short period of time, all of the systems began to function. The radar turned, the missile mounts began to rotate, signal flags were run up – it was one of the most exciting things that I have ever seen. From dead still in the water to a living, operating war ship, this was quite a transition. By 2:00 p.m. the ship was squared away and open to the public for tours. It was also open for tours on Sunday.

E. The Signing of the Constitution

In mid-1986, the Bicentennial of the Constitution chairmen for the Pennsylvania, Delaware, and New Jersey State Societies of the Daughters of the American Revolution came to my office to talk about doing a memorial to the signers of The Constitution in Independence National Historical Park. They thought that an appropriate monument could be designed and perhaps they could raise the funds nationally. I told them that the National Park Service had a general policy against monuments. Another idea they discussed was a book about the signers, but one had recently been completed. Films, exhibits, and celebrations had all been planned or already accomplished. I asked them to give me a couple of weeks to discuss the matter with my staff , and then we should meet again.

I discussed the idea with our Chief of Interpretation, Kathy Dilonardo, who brought in Ron Thompson and Russ Smith, and together they came up with an idea. There exist many paintings and illustrations of the signing of the Declaration of Independence but none of the Constitution. Furthermore, all of the paintings of the Declaration of Independence are inaccurate because of clothes, furniture, and the room itself. During the last two decades, the National Park Service had restored and refurbished the Assembly Room in Independence Hall. As part of the "Miracle at Philadelphia" exhibit, we had located a life portrait of all of the signers of the Constitution except one. All of the architects, historians, and curators who had done the research were still on our staff, so we had the knowledge to do an accurate depiction of the signing of the Constitution. All we needed was an artist who could take direction.

Kathy called the National Park Service Interpretive Center in Harpers Ferry, West Virginia, to see if they had used anyone who could do a project such as this. They recommended Louis S. Glanzman of Medford, New Jersey, an artist they had used to paint historic scenes for National Park Service exhibits. Since he lived only 20 miles from Philadelphia, we went to see him and were greatly impressed with the work he had done. I was particularly impressed because he had done several book covers for one of my favorite writers, Louis L'Amour. Lou Glanzman gave us a price of

$15,000 to do the job.

We met with the DAR ladies and told them that we would like them to commission a painting which would depict the signing of the Constitution in the Assembly Room of Independence Hall at 4:00 p.m. on September 17, 1987. We felt that this work would become the standard illustration for future publications about the Constitution. They asked if they could make prints of the painting to sell in order to raise the funds to pay for it. We agreed.

The project was turned over to Ron Thompson to manage. He assembled our appropriate staff to give direction to Lou Glanzman, and Lou returned in a month with a draft. The 3-foot by 6-foot painting was hung in an empty office and everyone reviewed it and made notes, which they gave to the artist. Lou made another draft, and we finally had the most accurate illustration of the Signing of the Constitution that could possibly be created.

The DAR ladies decided that they would like to unveil the painting and present it to us on September 16, 1987, because a large contingent from their National Society, Daughters of the American Revolution, would be in town to march in the Grand Federal Procession the following day.

The ceremony was set for one of the theaters in the Park Visitor Center and I was surprised at the large number in attendance. The President-General of the NS DAR and I were asked to unveil the painting, and did it look grand. A guide to the painting identified each of the 39 signers and some of the others who were there but did not

Image Courtesy of Independence National Historical Park

sign. Glanzman even included Jacob Broome of Delaware, of whom we had no portrait, but he is bent over the table signing so his face is not visible. I was asked to read the metal label attached to the frame:

"The Signing of the Constitution" by Louis S. Glanzman
Commissioned by the Delaware, Pennsylvania, and New Jersey State Societies, Daughters of the American Revolution in honor of Hobart G. Cawood, Superintendent of Independence National Historical Park. Sept. 16, 1987.

To say that I was surprised was an understatement. It was a great honor for me, and I owed another important moment to the DAR. Edward Piszek was so impressed with this painting that his

Liberty Bell Foundation distributed 23,000 prints of the painting to schools across America. After the bell-ringing program the following day, he commissioned Louis Glanzman to paint a scene from that ceremony.

Lou and Fran Glanzman became good friends of ours and we saw them socially from time to time. We even went canoeing together in the New Jersey pine barrens. After one of my National Park Service retirement parties in 1991, Lou gave me a wrapped package, and when I opened it I found the original art for the cover of Louis L'Amour's book *Kilkenny*. This was a treasure that I shared with my father until his death, when it came back to me.

The Signing of the Constitution by Louis S. Glanzman hangs in the east wing of Independence Hall, where tours of the building begin.

F. The Home Stretch:
September 9-18, 1987

On September 9, 1987, I should have known that the next 10 days were going to turn out well, because on that day I spoke at convocation at Thomas Jefferson University and my speech went very well. The school presented me with an honorary doctorate on the occasion. Barry and Lynn Wiksten, Tiff and Barbara Tiffany, Nancy Greytok, and Toni joined us at the ceremony and a luncheon. In my talk I reminded the aspiring medical doctors that they had a responsibility to their field of medicine, but that they also had the responsibility as citizens to the United States of American.

Bicentennial activities began in earnest on Sunday, September 13th, with a Hispanic Heritage Festival and a series of special church services. A program at Mother Bethel AME Church honored the congregation of this oldest independent black church in American. The service at Old St. Mary's Roman Catholic Church was a tribute to John Barry, "the father of the American Navy", who is buried in the church cemetery. The Old St. George's United Methodist Church program was a salute to the Bicentennial of the Constitution. Pastor Robert L. Curry was dressed in a costume of the type that would have been worn by the famous Methodist preacher Francis Asbury. I introduced the speaker, District Attorney Ron Castille. Old St. George's is where we had membership and I served as chairman of the Administrative Board.

Monday the 14th was quiet but with an obvious

Secretary of State George Schultz and Mrs. Schultz being given a tour of Independence Hall by Hobie

increase in visitation in the Park. On Tuesday there was a religious candlelight procession and interfaith convocation at the Constitution Pavilion at 8:00 p.m. There was a talk about "Female Federalism" at the Federal Court House and a musical show, *Let Freedom Sing*, by the American Music Theater Festival. Addie-Lou and I attended a cognac tasting at the First Bank of the United States sponsored by the Chaine de Rotisseurs, a well-known eating and drinking society. Their guests of honor were Mr. and Mrs. Maurice Hennessey, who brought along a significant amount of their product. The president of the "Chaine" was Roger Yaseen, the brother of our friend Barbara Tiffany. The Hennesseys presented me with a framed copy of a letter from their agent in Philadelphia dated December 17, 1787, in which he talks about the new government and what is necessary for its ratification.

My father, Pope Cawood, and his wife

Glenna arrived for a visit from their home in Middlesboro, Kentucky. I wanted my family to be in Philadelphia to enjoy the highlights of the bicentennial celebration. Toni came in from Boston, where she worked, and Stephen came from Wake Forest University in Winston-Salem, North Carolina, where he was in his third year. Since the men would be participating in two black tie events, I got their measurements in advance and rented their tuxedos. Daddy had never worn a tux before.

On the 16th at 10:00 a.m., the Daughters of the American Revolution held an unveiling ceremony for the painting, *The Signing of the Constitution*, in one of the theaters in the National Park Service Visitor Center. Even though this was a project of the Pennsylvania, New Jersey, and Delaware Societies, they invited Mrs. Fleck, President General of the National Society, to be present at the unveiling. Mrs. Fleck called me up front to remove the cover from the painting while Louis Glanzman, the artist, stood nearby. The painting was magnificent, and after the applause ended, she asked me to read the brass label attached to the frame which indicated that the painting was done in "honor of Hobart G. Cawood, Superintendent of Independence National Historical Park." Evfen with tears in my eyes I could see my father in the audience and I knew how proud he was. God Bless the DAR.

At noon I went to Market Street near the Liberty Bell to receive a shipment of gigantic rocks from three western states. This was a project called "Rocks Across America" which requested every state to send a rock the size of a filing cabinet to Philadelphia. We planned to incorporate the rocks into a memorial to the Constitution that could possibly be built into the future redevelopment of the second block of Independence Mall.

Problems on the Mall began with the complete demise of the Judge Lewis Fountain and included major water leakage in the underground parking garage. This, combined with cracked pavement and a general shabbiness that was developing, led me to believe that the whole block needed a facelift, so why not include a memorial to the Constitution in the work. With no more planning than that, we put our project on the "We the People--200" funding list, and the Knight Foundation gave us some seed money for it. We also put out the call to the states through their bicentennial offices to send us rocks of a specific dimension. The rocks had already started to arrive and we were putting them into storage.

On this occasion, a flatbed semi truck had started in California with a send-off by Astronaut Buzz Aldrin, and had picked up rocks in Utah and Wyoming en route to Philadelphia. They were presented to me and Bill Broome, the vice president of Philadelphia Newspapers, Inc., who represented the Knight Foundation. The truck was decorated with flags and signs and was at curbside near the Liberty Bell, so we had no problem in drawing a crowd. It was a beautiful sunny day and I was hopeful that we would have the same for Constitution Day.

Addie-Lou, Daddy, Glenna, and I walked to Washington Square to observe the honor guard that was on duty at the tomb of the unknown soldier of the American Revolution. We returned home and found a flatbed trailer parked in front of our house on Locust Street; on it was the Liberty Bell Foundation's replica of the Liberty Bell that was to be used the following day in the bell ringing ceremony. It could not be moved into place in front of Independence Hall until President Reagan had completed his remarks.

I went back to the office for a time, and later in the afternoon I went home to observe the formation of a procession of the Chief Judges and Chief Justices of the 13 original states on Locust Street in front of our house. They actually assembled in the Magnolia Garden beside our house and formed in the street. The procession included the We the People–200 Fife and Drum Corps, standard bearers from the First City Troop, a contingent of Revolutionary War soldiers, and the Chief Judges and Justices flanked by cadets from the Valley Forge Military Academy.

The group was made up of the chief judicial officer from every state except New Jersey, who was called away because of a family illness. A senior justice from the State replaced him. They paraded north on Fifth Street to Independence Square and into Old City Hall, where the Supreme Court of the United States had met from 1791-1800. A variety of speakers presented information on Constitutional issues. One speaker called to their attention the fact that a majority of U.S. citizens today could not have voted under the original document. That would have included Robert N. C. Nix, Jr., Chief Justice from Pennsylvania, a black man, and Ellen Ash Peters, Chief Justice from Connecticut, a female.

Two afternoon lectures took place before capacity audiences. Chief Justice of the United States Warren Burger spoke at the Park Visitor Center, and Justice John Noonan, Jr., of the U.S. Court of Appeals in San Francisco, spoke about religious freedom at Old St. Joseph's Catholic Church. The Pennsylvania Ballet performed *Rhapsody in Red, White, and Blue* at the Academy of Music at 7:00 p.m. Their performance included music by George Gershwin, Aaron Copland, and John Philip Sousa. The ballet and the gala following it at the Constitutional Pavilion on Independence Mall were attended by many of the dignitaries who were in town for the Constitution events of the week. The gala was black tie and the Cawood clan looked great. I thought that Toni and Steve looked so good that it was hard to remember them as children. Addie-Lou's camera recorded the event and her photos included two friends: Governor Michael Castle of Delaware and Secretary of the Army John Marsh.

It is hard to believe that one can meet all of the appointments that require your attention and participate in them in an intelligent manner. It would be impossible were it not for someone who covers your daily duties and organizes your time. I had two people in 1987 who knew me better than I knew myself. Bernie Goodman, who had been my assistant superintendent since 1977, knew my standards and thoughts so well that as I passed his door one day I heard him say to someone, "This is the way Hobie wants it done." Actually, we had never discussed it, but if we had, it would have been exactly the way Bernie wanted it done. We were good friends and across-the-street neighbors, and his loyalty was of the highest order. The other person who was key in organizing my time was Donna Reeves, the secretary/assistant to both Bernie and me. I shared everything with her and she was capable of making decisions on my behalf. I trusted her and was always rewarded with a quality performance. Donna kept my schedule, and one day I saw that I had an appointment with a doctor and I asked what it was about. She informed me that she and Bernie thought that I should have my eyes checked for glasses because of the way I was holding things that I read and because I was having headaches. I went to the doctor and did need glasses, which cured my problem. The three of us were like family.

At last came the day that I had been dreaming about for four years, Constitution Day, September 17, 1987. In my dreams it was always bright and sunny, but when I left home just before 8:00 a.m. it was overcast with a prediction of morning rain showers and clearing in the afternoon. Addie-Lou and I walked over to Chestnut Street, where the crowd was already gathering at the main parade grandstand across the street from Independence Hall. I walked east on Chestnut to the Second Bank, where chairs had been placed on the sidewalk and on the granite landing of the building. There I saw General Bob Arter, who told me that Army Secretary Marsh was on his way to the main reviewing stand. I offered him space there also, but he needed to be free to check on any Department of Defense problems that might arise.

I also talked at length with David and Joan Dutcher, who were wearing green knit shirts that identified them as a National Park Service Research Team that was recording the day's activities. David was Chief Historian at Independence and Joan occupied the same position at Valley Forge NHP. David Kimball and Coxie Toogood from Dave's staff and two people from Joan's staff were part of the team. Also included were two motion picture crews from the Harpers Ferry Interpretive Center, as well as two crews doing tape recordings. Eastern National Park and Monument Association provided some funds that made the project feasible. The collected materials were placed in the Park archives.

Just before the parade began at 9:00 a.m., Addie-Lou and I made our way into the main grandstand, which required us to go through tight security. Since I was in my National Park Service uniform, I had the ability to move about freely. We sat with Army Secretary Jack Marsh, across the aisle from Governor Castle of Delaware and Governor Sununu of New Hampshire. Nearby was U.S. Attorney General Edwin Meese. At the moment that the parade began, the first rain shower also began. Addie-Lou and most of the audience had umbrellas, but Secretary Marsh would not share with her because if his men were out in the rain, then he was going to be in the rain also.

The rain was in the nature of showers that came infrequently and was never hard enough to disrupt the parade or its audience. Almost everyone had an umbrella. During the parade I had the opportunity to observe one of the television monitors and even though it was raining it looked like a good day on television.

At around 11:00 a.m. I left the grandstand, crossed Chestnut Street, and entered Independence Hall through the rear door on Independence Square. I was there to greet President Reagan when he arrived at 11:15 a.m. The President was on time and was quickly briefed about his entry to the platform. There was some 20 minutes to wait and I asked him if he would like to visit the Assembly Room where the Constitution had been signed two hundred years before. He was thrilled to be in the room and was very attentive as I told him about both the Declaration of Independence and the Constitution. While we were standing on either side of the "Rising Sun Chair," he looked at the quill pens in the Syng Ink Stand on the table, and after I told him that the ink stand had been used in the signing of the Declaration of Independence, Articles of Confederation, and the Constitution, he said that the quills reminded him of a friend from Alabama. The friend owned a small chain of movie theaters, and years ago the film companies required the owners to sell novelties or souvenirs related to the film in order to be able to schedule it in their theaters. In his presence the theater owner's told the film company representative that he wished they would stop making those old fashioned movies because he had sold about as many of those turkey feathers as he could handle.

While President Reagan was telling this story, a White House photographer took our picture as we stood talking, and a couple of weeks later it was sent to me. The photo captures the comfortable and pleasant personality of President Ronald Reagan. Naturally it is one of my prize possessions.

At the appropriate moment, the parade paused and the President, escorted by Bill Rouse, walked out

of the front door of Independence Hall and onto the platform. After a musical presentation by the Mormon Tabernacle Choir and The We The People – 200 Band, President Reagan made a five-minute talk about the Constitution, its importance and its bicentennial. Upon conclusion, he and Bill returned to Independence Hall, where I escorted him to the rear door and with his security he left the Park. I found out later that Secretary of the Interior Donald P. Hodel was traveling with the President but he went to the grandstand instead of coming inside Independence Hall, so I did not see him.

At 1:00 p.m., while the parade continued past Independence Hall, "We the People--200" served a lunch beneath the Constitution Pavilion for our sponsors and special guests. The morning rain had ceased just before the President made his speech so the weather was perfect. Everyone who attended received a picnic basket with their food and eating utensils inside. Daddy, Glenna, Toni, and Steve joined us. Sitting near us was William Penn Mott, the Director of the National Park Service. With him were Pat and Jim Coleman, my Regional Director. There were a number of dignitaries at the picnic; Addie-Lou took a photo of Steve with Jessie Jackson, the civil rights activist.

While we were at the VIP picnic, the Great American Picnic began at Penns Landing. It featured $1.00 hotdogs and drinks plus a great variety of inexpensive food. The picnic lasted for three days, until 6:00 p.m. on Sunday, September 20th. There were four stages along the Delaware River providing a variety of free entertainment. During the evening of the 17th (Thursday), there would be hundreds of lighted boats parading along the waterfront, followed by the premiere of the new lighting of the Benjamin Franklin Bridge across the Delaware River. Several large screen televisions were set up to broadcast the Constitutional Gala from 9:00-11:00 p.m. Fireworks concluded the day. The Picnic continued on September 18th and 19th, noon to 7:00 p.m.; and on the 20th, noon to 6:00 p.m. The parade floats were on display on the 18th and 19th.

At 2:00 p.m. on Constitution Day, Director of the National Park Service William Penn Mott and I met Secretary of the Army Jack Marsh on the lawn behind the Second Bank of the United States to plant an oak tree that was a descendent of an oak tree that George Washington knew. Planting these oaks at various places was one of the U.S. Army's bicentennial projects. Just the three of us and an honor guard participated in this simple ceremony. The grounds staff of the Park had prepared a hole for the tree and we placed it and pushed in some soil. Our staff finished the job later. A plaque about the tree was given to me for placement later.

By 2:45 p.m. I was back at Independence Hall to greet Chief Justice Burger and Jacqueline Wexler, Director of the National Conference of Christians and Jews, to prepare for our 3:15 p.m. program, *Bells Across America*. The NCCI, along with the National Commission, had participated in a program called *Sign on to the Constitution* and it was to be part of our 3:15 p.m. program. I gave them both a tour of the Assembly Room; it provided inspiration before going out onto the platform for the program. The ceremony was

carried live on local television and nationally via radio. This allowed others to ring the bells in their community after our bells had given the signal. Youngsters from the National Conference of Christians and Jews delivered six million signatures from people who had participated in nationwide seminars about the Constitution and had signed a pledge of rededication to it. Actually, the plan was for the children to bring the signatures forward in the ceremony and Chief Justice Burger would ring the replica of the Liberty Bell, but in his enthusiasm for having the children on stage, he asked them all to grab the rope to the bell and help him ring. The children were thrilled. I stood by and counted off the seconds and also grabbed the rope. At 4:00 p.m. the replica bell rang, the Centennial Bell in the tower of Independence Hall rang, the Bicentennial Bell at the Visitor Center rang, and thousands of red, white and blue balloons were released. The program was concluded. We had just completed the Bicentennial of the signing of The Constitution of the United States of America.

After visiting with friends in front of Independence Hall, Addie-Lou and I walked home to dress for the Constitutional Gala. Addie-Lou wore a special red, white and blue gown that was designed and made for her by Laura Lou Bates. My father, at age 76, put on a tuxedo for the first time. The six of us posed in front of our house at 410 Locust Street for pictures. Since traffic and parking promised to be difficult, and since I needed to arrive promptly in order to host Chief Justice and Mrs. Burger, "We the People--200" arranged transportation for us. After arriving at the Civic Center, Addie-Lou and I went to the special box where we would be with the Burgers. Daddy, Glenna, Toni, and Steve had good seats in the audience.

The show was impressive and the Burgers were blown away. We enjoyed chatting during the show, and at one point he admitted that the events of the day, including the television show, were beyond his greatest expectations. We noticed that during the show, cameras would occasionally point toward our box, but we had no idea if we would be seen on television. Several people told us later that Addie-Lou and I sitting with the Burgers appeared on the actual broadcast several times.

After the conclusion of the taping of the television show, we collected our family and walked to the ballroom, where we joined 1600 people for a reception and dinner. During the reception I worked the crowd and greeted as many people as possible. Walter Cronkite and Diane Sawyer of CBS News acted as masters of ceremony during the evening. Our family had the opportunity to meet several of our friends, as well as performers in the television show. There were numerous toasts, so it was good that we were not driving. At the conclusion of the dinner, our van picked us up and we slowly worked our way toward Penns Landing and home. The fireworks began to explode over the Delaware River before we made it back. So we left the van on Third Street and found a site near Walnut Street where we could see the new lights on the Ben Franklin Bridge and the fireworks. There must have been more than a million people on both sides of the river. When the fireworks ended, we walked the three blocks home. It was 11:30 p.m. and we had enjoyed an exhausting and wonderful day. We were still too excited to sleep, so the six of us took off our shoes and ties and relived the day's activities.

On Friday September 18th, the celebration continued with Pennsylvania Day, which included a brief ceremony in which I participated and a meeting of the General Assembly beneath the Constitution Pavilion. This was the 200th anniversary of the Constitution being presented to the Pennsylvania General Assembly for ratification. It was a beautiful day and everything went very well. Chief Justice Burger had stayed in town to participate in the program. The session lasted for more than two hours and included several resolutions and patriotic speeches. The three branches of government participated: The Governor, the Legislature, and the Chief Justice. As would be normal, the Governor veered away from the celebration in order to chastise the Legislature for not passing a "super fund bill" that would clean up hazardous sites of environmental concern. The Great American Picnic continued at Penns Landing. It was obvious that the celebration continued to increase the number of visitors to the Park and the City.

In the late afternoon our family went to Dickens Inn to visit our English friends, Pat and Michael Harwood and Elizabeth and Cedric Dickens. With a pint of ale and a clay pipe in hand, I was beginning to feel relieved of all of the pressures of the past year.

G. The Grand Federal Procession

From the beginning, a parade on Constitution Day was an important part of our plan. Our first concept was to start the parade from four different points in the City and others would join the four parts as it passed them. The four parts would become one as the parade converged on Independence Mall, where the leaders of three branches of government, the President, the Congress, and the Supreme Court would be assembled. Together the multitude would have a rally honoring the government under the Constitution. We talked about this concept a great deal, but the more we thought about it, we realized that it would be extremely difficult to carry out.

In 1985, Dr. J. Whitfield Bell, Jr., Librarian Emeritus of the American Philosophical Society, gave me a booklet, "Francis Hopkinson's Account of the Grand Federal Procession Philadelphia, 1788." A number of "federal processions" had been organized in 1788 in an effort to encourage ratification of the Constitution. In order for government under the Constitution to be adopted, nine states had to approve it, and anticipating that that would happen in late June, Judge Francis Hopkinson organized a committee to plan a federal procession in Philadelphia for Independence Day, July 4, 1788. Hopkinson recruited the artist Charles Willson Peale, and with the assistance of hundreds of others, they produced a massive parade with some 88 units. The length of the parade was a mile and a half and the route that it covered was three miles. It had floats and bands, tradesmen and ordinary citizens, and great symbolism to explain the new government.

This was a perfect pattern for a parade on the Bicentennial of the Constitution.

The 1788 parade had five troops of dragoons, two Corps of Infantry, and an artillery battery scattered throughout the procession. Representatives of foreign States in alliance with America, France, Sweden, Prussia, and Monaco, participated. Organizations such as the Pennsylvania Society of the Cincinnati, the Agricultural Society, The College of Physicians, The Manufacturing Society, The Marine Society, the Clergy, the Supreme Executive Council of Pennsylvania, and many more marched together and some even had floats. Trades and professions such as cordwainers (shoemakers), cabinet and chair makers, brick makers, coopers, blacksmiths, distillers, printers, and 25 more had floats that featured these trades at work.

Two major floats are worthy of mention:

1. Grand Federal Edifice – a domed building with 13 Corinthian columns (10 completed and 3 incomplete representing the States yet to ratify the Constitution). On top of the dome was a cupola with a figure of plenty and the whole float was 36 feet high. The building was 10 feet in diameter and was on a carriage pulled by 10 white horses. Four hundred and fifty architects and carpenters followed the float.
2. The Federal Ship Union – a float 33 feet long and her width and masts with sails in proportion. She mounted 20 guns and was manned by a crew of 25 sailors. She was on a carriage pulled by 10 horses, and a canvas the

color of water was draped from the water line to the ground to hide the wheels. The pilots of the port followed the float.

These few examples of this magnificent parade will let you understand why I became so excited about using the 1788 Grand Federal Procession as the pattern for our parade for the 1987 celebration. Our budget for the parade was $6 million. We put out a request for proposals to organizations that produce major parades, and after serious investigation selected Radio City Music Hall Productions to design and produce it for us. I went to New York with a group to meet with Barnett Lipton of Radio City Music Hall and his team to begin the planning process. I gave him a copy of Whitfield Bell's booklet and made a plan to consider it as a pattern for our parade.

After our meeting was concluded, we had some extra time before taking the train back to Philadelphia, so Barnett gave us a tour of the Music Hall. We rode up to the stage on the elevator and stood on the edge and looked at the empty red seats. On the spur of the moment I did a little dance and everyone applauded. My wife, Addie-Lou, grew up in Brooklyn, and as a young girl she dreamed of being a Rockette and dancing on the stage of Radio City Music Hall. She did take dancing lessons and danced all through school, including college. So when I went home that evening, I told her that I had danced on the stage of Radio City Music Hall. I made a mistake; she did not think that it was very funny. I even thought that I would have to prepare my own dinner that night. I learned a lesson and have kept my mouth closed about that experience ever since.

As the planning for the parade went forward, it became apparent that the idea of the Grand Federal Procession could be an element, but our parade had to be much more. As it worked out, the first part of our parade would be a recreation of some of the floats and marching groups of the Grand Federal Procession. The second part was to be 24 Rose Bowl-type floats themed around the Preamble of the Constitution. The third part was to be called "The Parade of America's People" and would involve such diverse groups as anti-abortion, gay and lesbian, veterans, essay contest winners, virtually anyone who would like to be involved. So the parade would not be exactly like the Grand Federal Procession of 1788, but in spirit it was exactly the same.

CBS agreed to cancel its usual morning programming and carry the parade live from 9:00 a.m. to noon. At 11:45 a.m., after the first two parts of the parade had passed Independence Hall, President Ronald Reagan would come to the platform in front of Independence Hall and make a five-minute speech. This would allow CBS to sign off at noon, but the third part of the parade, "The Parade of America's People," would continue until completed.

The Mormon Tabernacle Choir kicked off the television broadcast in front of Independence Hall and then the parade began:

Division 1
- A town crier preceded the U.S. Army Old Grand Fife and Drum Corps
- Two oxen named Anarchy and Confusion

- Members, Pennsylvania Society of the Cincinnati
- Colonial Williamsburg Fife and Drum Corps
- 39 descendents of the Signers of the Constitution
- Coopers and wheelwrights float featuring wheelwright and barrel making equipment
- The *Federalist*, a 15-foot replica of an 18th-Century ship with three masts and sails
- Blacksmith, whitesmith, and nailors float with working forges and several tradesmen at work.
- 130 members of a handbell choir
- Boat Builders float with working carpenters, sail makers, rope makers, and other trades of the boat building trade
- Bread and Biscuit Makers with baking in progress
- Baked goods were passed out courtesy of Stroehmann's Bakery
- The Grand Federal Edifice, an exact replica of the float in the 1788 parade, recreated by the Carpenters Company. Leon Clemmer, President of the Carpenters Company, was the force behind this project. I thought it was the best float in the parade.

Division 2

WE THE PEOPLE OF THE UNITED STATES

The We the People float began the theme of using the Preamble to tell a story. The float's 40-foot-long parchment scroll had 5 portraits of fathers of the Constitution and a giant quill and inkstand, and riding on it were the two honorary grand marshals, Coretta Scott King and Walter Cronkite.

Division 3

IN ORDER TO FORM A MORE PERFECT UNION

Three floats representing all 50 states including their seals and flags. Between the floats were a brass band, a New Orleans band, and the Afro-American Dance Ensemble of Philadelphia.

Division 4

ESTABLISH JUSTICE, ENSURE DOMESTIC TRANQUILITY

A float with replicas of the White House, the Capitol, and a giant set of scales calling attention to the separation of powers among the Executive, Legislative, and Judicial branches of government. Following the float were the Valley Forge Military Academy cadets carrying portraits of all of the presidents; also, the Emerald Society Bagpipe Band.

Division 5

PROVIDE FOR THE COMMON DEFENSE

Five floats honoring veterans. The World War I float had a biplane and two Medal of Honor recipients riding on it. Included was a replica of the Iwo Jima Memorial and a sculpture of Vietnam era soldiers.

Division 6

PROMOTE THE GENERAL WELFARE

This was the largest collection of floats. One was 50 feet high with a skyscraper under construction; another was the yacht *Stars and Stripes* with its crew and the America's Cup on its bow. Other floats were about inventions; agriculture with dancing flowers; and entertainment, with giant comedy and tragedy masks, and Colleen Dewhurst and Grover Washington, Jr. riding on it. A sports unit and education concluded the section. The Brief Case Drill Team was a hoot, and bands were interspersed in between floats.

Division 7

SECURE THE BLESSING OF LIBERTY TO OURSELVES AND OUR POSTERITY

Our freedoms under the first ten amendments to the Constitution were featured with a working 18th-Century printing press and gospel music (freedom of religion) provided by the Fellowship Tabernacle Choir.

Division 8

CLOSING CEREMONY

A large replica of the Liberty Bell. It was at this point that President Reagan came from inside Independence Hall and took the platform. The Mormon Tabernacle Choir sang "America" and President Reagan spoke for five minutes.

Division 9

PARADE FINALE

The American Eagle, 15-½ feet high, 37 feet long, 15 feet wide. As this float passed, 1500 white doves and thousands of red, white and blue balloons were released. Four National Guard fighter jets flew overhead. This concluded the national television coverage on CBS.

Division 10

THE PARADE OF AMERICA'S PEOPLE

This last section of the parade included 15,000 people who wanted to be involved: the Daughters of the American Revolution, AFL-CIO, several veterans groups, school classes, churches, gay and lesbian, fraternal, etc.

Raul Rodriquez of Pasadena, California, designed most of the large floats for the parade. It lasted for four and a half hours and stretched from Penns Landing to the Philadelphia Museum of Art. Grandstands for viewing the parade were erected at Independence Hall and at several other locations along the route. Over 20,000 people were in the parade and a million saw it live along its route.

I have not mentioned many of the musical groups that were mixed in between the floats. The Army, Navy, Air Force, Marine Corps, and Coast Guard Bands were there, as was a unit of cadets from each of the service academies. The We the People--200 Band was made up of 200 college students from 50 states. There were also some exceptional high school and college bands marching.

It was a parade to remember; a parade of *We the People.*

H. We The People – 200 Constitutional Gala

It seems that no celebration worthy of its salt is complete without a television special that shares the event with millions of people throughout the world. Our planning included such a program, but there was little we could do about it because our celebration was not something that was on everyone's mind. It all came together as part of a package deal with CBS to do both the parade and a television special on Constitution Day. It also made sense to the producers that there was some economy in having celebrities and entertainers who could participate in both programs.

The gala was to be filmed in the Philadelphia Civic Center before a live audience between 6:00 – 8:00 p.m. and would be broadcast 9:00 – 11:00 p.m. the same night. The public could purchase tickets for the taping of the show. Following the taping, there was a Constitutional Gala Dinner for 1600 invited guests. The black tie, invitation-only gala was the way "We the People--200" thanked the performers, our special guests, and our major sponsors.

The two-hour program was hosted by CBS anchor Walter Cronkite and opened with Sandi Patti and the Mormon Tabernacle Choir singing "The Star-

Spangled Banner." The show was about equal parts music and skits, with a high point being the performance by Barry Manilow of the song "Let Freedom Ring," which he wrote for the occasion. The all-star cast included Cicely Tyson, Marilyn McCoo, Patti LaBelle, Ned Beatty, Dean Jones, Rich Little, Dorian Harewood, Barry Bostwick, Lee Greenwood, Wayne Rogers, Rex Smith, Yakov Smirnoff, John Schneider, Stephanie Powers, and John Raitt.

It was a great evening of entertainment, but also a tribute to the Constitution. Actors such as Gregory Peck, Eli Wallach, and George Peppard dramatized a number of landmark Supreme Court decisions that reminded viewers of how important the Constitution is to our daily lives. Addie-Lou and I sat in a box with Chief Justice of the United States and Mrs. Warren Burger, and from their reactions and remarks, you could tell that they were emotionally moved by the show.

As soon as the television taping was completed, we excused ourselves from the Burgers and joined Daddy, Glenna, Toni, and Steve and made our way to the ballroom for dinner. Several of the stars who had participated in the taping were seated at a table next to ours, so we had a chance to visit with Stephanie Powers, Rich Little, and Walter Matthau. Glenna was a fan of Lee Greenwood, who sang his "I'm Proud to Be an American," so Addie-Lou got her trusty camera out and everyone posed for pictures.

After a champagne reception, we were seated and Walter Cronkite and Diane Sawyer led us through a 13-toast dinner, with cognac afterward. It really was a star-spangled evening and gave our family an idea of the kinds of activities in which Addie-Lou and I commonly participate.

I. Constitution Day Bell Ringing

At approximately 4:00 p.m. on September 17, 1787, the delegates to the convention gathered to sign their names to the Constitution that would be recommended to the States for ratification. Therefore, working with the Commission on the Bicentennial of the United States Constitution, Independence National Historical Park planned a special program to observe this significant moment.

The Commission thought that a national bell-ringing program would be appropriate, and since the Park had participated in this kind of program for years on Independence Day, we were comfortable with the event. Called "Bells Across America," it would begin with a bell ringing at Independence Hall, which would trigger bells ringing throughout the country (even worldwide). The Commission spent several months notifying churches, synagogues, educational institutions, carillon and bell ringing societies, bell manufacturers, and other interested organizations. Even the Defense Department rang bells at their bases and the State Department secured participation in London from Westminster Abbey and Saint Paul's Cathedral.

The Commission had another program which included a special curriculum for elementary and secondary schools. Called "Sign on to the Constitution," it was a course of study that concluded with the students signing a copy of the Constitution. Since we were commemorating a signing, then why not bring some of the signatures of the next generation pledging support of the Constitution? The Chief Justice called on Jacqueline Wexler, Director of the National Conference of Christians and Jews, to recruit a group of young people representing a cross-section of our nation in the future to carry the signatures onto the stage. They would also participate in the bell ringing.

I suggested that instead of using the Centennial Bell in the tower of Independence Hall, which could not be seen, that we use a bell at ground level which could be seen. I told them that Edward Piszek of the Liberty Bell Foundation had a replica of the Liberty Bell that could be mounted adjacent to the program platform. We used the same stage, with some modifications, that President Reagan had used earlier.

At 3:00 p.m. the "We the People--200" Fife and Drum Corps and a handbell choir alternated in entertaining the gathering audience. At 3:15 p.m. Chief Justice Burger, Mrs. Wexler, and I came onto the platform from the front door of Independence Hall. The grandstand across Chestnut Street was filled to capacity.

I welcomed the audience and spoke about the Liberty Bell, particularly about the origin of the inscription on its crown. Then I explained that the replica was the same size and weight as the original, and had even been cast at the same foundry in England. I spoke for some 15 minutes and then introduced the handbell choir for a brief performance. Then Chief Justice Burger talked about the importance of the Constitution and the significance of our ceremony today. He introduced Mrs. Wexler, who brought the children on stage one at a time with baskets filled with signatures, over six million altogether.

We kept a close watch on the time, and when it neared 4:00 p.m., we spread the rope that was attached to the bell's clapper across the platform. I had given them some instruction on pulling the rope before the program began. Chief Justice Burger, the children, and I held the rope and pulled in unison on my signal. We rang the bell several times, thousands of balloons were released, and in the background I could hear the Centennial Bell, the Bicentennial Bell, and the bells of Christ Church. The audience applauded and the fife and drums played. After a few minutes, I thanked the crowd for their attendance and we left the platform. The ceremony was so impressive that Edward Piszek had the Liberty Bell Foundation commission Louis Glanzman to make a painting of the moment. In one year, Glanzman had made paintings of the Signing of the Constitution (1787) and the bell ringing ceremony celebrating the Bicentennial of the signing of the Constitution (1987).

The ceremony was carried live on local television.

Members of the U.S. Supreme Court in the Assembly Room in Independence Hall with Hobie: Justice Byron White, Justice Sandra Day O'Connor, Chief Justice William Rehnquist, and Justice William Brennen

J. The Supreme Court

We had dreamed from the beginning that the Bicentennial of the Constitution in Philadelphia would include the involvement of all three branches of government. On October 2, 1987, Chief Justice William H. Rehnquist, Justice Sandra Day O'Connor, Justice William J. Brennan, Jr., and Justice Byron R. White came to Philadelphia to make the Supreme Court Bicentennial of the Constitution official visit.

It was a beautiful morning. The Justices arrived at the West Wing Reception Room in Independence Hall at around 10:45 a.m. A few of the local Federal judges from the district and appellate courts were on hand to greet them, including Judge Ed Becker, who was involved in the arrangements for the day. Our friend A.B. Dick Howard from the University of Virginia Law School was also in attendance. After coffee, I took the group into the Assembly Room in Independence Hall and afterward to the Mayor's Court Room in Old City Hall, where the Supreme Court had heard its first case, and which served as its home 1791-1800.

Each justice made comments from the bench in Old City Hall:

> "It is one thing to read about these things in books and even see pictures of them, but to see them right here … is a very moving experience."
>
> Chief Justice William H. Rehnquist

> "This indeed is a hallowed place. For me it causes a shiver to stand in the room where the Declaration of Independence and The Constitution were forged."
>
> Justice William J. Brennan, Jr.

> "[The Constitution's bicentennial celebration is a] great educational process, not only for the people of the city and state, but for the people of the country. You have done extremely well and should be congratulated."
>
> Justice Byron R. White

> "[Philadelphia] has been playing host for 200 or more years now for all the activities that established us as a nation, and you are still playing host today to another meeting which we treasure.
>
> Justice Sandra Day O'Connor

After the ceremonies at Old City, we walked to the Public Ledger Building across Sixth Street from Independence Square and went to the Downtown Club on the top floor for a special luncheon. The Chief Justice of the Supreme Court of Ireland, who I had arranged to be present, sat beside Chief Justice Rehnquist. There were probably 200 people invited and the Supreme Court Justices spread throughout the tables. I was at a table with the distinguished U.S. District Court Justice John P. Fullam. There was a large pot of ferns as the centerpiece, and the person on my right asked me what the brown spots were on the underside of the fern leaves. I told him that I thought they were spores and that is the way ferns reproduce. I then turned to Judge Fullam to see what he thought. He said, "Hobie, this may be the only thing that you and I have ever agreed upon." He was referring to several legal decisions he had made that decided against the National Park Service.

After the luncheon, the members of the court went to the Friends Meeting House at Fourth and Arch Streets for another program honoring The Court. State Supreme Court Chief Justice Robert N. C. Nix introduced the Justices to about 200 people assembled, and Mayor Goode gave them Liberty Bowls. Chief Justice Rehnquist gave an impressive talk about paper charters: "no matter how skillfully written or beautifully phrased do not of themselves create a system of government. …but it takes men and women interpreting the terms of those charters and operating under them to breathe life into them and make them effective in our daily lives."

After this program was completed, the members of

the U.S. Supreme Court returned to Washington. The three branches of our government had participated in the "We the People--200" Bicentennial Celebration.

K. Ratification

When the Constitution was written and signed, it was passed to the Congress, which was operating under the Articles of Confederation, for approval. The new Constitution itself said that it must be ratified by nine states before it would go into effect. Since Congress only authorized the Philadelphia Convention to make the Articles of Confederation "adequate," some members of Congress argued that they had exceeded their authority by creating a completely new government. Nevertheless, on September 28, 1787, the Congress voted to send the Constitution to all of the state legislatures for ratification.

Thus began the debates between the Federalist (advocates) and the Anti-federalists (opponents). The principal issue was whether to have a strong central government or should the states remain sovereign. The Federalists, Alexander Hamilton, James Madison, and John Jay, argued that the Articles of Confederation did not work so it should be replaced by the Constitution. The Anti-Federalists were mostly from the rural areas and were led by Patrick Henry of Virginia and Sam Adams of Massachusetts.

On December 7, 1787, Delaware became the first state to ratify the Constitution. Pennsylvania followed on December 12th, and New Jersey on December 18th. The other states approved it in the following order:

Georgia	January 2, 1788
Connecticut	January 9, 1788
Massachusetts	February 6, 1788
Maryland	April 28, 1788
South Carolina	May 23, 1788
New Hampshire	June 21, 1788
Virginia	June 25, 1788
New York	July 25, 1788
North Carolina	November 21, 1789
Rhode Island	May 29, 1790

Many of the States had heated debates and close votes regarding ratification. Massachusetts appeared to be favoring a negative vote, but the Federalists were able to delay a vote for a month, which gave them more time to work for approval. Rhode Island rejected ratification in March 1788, and did not approve the Constitution until after George Washington had been sworn in as president. Virginia and North Carolina approved it with the condition that a Bill of Rights be added to the Constitution.

On July 2, 1788, the Congress recognized ratification and appointed a committee to prepare for the new government. In September, they adopted an ordinance that the new government would be located in New York and that the first Congress would meet on March 4, 1789.

Since we were celebrating a full bicentennial era, the Park's programs continued on into the ratification process. It was also a fact that we had become known for bicentennial celebrations beginning in 1974, so we were often invited to participate in the ratification activities of the states.

Ed Piszek had acquired the replica of the Liberty Bell that rang on July 4, 1976, and frequently it rang for other celebrations through the years. Most recently it had been used at the bell ringing ceremony on Constitution Day, 1987. Mr. Piszek had created the Liberty Bell Foundation and used it to transport the replica bell to appropriate celebrations and for other educational purposes. He had the idea that he would make the replica bell available to the states during the bicentennial programs of their ratification of the Constitution. He asked me to accompany the bell and make a 5-minute presentation about the Liberty Bell and the replica during the states' ratification ceremonies. I agreed to do it when it was convenient; otherwise, the bell would be available without me.

The first ceremony was in Delaware on December 7, 1987. During the afternoon, there was a ceremony in downtown Dover where Chief Justice Burger spoke and I did the bell ringing program, with Governor Michael Castle ringing the bell. The U.S. Postal Service had a first day of issue postage stamp program as they had on the anniversary of the ratification of the Constitution by each of the 13 original states. There was a major parade and at night there was a major gala at Dover Air Force Base. Delaware was first to ratify and their bicentennial celebration was worthy of that position. The other state directors of bicentennial committees were in attendance, and the outstanding job done by Delaware probably made the other programs better.

The Pennsylvania ceremony was planned by the Pennsylvania Historical and Museum Commission and took place in Harrisburg on December 12, 1987. The program was appropriate but it was not of the magnitude of the programs they had been involved in during the summer. The Liberty Bell Foundation sent the replica bell but I was unable to attend.

The New Jersey celebration on December 18th was held in downtown Trenton. It was so cold that the program was moved inside a large downtown commercial building, but the attendees went outside for the bell ringing in which I participated with Governor Keane.

I did not participate in Georgia (January 2nd) or Connecticut (January 9th), but the bell went to Savannah, and also to Hartford, Connecticut, on February 6th. The Massachusetts ratification was also an extremely cold day, but that did not deter the hundreds of high school students from Massachusetts and Maine who heard historical lectures in the chambers of the statehouse. Again, we went outside to hold the bell ringing ceremony, which included a fife and drum corps. The cold weather required us to keep the program to a minimum.

Although Maryland ratified on April 28th, the bicentennial programs did not take place in Annapolis until April 30th and in Baltimore on May 1st. The Annapolis bell ringing took place at the historic State House and included the Governor and Congressman Tom McMillan. The Baltimore program took place on Fort Hill and involved Mayor Schmake. The celebration also included a parade.

While we were in Baltimore, Addie-Lou and I visited Lovely Lane Methodist Church. This is the site where the Methodist Church had been organized in 1785.

I did not attend the South Carolina ratification on May 23rd, but we turned the New Hampshire program in June into a vacation. Our friends Peggy and Gene Slough from Findley, Ohio, came to Philadelphia and together we went to visit Beth and Lalle Wicander in Exeter, New Hampshire. The six of us went to Concord for the ceremony. New Hampshire's ratification on June 21, 1788, made it the ninth state to ratify, which meant that the new government under the Constitution was approved. The State planned a day-long celebration with a New England Clambake, the first day of issue of a postage stamp, a concert by the U.S. Army Band from West Point, and our bell

ringing ceremony. Governor Sununu and Chief Justice Burger participated in the activity.

After the ceremony, Gene Slough told Ed Piszek that I had given him a plate on which an Indian was painted. Mr. Piszek had given me the plate a few months before and I thought that it would be nice for Gene's western collection, since I had no use for it. My concern was that Ed Piszek would be offended, because I gave away a gift that he had given me. The only thing that Ed said to Gene was that you must be a good friend of Hobie's. When Gene told me the story, I was afraid that Ed would be mad, but he said nothing. About a month later, Ed Piszek called and invited Addie-Lou and me to lunch at Emlen House in Fort Washington. This usually meant that he had something on his mind to talk about. After lunch, we walked to his indoor tennis court where he had some six to eight Frederick Remington bronze statues on a table. He said for us to pick out the one that we liked and he would give it to us to replace the Indian painting that I had given Gene Slough. We selected the 27-inch-high bronze called *Mountain Man*, which is displayed in my home today.

The Virginia ratification celebration was the last one in which I participated. The program was held in Capital Square in Richmond and included music, living history displays, and a ceremony. It included an address by

Harri Holkeri, Prime Minister of Finland, and Mrs. Holkeri with Hobie (May 6, 1988)

Secretary of the Army Jack Marsh, remarks by Governor Gerald Baliles, and me doing the bell ringing. The celebration also included tours of the Executive Mansion, which was 175 years old. A few blocks away, the Museum of the Confederacy had a grand opening to show off a major renovation of their building and new exhibits. The afternoon was filled with dramatic presentations about the Constitution, choral and band concerts, and the first day of issue of the Virginia ratification postage stamp. The whole celebration was coordinated by Tim O'Rourke, director of the Virginia Constitution Bicentennial Commission.

VII.

AFTERWORD

A. National Constitution Center

In 1985, when "We the People--200" first began meeting, we had great discussions about what should be left behind after the celebration was over. I appointed a committee chaired by Craig Eisendrath, and including Jeff Garson, Stuart Feldman and Pepe Wistar, to work on this issue. The group put in many hours on their assignment and concluded that since the celebration mission was to educate people about the Constitution, then we should do something that would educate people after the celebration was over. The answer was a non-profit organization called The National Constitution Center.

The organization was incorporated after the celebration. I served on its board until I retired in 1991, but for several years it was able to muster little support. We had used so many of the community resources for the celebration that there was little left for afterward. I am certain that had it not been for Ted Wolfe, an area businessman, the Center would have died. As time passed and community leadership got involved, the National Constitution Center began to gain momentum.

Under the leadership of nationally-know economist Jack Bogle and the effective fundraising by a new president and staff, the National Constitution Center began to receive its place in the scheme of things. Just as I was leaving Philadelphia, I recommended to the National Park Service that a building for the Center should be built on the little-used third block of Independence Mall. Today a very impressive structure there hosts thousands of visitors each year. Everyone who goes there leaves with more knowledge and appreciation for the American Constitution.

B. Media Relations

From the beginning of my tenure as Superintendent, the news media had a great interest in Independence National Historical Park, and I maintained a good relationship with them. Anytime a reporter called me, I answered the phone, and if I was not available, I called them back as soon as possible. This included calls I received at home and at other places before and after work. I never lied to them, and even if I could not share information with them, I usually gave them enough background so that they could understand the situation. At no time was I betrayed by anyone to whom I gave information off the record.

In particular, the Park had great support from the Philadelphia newspapers. Publisher Sam McKeel at Philadelphia Newspaper Inc. (*Inquirer* and *Daily News*) and Gene Roberts, editor of the *Inquirer*, became personal friends. However, Creed Black of the *Inquirer* editorial page and Rolfe Neill of the *Daily News* were southerners who were ready to assist another of their kind. Black even did an editorial in support of major increases in the Park budget during a time when the Director of the National Park Service was meeting with his Regional Directors in the Park conference room. I purchased a paper for each of those involved and had it laying open to the editorial at their seat at the conference table. The *Inquirer* reporters and columnist I knew best were

Former President Jimmy Carter with Hobie and Addie-Lou (July 4, 1990)

Edgar Williams, Walter Naedele, Dorothy Storch, Joe Slobodzian, and David Boldt, editor of the Sunday Magazine.

The *Philadelphia Bulletin* was owned by publisher William McLain, who, along with editor Dale Davis and editorial page editor John McCullough, were friends and also supportive. Dorothy Byrd was the reporter that I talked to most. The *Bulletin* ceased to operate after 1976.

The editors and newsmen were always interested in our construction projects, special events, demonstrations, and visitor statistics, but if very little was happening of news value, we were often covered by the society columns. The queen of society pages was Ruth Seltzer of the *Inquirer*. Ruth liked the Friends of Independence and, I think, me personally as well. She always called

to double check her facts and make sure that the names and titles were correct. Many times, when we would go to Washington or New York, such as to Set Momjian's reception for his appointment as ambassador to the United Nations, we would give Ruth a ride. After Ruth died, David Iams wrote the column, and he also was supportive. The *Bulletin* society articles were written by Joseph X. Dever. He was a regular in covering the Friends and Park activities. Carol Springer reported for the *Main Line Times*, where many of our Friends of Independence lived.

We were also able to maintain excellent relations with the radio and television stations. Naturally they were always interest in covering our major activities, such as moving the Liberty Bell, July 4, 1976 and September 17, 1987. Actually, the national and international media were interested in those three days. Every Independence Day, demonstrations, visiting dignitaries, and the opening of new exhibits and facilities were always covered by the local stations. Channel 6, the ABC affiliate, had the better reputation for local news coverage and was often the first to respond. The NBC affiliate was on Independence Mall and was physically the nearest station but often the last to respond. However, their radio station, KYW, was a news station and always present in the Park. In my early years, Andrea Mitchell was a reporter we saw often, and also Richard Maloney.

Herbert Lipson, owner of *Philadelphia Magazine*, frequently said something favorable about the Park in his "Off the Cuff" columns. In June 1985, Samuel Hughes wrote a major article for the magazine, "The Friends of Hobie Cawood," that was very flattering to me.

I know that some people in public life tend to

distrust the media and try to dodge them whenever they can, but I always felt that I could trust the individual reporters, and they helped build the image of Independence National Historical Park.

C. Retirement

During my two decades as Superintendent, Independence National Historical Park, I had dodged other assignments to Parks and Regional Offices, and I even had a discussion with the Secretary of the Interior about the Director of the National Park Service position. I was always able to convince everyone that I could be more effective for the Service and the country by continuing my work in Philadelphia.

In my own mind, I had always imagined that I would be at Independence until I retired and then I would try to get a part time job with the Philadelphia Phillies. I had even mentioned my dream to Bill Giles, President of the Phillies, and he said that he could use me when I was ready.

I became eligible for retirement on June 15, 1990, when I celebrated my 55th birthday. Two months later, I received a call from a head hunter who was recruiting for a President of Old Salem, a restoration of the 18th- and 19th-Century village that was beginning

The Dalai Lama with Hobie, Philadelphia Mayor Wilson Goode, and Archhbishop Anthony Bevilacqua

in the city of Winston-Salem, North Carolina. I knew Old Salem because we had visited there when we came to see our son, who had graduated from Wake Forest University, which is located in Winston-Salem. I had even said to Addie-Lou as we walked down the streets of Old Salem that working at a place like this might be worth checking into after I finished my career with the National Park Service. I told the head hunter that they could put my name on the list, and I sent them a brief biographical statement that I usually sent to people who would introduce me as a speaker.

Time went by, and I got a telephone call just after Thanksgiving informing me that I was one of the four finalists and asking if I could come to Winston-Salem for an interview. I made the trip at their expense and stayed with my cousin, Campbell Cawood, who admitted that he might have let my name slip to a member of the search committee. I still wasn't sure if I was interested in leaving the NPS.

I got another call just after the first of the year inviting me and Addie-Lou to come for a follow-up visit to Winston-Salem. We now knew they were serious.

Upon arrival, Addie-Lou was taken on a tour while Old Salem Chairman Frank Driscoll and board member Ann Ring took me into an office and offered me the job. I asked for a week to consider it. That night, a group of board members and their spouses entertained us at the Old Town Country Club. Needless to say, we had a sleepless night, and Campbell was aware of our red eyes the following morning.

Two days after returning to Philadelphia, I had to go to a planning meeting for the 75th anniversary of the NPS celebration. Addie-Lou took me to the airport, and I told her on the way that I thought it was time for me to retire from the NPS. I had come to a point where I had accomplished my goals, and after what I had been through, I was concerned that I might get bored. But I said I would leave the decision with Addie-Lou, because Philadelphia had been her home longer than it had been mine. The next day I returned to Philadelphia and a ranger met me at the airport. When I walked into the house, I saw a bottle of champagne sitting in an ice bucket on the coffee table. I asked Addie-Lou what was the occasion and she said, "We are celebrating; we are moving to North Carolina."

APPENDIX A:

Awards 1971-1991

Awards 1971 – 1991

Commissioned a Kentucky Colonel, April 5, 1976

Chesnut Street Association, Man of the Year, May 20, 1976

Philadelphia Bowl, Mayor Frank Rizzo, May 20, 1976

Tribute by the Law Enforcement Square Club, May 24, 1976

Franklin Medal, Poor Richards Club, September 28, 1976

Legion of Honor, Chapel of Four Chaplains, October 17, 1976

St. Georges Gold Medal, St. Georges Methodist Church, October 22, 1976

Liberty Bowl, Colonial Philadelphia Historical Society, February 13, 1977

Certificate of Achievement, Haym Solomon Lodge 663, March 8, 1977

Meritorious Service Award, Department of the Interior, May 6, 1977

Distinguished Alumni Award, Emory and Henry College, May 7, 1977

Distinguished Service Award, Philadelphia Flag Day Association, June 14, 1978

In Appreciation, South Carolina Exchange Building Commission, March 1979

Distinguished Service, Cruiser Olympia Association, May 26, 1980

Honorary Doctor of Humane Letters, Pennsylvania College of Podiatric Medicine, June 1, 1980

Selected for English Speaking Union Exchange Program, April 24, 1981

Selected to go to the USSR to accompany an Exhibition, February 13, 1983

The New Philadelphia 400, Philadelphia Magazine, December, 1983

Philadelphia Bowl, Pennsylvania Society, Sons of the Revolution, April 11, 1985

Honorary Doctor of Law, Drexel University, April 27, 1985

Award for Achievement in Equal Employment Opportunity, Department of the Interior, 1985

In Appreciation, Society of the Sons of St. George, April 19, 1986

Gold Medal, Philadelphia Public Relations Association, May 22, 1986

An Emmy, National Academy of Television Arts and Sciences for one of the programs of "The Constititution, That Delicate Balance", May 1986

Boy Scout Award, September 24, 1986

Recognition of Work, Welsh American Foundation, October 21, 1986

Award by Hellenic University Club, October 24, 1986

Recognition for serving as Chairman of the Advisory Board, Eastern National Park and Monument Association, January 26, 1987

Service to America, Virginia Highlands Community College, May 5, 1987

Contributions to the U.S. Marshals Service, May 1987

Humanitarian Award, Mac Sanders Brotherhood Lodge, June 3, 1987

Plank Owner, U.S.S. Thomas S. Gates, August 22, 1987

Honorary Doctor of Law, Thomas Jefferson University, September 9, 1987

Painting "Signing of the Constitution" in honor of Hobart G. Cawood, Pennsylvania, New Jersey and Delaware Societies, Daughters of the American Revolution, September 16, 1987

Award of Merit, Association for State and Local History, October 5, 1987

Honorary Doctor of Law, Emory and Henry College, May 28, 1987

Award for Service, Baronial Order of Magna Carta, June 12, 1987

Civilian Service Award, U.S. Army, October 1987

Philadelphia St. Andrews Society Speakers Award, November 11, 1988

Columbia Lodge 91 Award, April 24, 1989

Award for Service, Philadelphia Federal Executive Board, May 10, 1990

Middlesboro (KY) High School Sports Hall of Fame, September 14, 1991

Service to Seniors, NE Senior Citizens Council, April 7, 1991

Support for Savings Bonds, U.S. Treasury, April 1991

Philadelphia Bowl, Mayor W. Wilson Goode, April 12, 1991

For Years of Service and Friendship, Philadelphia Federal Executive Board, April 20, 1991

Recognition for Service, Philadelphia Chamber of Commerce, April 20, 1991

Honorary Doctor of Law, Philadelphia College of Textiles and Science, May 19, 1991

Friends of the Wistar Institute, Medal of Achievement, November 11, 1991

In Appreciation of Service, National Constitution Center, December 1992

Distinguished Service Award, Department of the Interior, May 5, 1992

APPENDIX B:

Distinguished Visitors
To
Independence National Historical Park 1971 – 1991

Distinguished Visitors
To
Independence National Historical Park 1971 – 1991

Mrs. Eleanor Spicer, President General, National Society, Daughters of the American Revolution, October 10, 1971

Patrick Gray, Director of the Federal Bureau of Investigation, July 4, 1972

President Richard Nixon, October 29, 1972

Vice President Spiro Agnew, October 29, 1972

Gerald Ford, Speaker of the House of Representatives, October 29, 1972

Nelson Rockefeller, Governor of New York, October 29, 1972

Ron Walker, Director of the National Park Service, February 13, 1973

Jack Palance, Actor, July 4, 1973

Princess Margaret of Great Britain, June 1974

Kurt Waldheim, Secretary General, United Nations, June 1974

President Gerald Ford, September 6, 1974

Secretary of the Interior, Rogers C. B. Morton, October 14, 1974

John Huston, Actor and Film Director, June 19, 1975

Eli Wallach, Patrick O'Neil, Pat Hingle, Ken Howard, Anne Jackson, Actors, June 1975

Bob Hope, Comedian, July 4, 1975

Gary Everhardt, Director of the National Park Service, October 4, 1975

Vice President Nelson Rockefeller, November 12, 1975

Betty Ford, January 13, 1976

Yitzhak Rabin, Prime Minister of Israel, January 26, 1976

Count and Countess Phillippe de Lafayette, January 26, 1976

Stan Musial, Baseball Player, February 4, 1976

150 Diplomats from the United Nations and 95 Diplomats from Washington, DC, February 26, 1976

Liam Cosgrave, Prime Minister of Ireland, March 19, 1976

Carl XVI, King of Sweden, April 6, 1976

Betty Ford, First Lady, May 14, 1976

Valery Giscard d'Estaing, President of France, May 19, 1976

Crown Prince Harold of Norway, June 1976

President Gerald Ford, July 4, 1976

Charlton Heston, Actor, July 4, 1976

Queen Elizabeth II of Great Britain, July 6, 1976

Helmut Schmidt, Chancellor of West Germany, July 17, 1976

Princess Grace and Prince Ranier of Monaco, July 1976

President Tolbert of Liberia, August 1976

President Carlos Andres Perez of Venezuela, July 1, 1977

Crown Prince Akahito and Princess Michiko of Japan, June 26, 1978

John Cardinal Krol, July 4, 1978

Archbishop of Cyprus May 30, 1979

General Alexander Haig, July 4, 1979

Leonard Nimoy, Actor, April 1980

Vice President Walter Mondale, July 4, 1980

Leslie Neilson, Actor, September 3, 1980

Dr. Sheldon Hackney (President, University of Pennsylvania), Emlyn Williams (British Actor), Arlen Specter (U.S. Senator), March 1, 1981

Rod McKuen, Performer, March 1, 1981

Lt. Governors of Thirty States, September 24, 1981

Joan Mondale, wife of the Vice President, November 12, 1981

Queen Beatrix of the Netherlands, April 22, 1982

Barbara Eden, Actress, June 14, 1982

Drew Lewis, former Pennsylvania Governor and Secretary of Transportation, November 11, 1982

James G. Watt, Secretary of the Interior, April 21, 1983

Rosalynn Carter, wife of President Carter, Apr8il 25, 1984

Mr. and Mrs. Fred Friendly, May 12, 1984

William Penn Mott, Director of the National Park Service, September 17, 1985

Bishop Desmond Tutu, January 15, 1986

Anthony Quinn, Actor, July 4, 1986

Chief Justice Warren Burger, September 16, 1986

Mary Martin and Carol Channing, Actors, September 16, 1986

President Ronald Reagan, April 1, 1987

Governor Robert Casey of Pennsylvania, April 1, 1987

Eighteen Diplomats, Organization of American States, April 3, 1987

Princess Alexandria of Great Britain, May 1, 1987

Ambassador Walter Annenberg, Ross Perot, Attorney General Edwin Meese, President of the American Bar Association, British Ambassador, May 1, 1987

Governors from the First Thirteen States May 24, 1987

Vice President and Mrs. George Bush, May 25, 1987

Governor Baililes and Lt. Gov. Wilder of Virginia May 29, 1987

President Alfonsin of Argentina, June 19, 1987

Governor Michael Castle of Delaware, June 27, 1987

Patrick Duffy, Actor, Senator Arlen Specter, David Eisenhower, July 4, 1987

220 Members of Congress, July 16, 1987

Governor O'Neil of Connecticut, July 16, 1987

Admiral Zumwalt, August 1987

Chief Justices of the First 13 States, September 16, 1987

President Ronald Reagan, September 17, 1987

Warren Burger, former Chief Justice, September 17, 1987

Chief Justice Renquist, Justices White, O'Connor and Brennen, October 2, 1987

Prime Minister of Finland, May 1, 1988

Prime Minister of Malta, July 14, 1988

Vice President George Bush, August 8, 1988

Mrs. Lech Walesa, wife of the President of Poland, July 3, 1989

President Lech Walesa of Poland, November 19, 1989

Former President Jimmy Carter, July 4, 1990

Secretary of the Interior Manuel Lujan, September 6, 1990

The Dalai Lama, September 22, 1990